T0352537

BIG MOUTH

Matt Preston is an award-winning food journalist, radio presenter and international TV personality. Over eleven years on *MasterChef Australia*, Matt reached an audience of more than 180 million people across 110 countries. Matt writes a weekly column for *Stellar* in the News Corp metro mastheads, seen by over 4 million Australians every week. He is also a senior editor for *delicious.*magazine, and contributes to taste.com.au, one of the world's most-read recipe websites. Since 2012 he has published eight bestselling cookbooks, most recently *Matt Preston's World of Flavour* in 2021.

Also by Matt Preston
Cravat-A-Licious

Cookbooks
Matt Preston's 100 Best Recipes
Fast, Fresh and Unbelievably Delicious
Cook Book
The Simple Secrets
Yummy, Easy, Quick
Yummy, Easy, Quick: Around the world
More: More recipes with more veg for more joy
Matt Preston's World of Flavour

Matt Preston

a memoir

BIG MOUTH

VIKING

an imprint of

PENGUIN BOOKS

VIKING

UK | USA | Canada | Ireland | Australia
India | New Zealand | South Africa | China

Viking is part of the Penguin Random House group of companies
whose addresses can be found at global.penguinrandomhouse.com

Penguin
Random House
Australia

First published by Viking in 2023

Copyright © Matt Preston 2023

The moral right of the author has been asserted.

All rights reserved. No part of this publication may be reproduced, published, performed in
public or communicated to the public in any form or by any means without prior written
permission from Penguin Random House Australia Pty Ltd or its authorised licensees.

Every effort has been made to acknowledge and contact the copyright holders for permission to
reproduce material contained in this book. Any copyright holders who have been inadvertently
omitted from acknowledgements and credits should contact the publisher and omissions will be
rectified in subsequent editions.

Cover photography by Julian Kingma; neon letters by Alhovik and tray
and cloche by Pixel-Shot courtesy of Shutterstock
Cover design by Adam Laszczuk © Penguin Random House Australia Pty Ltd
Typeset in 12.5/17.3 pt Adobe Garamond Pro by Midland Typesetters, Australia

Printed and bound in Australia by Griffin Press, an accredited
ISO AS/NZS 14001 Environmental Management Systems printer

A catalogue record for this
book is available from the
National Library of Australia

ISBN 978 1 76104 445 8

penguin.com.au

MIX
Paper | Supporting
responsible forestry
FSC® C018684

We at Penguin Random House Australia acknowledge that Aboriginal and Torres Strait Islander
peoples are the Traditional Custodians and the first storytellers of the lands on which we live
and work. We honour Aboriginal and Torres Strait Islander peoples' continuous connection
to Country, waters, skies and communities. We celebrate Aboriginal and Torres Strait Islander
stories, traditions and living cultures; and we pay our respects to Elders past and present.

Dedicated to all Jennifer's grandchildren.
May they have all her good traits – and
a few of her naughty ones.

Prologue

It's the Spring of 2008 and I'm standing in a teaching kitchen at Box Hill TAFE with a couple of Melbourne chefs, Guy Grossi and Gary Mehigan, as a hapless kid cooks for us. I'm here for an audition for a new cooking show but am already a little off-kilter as I'd shown up to find Gary wearing *exactly* the same pin-stripe suit that I'd planned to wear. So I'm in my street clothes. I leave thinking Guy's got the gig for sure. I don't know if he sang opera to the fake contestant but that's the sort of showmanship that TV likes, right?

At the next audition in Sydney I try a dish that is so over-seasoned it burns my lips. I'm talking the sort of burn you get after four days by your broken-down Landcruiser on the Tanami Track – without a drop of water. Later a journalist will carp about how I got the role instead of him because I was 'pantomime-over-the-top'. The real reason was because he couldn't taste the salt – or was too cowed to comment. Apparently I was wearing a red velvet jacket too. More fantasy. I didn't own one back then. Now . . .

*

The long-running UK show on which *MasterChef Australia* was to be based featured just two judges and a female voice-over. And that was originally what Network Ten were looking for. I knew this because the woman who cast the host and judges, Henrie Stride, subsequently became both my manager and a friend. She'd earlier rung for advice about what chefs were good talent given my experience at the Melbourne Food and Wine Festival. About halfway through the conversation she asked me to send her a photo of myself. I thought little of it, but behind the scenes the wheels were in motion. It turned out Henrie quite liked the photo of a slightly dishevelled me looking disapprovingly at a salad and passed it up the Fremantle/Network Ten chain of command. Eventually the head honcho exclaimed, 'If this mug can string a sentence together we'll write another judge role for him!' Okay, he probably said something ruder than mug, but I digress. They also didn't mind the scrappy piece of material tied round my neck. But as I say, I didn't give it that much thought. The day after the second audition my wife Emma and I boarded a flight to Europe to file a story for *Vogue Entertaining + Travel*.

Back in Sydney, the *MasterChef* producers continued their deliberations, cycling through a number of different combinations of female host and pairs of chef judges. It could have been Gary Mehigan and Manu Feildel but in the end George Calombaris was teamed with Gary instead of the Frenchman. I heard that George's unconventional approach to language and the fact that he'd been Gary's apprentice but had now eclipsed the master with multiple restaurants and awards were pluses for his appointment.

*

I was eating blanquette de veau in a little bistro in Paris's 15th arrondissement with a couple of French food writer mates when Emma burst in. Somehow she'd tracked me down across town when she was supposed to be resting. She told me I needed to talk to the *MasterChef* producers as soon as possible.

Later that night, lounging around in a bathrobe in our rather nice room at Le Meurice – it's where Salvador Dalí liked to stay, you know – while eating one of Pierre Hermé's angelic-looking white truffle and hazelnut praline macarons, I got the call. The producers offered me the job alongside Gary and George.

Two days earlier I'd found out that I'd been overlooked at *The Age* for the role of chief restaurant reviewer. It was a stinger as I foolishly expected I was the next cab off the rank. So what did I have to lose?

Well, for one, my job as a food and travel journo that had landed me in a five-star hotel opposite the Tuileries eating what had to be the coolest pastry in the world! I was already in the most blessed place imaginable. And I'd done a bit of TV in the past and found it a small pond of hungry sharks. I'd deliberately shied away from roles that called for the usual reality TV scorched-earth, nasty judge criticism, but there was something about UK *MasterChef* that I liked. Judging the Australian version with a couple of pals seemed like a bonus.

So I said yes.

The complication was the fact *MasterChef* was shooting in Sydney and my family and I lived in Melbourne. I'd need to relocate for seven months a year. (This would later increase to about nine months when variants like *Celebrity* and *Junior MasterChef* were added but that wasn't in anyone's wildest dreams at that stage.) Emma and I had three little kids. Friends who were veterans of such arrangements warned about the dangers to our relationship. It would be hard on Emma, but she pushed me to do it. She thought it'd be good for me. Anyway, it wasn't as though it was going to go to a second series. What's the point of a cooking competition where you can't smell the food or taste the dishes?

In order to understand how I came to be at that audition at Box Hill TAFE, I ought to tell you about growing up in the UK, the monks at school, joining the army, my beloved Chelsea FC and, of course, my family.

Oh my, my family. A mismatch of bad behaviour, glamour and scandals . . . but we'll come to some of that later. Suffice to say, I am delighted to reveal that the later generations are now, so far, better behaved. However, you'll be pleased to know that most of the people in the pages that follow are much more interestingly flawed.

Too
Many
Introductions

Introduction 1

'Why have you got two birth certificates? Are you adopted?'

This is my seventeen-year-old daughter, whip-smart with a street fighter's insight. Standing among a thousand holiday-makers near the chaotic and slightly frantic Jetstar gates at Melbourne Airport seems a less than ideal spot to start revealing lifelong family secrets . . . but then again, where could be better, where could be less likely, and more perfectly inappropriate, than surrounded by the piled hand luggage and all the howling, the collective stress of holiday travel on a no-frills airline thick in the air? It is strangely right.

I nod.

'So your dad wasn't your dad? And your sisters – our aunts – aren't really your sisters?'

Not quite . . .

It's complicated . . .

'Well, yes and no. And they're actually my half-sisters.'

You can see the world reordering in her eyes.

'But to me they've always only ever been my sisters.'

At this, you can see things start to right.

My boys look on, not sure if this is a joke or not. The woman I love just nods. Realisation spreads among us.

'Oh, Father,' says Sadie. 'Don't we have a lot to talk about?'

Introduction 2

The strange thing about memoirs is that they really have to start before the memory of the writer actually kicks in.

If that wasn't the case, we'd be talking about Bossy Bell, the pull-along cow that I dragged around the loungeroom from the moment I could move; the cow bell round her neck dinging with every rotation of her front wheels, frustratingly for adults, but much to my apparent delight. Or perhaps the squeaking rubber elephant that was a constant, drool-covered companion during my months of teething. These would be my earliest memories – not so much vivid recollections but shadows and stains on my hippocampus and prefrontal cortex. I'd expect the squeaking rubber elephant to hang out in the hippocampus, obviously, with the other large African beasts.

Holding these toys once again sixty years later ignites these deeply buried memories like a blue light wand waved over a crime scene. These are underwater memories, soft and shifting, but I feel an emotional connection with them that can only be explained by the earliest imprint. I am sure I can even hear my happy gurgling and feel the wet slipperiness of squeaking rubber elephant's trunk between my chubby little fingers.

I am not sure who gave either toy to me, but I know the desire to make the noise they delivered was a constant in my life even before I could vocalise my demands.

The whole complexity of family gift-giving lifts a notch, however, when you've got three grandmothers and two grandfathers trying to compensate for the absence of one father.

Whoa! I'll pull myself up here. There's a danger of imbuing the past with memories that aren't. Things pop up like kneejerk reactions, learnt over the years but never really experienced.

I should say first of all that I never felt unloved – anything but – and that when I was adopted by the man who would marry my mother, I never felt any resentment towards him or my natural father.

In fact, the words 'natural father' have always sounded totally alien to me. It wasn't like there was a father-sized hole in my life that was clearly visible to me, or that needed to be filled. Life was just as it was. I got on with living it. This is perhaps emotionally shallow of me – and maybe I need to explore this with some therapy – but not having someone to call 'Dad' only bothered me once a year, at the annual prep school sports day, when the tannoy boomed out the request for fathers and mothers to gather for the parents' race. It was then that I quizzically noted the difference, in a school environment where divorce was rare and single mothers rarer.

Later on, when I met Michael, the man who got my mother pregnant (oh, how dated is that concept! Let's just call him my grandmother's son), I was interested but not haunted by any primeval desire to develop a bond with him. In part this was through a sense of loyalty to the man who had played the role of my father for thirty years or so, but also because there was a strange feeling of taking sides here. Of declaring that I was my mother's son.

This was perhaps unfair, as, somewhat strangely for those times back in the early 1960s, sides were not taken when it came to my arrival as a baby. Or that's how it looked from my perspective, but equally, I'm not sure that the parents siding not with their son but with the unborn child and his mother wasn't in its own way taking a side.

At this point I should point out two things. First, I had an incredibly close relationship with my paternal grandmother. She was a complex woman and one who largely lacked a filter where I was concerned. She told me everything she knew – even if much of it wasn't suitable for a young, wide-eyed child. Certainly, these things were told as her stories and I'm mindful of that as they were at times tinged by her sadness, her experience and her anger.

She was also a vivid storyteller. Drawing hard on a perpetual cigarette, she'd regale me with tales . . . of the time she had a lump removed from her breast under only local anaesthetic in a Rome hospital . . . of the time Admiral Doenitz's wife came to her house in postwar Germany begging for a menial role; anything so she could feed her daughter . . . and then her endless tales of her only child, her son.

If there is a tragedy in this part of the story it is how I fear my arrival must have been a rift between them, and while I know that my grandmother felt this, she was a tough character from a world where you didn't complain and you seldom apologised. She called it the stiff upper lip, and it was expected.

While there was softness and no little concern when she slammed my fingers closed in the boot of her impossibly sporty grey 1968 Ford Capri, the fact I never cried was almost of more importance when we sat together at the casualty department waiting for the result of the X-rays.

The other thing you need to know is that I have a horrifying ability to remember details and events, even if I struggle with names of people I've met many times before. And my grandmother Vivienne liked to talk a lot. So, there is much to remember . . . so much that I have the arrogance to feel that I might know the full extent of her story better than anyone else living.

It seems strange to start this book by talking about a man I've only met once, but it seems as if I should mount some form of defence for him before what comes next. 'The man who deserts the pregnant woman' seldom gets the best hearing.

Before we do that, however, I need to introduce you properly to his parents, Boy and Vivienne, which you may find instructive . . .

ONE

Soft-handed, Plump-cheeked and Spoilt in Old Blighty

1

When I think of my paternal grandmother, Vivienne, the most vivid picture that comes to mind is of her with a cigarette in one hand and an Americano (vermouth and Campari on ice, with a twist of lemon or a wheel of orange) in a crystal-cut tumbler in the other.

The only child of a fairly loveless, wealthy couple, she was raised by her nanny, someone she spoke of more warmly than her own mother. Vivienne's father had been wounded at Gallipoli, and mentioned in dispatched landing troops as a member of the British Merchant Marine. He was gutted that his family name would die with his daughter, his only offspring. To compensate, he indulged her, at least as a child.

At boarding school, she was a tearaway. Later she flirted with the new craze, films; Alfred Hitchcock pursued her; and everyone was having fun at parties with nitrous oxide. In her twenties, a romance with a dashing Colombian led to a secretive pregnancy and an even more clandestine solution at a clinic in London's Harley Street. The last thing she remembered was the surgeon arriving from dinner in his white tie and tails – silk scarf wrapped around his face for anonymity – to perform the illegal procedure. It was twins, a boy and a girl, she was later told. The abortion was one of her lasting regrets. She cried talking about it.

She fell in love with my grandfather, 'Boy', when she saw him working his horse on the parade ground of the old Brighton Barracks. They married towards the end of the 1920s, and as he was with the artillery they were immediately posted abroad – to the one-time pirate haven of Port Royal in Jamaica.

Boy had been born in Rome. His Scottish father was the British Consul in Italy and lived on the Via Condotti. According to my grandmother, Boy's dad was the 'biggest bore' in Rome.

Boy had two older sisters and as the youngest child he was spoilt – the nickname 'Boy' came from the fact my grandmother teased him as being the 'golden boy' of the family. His real name was Maurice Rapinet, but everyone called him Boy . . . or the Brigadier.

His severe Scottish exterior concealed the volatile gesticulations and rapid-fire speech that erupted in a flurry whenever he spoke Italian. Teased about his Roman birth during his first week at an uptight English boarding school, that volatility surfaced. He broke the other boy's nose.

I only ever witnessed his dour Scottish side, but I relished the idea that an Italian-born grandparent meant that I could represent Gli Azzurri, should they one day need me for the World Cup.

My grandparents' posting to Jamaica was a whirlwind affair. These were the days of nightclubs and balls and sailing to deserted cays for languid picnics. Boy had the rakish movie star looks of a Clark Gable – and he used them. Some nights he'd come in from an innocent smoke on the balcony with not-so-innocent grass stains on the back of his white mess jacket. Furious fights ensued. After one such altercation, Vivienne found herself pregnant. About the same time, Boy was posted to the North-West Frontier (the area between north-west Pakistan and Afghanistan). Here he spent his days gathering intelligence in the markets of what the servicemen called 'The Grim'. With his skin dyed dark with walnut juice, the Scot with the Italian temperament pretended to be a 6'2" Parthan with piercing blue eyes.

Back in London, meanwhile, Vivienne gave birth to a son who was christened Michael.

Boy returned from the North-West Frontier with little interest in his new child. To Vivienne's lasting anger, when he first met him, he described him as 'quite a bloody little mess' and seemed more worried about the kid dirtying his dress boots. This was not auspicious.

The couple separated at the start of the Second World War. Living on an allowance of £500 a year from her father, Vivienne received permission to stay in the general evacuation zone of East Sussex. The proximity to invasion beaches made property cheap. And it was all she could afford.

While they were there, Michael contracted meningococcal disease and nearly died. Vivienne meanwhile captured a downed German fighter pilot with a sword. She spotted a young downed Luftwaffe pilot floating over the next-door field and was there to meet him as he landed, brandishing her husband's ceremonial sabre. She could be a frightening woman when roused. She did gain a certain notoriety in the area for marching the German pilot into the local police station in the village at sword point as the local villagers applauded loudly.

There was no love lost down this way for an enemy air force that would jettison bombs on their way home from lighting up London or Coventry, or strafe shoppers on the nearby seafront in Eastbourne. My grandmother would observe when we were there for cream cakes at Bondolfi's how she'd hugged every inch of the concrete pavement of the beachside promenade as ricochets pinged and fizzed around her.

Like her son, she too fell ill, picking up a nasty type of gingivitis known as 'trench mouth' – possibly while dating a dashing American pilot from the Flying Tigers. When she found out how much it would cost to 'civilly' treat the disease under anaesthetic, she opted instead to have her gums cut away over four painful visits.

Although she'd filed for divorce before the war, she told me each time the papers came around she'd send them straight to the bottom of the pile. Her thinking was that if her husband was killed, as a war widow she'd be entitled to his pension. Like I said, no filter.

My grandfather never spoke about his war experiences – but my grandmother certainly did. She told of the hand-to-hand combat with a German officer who was also looking for a forward observation position to direct gunnery for his battalion, and how my grandfather was the only one who walked away. There was no time to draw a weapon, so they fought like animals for their survival. It was chilling to realise that the wiry fingers that incessantly tickled me as a small child had fastened round another human's neck and choked the life out of him.

I never asked him if he had a death wish during the war and after splitting with Vivienne, but he acted with a bravery that suggested that he did. In one European skirmish he was rescuing wounded Canadian troops while their officers apparently cowered in their foxholes when he stood on a landmine. It pretty much blew off his arm, but that didn't stop him – he bent down, grabbed the limb, which was dangling but still attached by sinew, skin and muscle, and carried it back to the field hospital. He argued violently, and with ugly threats, with the surgeon to keep the limb. The surgeon eventually agreed. After a year of rehabilitation and with his arm reattached and fully functioning, he was offered a desk job but preferred to take a demotion and a cut in pay to return to the action with a command in the field, now fighting the Japanese in South-East Asia. He arrived there with another medal, the DSO, on his chest for the men he'd saved on the fateful day.

At the end of the war, as a colonel, he had to accept the surrender of a Japanese regiment. The process was simple; the Japanese officers would walk up to him and hand over their swords. Many of these weapons were family heirlooms of great antiquity and artistic value. However, one man was so distraught that my grandfather took pity on him and gave him back his sword. It was the wrong thing to do. The soldier took it as a mortal insult and committed impromptu seppuku there and then, ruining, my grandfather said, another perfectly good pair of boots. Not much love lost there either.

After the war my grandparents reunited – one of the first couples in the UK to file for divorce and then subsequently remarry – and were transferred to Germany, where my grandfather oversaw a region of the conquered country, replacing the deposed gauleiter. Shocked upon visiting one of the concentration camps and witnessing first-hand the horrors that had taken place, my grandfather hired cinemas in the area and compiled a list of all the local German survivors. Each was checked off once they had watched gruelling newsreels of the liberation of the camps so there could be no denial at a later date of the atrocities committed.

On a lighter note, I still have a beautiful painted Bavarian bread-proving cupboard my grandmother bought for 5 deutsche marks.

Boy returned to the UK as a decorated brigadier and went on to do something shadowy with a right-wing organisation known as the Economic League. If you've seen the TV series *Peaky Blinders*, you'll know the sort of things they got up to. I remember there was a big chart on the wall of his London office that featured known communists and trade union activists – and their whereabouts. As a child I would wait quietly studying this blacklist before we'd cross the road to Victoria Station and the trip down to the thankfully agitator-free East Sussex.

Here he was the perfect doting husband and the best grandfather a lad could hope for. The anger and offhand nature had deserted him. He made a breakfast tray for my grandmother every day, and provided the sweat and muscle that enabled her to pursue her lifelong love of gardening. The lush, lined lawns and herbaceous borders packed with height and colour were in large part down to him.

I'd follow him around the garden asking endless questions. Whenever I disappeared for too long he'd sing out, 'Mr Chatterbox, where are you?' and I'd come running.

We'd go for long walks over the Downs no matter the weather, and careen down the slopes of the garden in fertiliser bags or on kitchen trays when it snowed. He taught me skills that I still use today, like how to split a log with a sledgehammer and wedges, how to chip for kindling and how to swing a lawnmower down a steep, grassed slope with a rope. In many ways, he was the father to me that I'm not sure he ever was to his own son.

2

On the other side of the family, my maternal grandmother, Joan, experienced her own tragedies. One of her brothers committed suicide in the London Underground. He was an actor with an elfin beauty that my grandmother, with her gamin haircut, shared. She suspected he was gay and that he was tortured by this.

Joan was the daughter of a British naval officer and a wealthy American of Revolutionary/Founding Father heritage, but she never spoke of her own childhood or her life before grandchildren. I later found out she'd spent time in Paris in the late 1920s with her sister (and her sister's female companion) in their apartment on Rue Bonaparte in the fashionable 6th arrondissement. The significance of this will only be seen much, much later in this book. It came as a shock to me.

Joan was a quiet practical woman. She could rewire a lamp, build and paint scenery for the award-winning amateur dramatics company she founded with her two best friends, and knew her way around the punt and the football pools. Given her privileged background, this was highly unusual.

She married a dashing 6′6″ adventurer and rake, Larry, and gave birth to my mother Jennifer in 1933 – the year Hitler came to power. Sadly the marriage didn't last, but Hitler did.

During the war Joan trained as a nurse and was part of the Women's Land Army, where she added further to her skills, learning how to fix cars and trucks. She later worked among the 'boffins and debs' at the secret service facility at Bletchley Park in Milton Keynes where the Germans' Enigma code was cracked. Here she helped run spies into France to work with the Maquis (French resistance) – young men and women who would often never return, dying in some corner of a foreign field or more likely in the basement of a Gestapo interrogation centre.

While adept in so many other areas, she was a ghastly cook and venturing into her fridge or pantry was an exercise in archaeology. There were always cans of Long Life lager and tomato juice as thick as velvet. Lunch might be cheese and slices of apple dipped in salt. When we stayed with her she'd make us salads of grated cheese and hard-boiled eggs with Hellmann's mayo; a witlof and ham gratin; and desserts like chocolate semolina or an airy lemon mousse set with gelatine.

No great culinary feats, and yet, when I wrote my first cookbook there were more recipes in it from this grandmother who couldn't cook than the other one, Vivienne, who could. Perhaps this was because down in Joan's little pink 1950s Barbie bungalow, in the lee of the woods and so near to where the River Rother slowly winds across the meadows and past the old Swan Inn, I'd usually be with my brother and sisters – while trips to visit Vivienne were made solo.

Joan doted on my little brother William. I always wondered if this was because he came along pristine and unsullied, the result of a church marriage rather than some dodgy one-night stand. Or maybe there was something more to it. You'll find out later but don't get your hopes up as it probably *was* because he was a cuter baby and a nicer child!

Visits to Joan's house were interspersed with running wild in the woods and across the fields, and damming the ditches that tripped the deer when they wandered blind out of the woods at night.

You'd be right in thinking that apart from a love of cigarettes, my two grandmothers were very different. Joan's nickname was 'Mouse' and she was as careful with her money as she was generous with her love. Both women wore their hair up but with Joan there were always a few strays that escaped the bobby pins and Kirby grips. Vivienne's wouldn't dare fall out of line.

It's an odd feeling realising you will never be as courageous as one grandfather nor as cool as the other. Joan's husband Larry was born in Cork in the south-west of Ireland and lived a *very* cool life. For starters, his family was from one of the twelve tribes of Galway and his father Patrick Kirwan was a renowned actor and theatre impresario who started Shakespeare in London's Regent's Park.

Larry went to Oxford and wanted to be an archaeologist. He was sent to Cairo to work in the Egyptology department of the Cairo Museum. He told me his first job was helping unpack treasures from Howard Carter's excavation of the tomb of Tutankhamen! Digging a little deeper, it appears that he in fact helped Carter *reassemble* Tut's tomb. Whatever the case, he was on his way. It also made me think he was freaking Indiana Jones.

Leaving my grandmother after the birth of his only child, my mother Jennifer, was one of the *less* cool things Larry did – but it did mean he wound up stationed in Alexandria for part of the war where he and his new wife Stella befriended the one and only Elizabeth David. This meant nothing to me when I first learnt of it, but came to mean so much more when I began writing about food. A pilaf my step-grandmother cooked was allegedly one of Elizabeth David's.

Shortly after, Larry was called up to work in intelligence for Winston Churchill in the Cabinet Office, where he rose to the rank of lieutenant colonel.

After the war, he devoted his life to championing more archaeological sites in East Africa and became a leading expert in the Twenty-Fifth Dynasty (or Nubian Dynasty) of Egypt. He had compounded his Indiana Jones status as a young man, riding mules into the middle of what is now Sudan with a mate on a hunch they could discover Nubian tombs from 680 BC. Digging a hole into a suspicious mound, he lowered his smaller, lighter mate by the ankles into the void their shovels had revealed. The flashlight the mate was clutching lit up sandstone blocks decorated with bas-relief sculptures of Amun-Ra. Here they'd found their first temple at Kawa on the east bank of the Nile. Or that's the way he told it. All very Boy's Own adventure.

After the war Larry also became the director of the Royal Geographical Society. Here he managed the 1953 ascent on Mount Everest led by John Hunt and finally achieved by Tenzing Norgay and Sir Edmund Hillary. Before he died, he gave me a pocketknife that had been issued for the Everest expedition. I'm not entirely sure it was Sir Edmund Hillary's, as these knives were standard army issue . . . but this was always the inference so that's the story I'm sticking to, and it's a very precious thing indeed.

In those years at the Royal Geographical Society, Larry organised several polar expeditions, but more important to me back then was the summer of 1969 when the first man landed on the moon – and then visited the RGS as Larry's guest for a lecture, and I got to meet him!

It's hard to convey just how excited I was as a ten-year-old meeting the legendary astronaut Neil Armstrong – certainly I was so excited that I brushed down my bowl haircut especially nicely. I suppose now it would be a bit like Harry Styles and TayTay turning up for school sports day.

I should note that the blond cousin in the middle of the photo I have with Armstrong looks a little less excited than me . . . probably because I am apparently – but I don't believe this – standing on his toe. He's now something very important in the International Monetary Fund so it clearly didn't set him back too much.

Larry was knighted with the KCMG in 1972, which meant he got to wear a grand blue velvet cape and a huge silver star. When he died, his obituary was carried in the *New York Times*, the *Washington Post* and the UK broadsheets, which is why you'll find more actual facts and dates in this chapter than any other in this book. Relish them but don't get used to it.

All this standing so close to history was definitely cool but possibly the coolest thing of all is that he has bits of Antarctica named after him. Being on the most successful TV show in Australian history seems a tad shallow and unimportant compared to that. Probably . . . because it is! But hey, you can't knock it . . . we had so much fun and met so many cool people ourselves. I even ended up on doof sticks at drug-fuelled music festivals, which is pretty elite.

More of that later.

3

I have most of my grandmother Vivienne's diaries dating back to 1939. I don't know why she kept them all, it's not as though they're particularly profound journals, more just the blandest notes: hair appointments, whist drives, tea and lunch dates. There's nothing even to tell you that there was a war going on.

It is in the seemingly mundane, however, that truth so often resides. While she saw her husband Boy a lot in 1940 (most weekends in fact), in the latter years of the war he is absent, his place taken in 1941 by a 'Freddie' and then in 1943 by a 'Bob'.

With most of the witnesses long gone, her diaries for 1960, 1961 and 1962 must also provide me with a skeleton key to the events of my birth – and the necessary deliberations to sort out the little bundle of a problem that was on his way.

I know that I was conceived on a weekend away in Kent, at a house overlooking the Royal Military Canal. This would have been around October 1960. As to the circumstances, my grandmother always claimed that my mother, uninvited, clambered into bed naked with her son Michael, 'so what could you expect?' As this was after Vivienne had started a slow decline into dementia and catatonia, it's hard to know if it was fantasy or truth.

Michael is not around his mother's house much in the second half of 1960 but the start of 1961 sees a flurry of visits. The first hint of my arrival are the simple words 'Lunch Stella' (my step-grandmother) on 5 July. It appears that my grandmother and step-grandmother were getting together to talk about the slight problem of an illegitimate child in the family.

Fifteen days later, on 20 July, I make the first of many appearances in Vivienne's diary – 'Matthew's birthday' – and on Saturday 5 August she gets to meet me (and my mother) for the first time. On Sunday 3 September we have 'Matthew's christening, 3 o/c, the Servites in Fulham Road', and at the start of December my mother and I make the first of numerous visits to Vivienne and Boy's place in Sussex.

From what I can gather the meetings about my future were fraught and not all the behaviour was the best. Both my grand-fathers were proud and patrician. Both were angry about the situation. An offer of marriage was, apparently, made, but it was one that came with its own proviso: that it would be a marriage in name only. This was never going to fly with a young woman from a church that didn't accept divorce, especially when marrying anyone else later on for love would have been seen as bigamous.

It all ended with baby me taking my father's surname, and Michael's parents – Boy and Vivienne – recognising me as their grandchild. So, all in all a win for the chubby little kid in the swaddling clothes. The alternatives were far less attractive, as we'll see.

I've grown up believing that in this life you can only be judged on your actions, and judging others on theirs is a waste of time unless you can help them to a better path. You must realise, and act on, the power you have to influence others positively. I have a profound sense of gratitude for the vast majority of people who have surrounded me, and no little happiness at where I've ended up. Whether I have done any good is for my children, and to a lesser extent for my friends, to decide.

Now enough of that – let's get on with the story . . .

4

'I was born behind a brewery.'

That was supposed to be the first line of this memoir. It just seemed to work so well with the second line, 'We were poor but we were happy.' I felt this combo made me sound street-wise and like a bit of a battler, when I was actually soft-handed, plump-cheeked and spoilt.

I wasn't born in a narrow suburban street between two highways in a shit part of London, but in a grand hospital up on Marble Arch that's now a five-star hotel. I was a big baby, in part because my perennial lateness was already hardwired into my DNA. I missed my due date of American Independence Day by two weeks. But first babies are often late and my birth was fairly typical, aside from the fact that my mother received one of the first epidurals ever given in a UK hospital – like I said, I was a big baby.

The brewery isn't actually that much of a lie. When I was a baby, after leaving the hospital we did move back to my mother's basement flat behind the Watney's bottling plant. The soundtrack of my early years was long-neck bottles rattling in wooden crates and the wooden clogs of the workers crunching on the broken brown glass that lay thick across the bottling line and loading dock.

There was a whistle at clocking-off time and the women in blue-grey warehouse coats with headscarf turbans would stream back over the border to the warren of streets around the gasworks and the Lots Road Power Station. It was a part of London we'd later dare each other to ride through. Some houses were so rough they'd sold their doors. We'd hear lurid stories about how the bloke who got stabbed outside the fish shop was also involved in a shooting.

These days you won't get much change from $5 million (around £2.6 million) for a house there. But back in the 1960s, this bit of London was a netherworld – a no man's land between suburbs rich and poor – and as such it earnt the moniker 'World's End' after a pub of the same name. I didn't know it at the time but the penniless Rolling Stones lived in a basement flat just round the corner from us in digs so dire and dank that Keith Richards was reduced to sleeping in the bath. Other than having a spare tyre stolen when I moved back there twenty-five years later, I never had much trouble.

Well, at least what trouble there was, was of my own making . . .

When you're five years old you really don't want a policeman coming around to your house to question you. The problem was, I'd swung my new cricket bat at a bigger, older kid who wanted it, landing them in the local casualty department.

I can still feel the sting on my chubby little thigh from my mother's hand and the wild fury in her eyes after she heard the ambulance bells. Fainter is the horrid realisation of how much damage I could have done with that bat – even if, the next day, the kid looked just fine running along the footpath on the other side of the street.

I don't remember what the policeman said exactly but I do remember thinking that his heavy serge uniform must have been very hot and itchy on that sweltering summer's day and perhaps *that* was why he seemed so cross.

Given this inglorious beginning, it may not surprise you that as a child I was, quite frankly, a bit of a shit.

When a friend of my mother's – a very correct gentleman who would go on to be something to do with heraldry in the royal household – came around for tea one afternoon, I offered him lemonade. When he accepted, I instead gave him a glass of my freshly squeezed urine. He was somewhat unimpressed. Thankfully, his younger brother, a far less stitched-up individual, thought the idea repulsive, but also somewhat delightful. He'd retell the story at Christmas with glee and a rolling belly-laugh.

When I mentioned this incident to my mother years later she couldn't recall what my justification was, only that I had a rather unusual belief in the magical power of my pee. On one of our regular walks in the park she caught me pissing on the biggest tree chanting, 'Die tree, die.'

I also hated not getting my own way.

I proffer as proof a series of pictures of me on the beach in tears of anguish, snarling wild-faced at my grandmother,

Vivienne. I have just latched on to her inner arm with my teeth and hung there like a determined bull terrier until she slapped me off. Again, I'm not sure of the affront but I clearly remember my grandmother showing me the tooth marks that remained imprinted in her soft, loose flesh a month later.

It was probably something to do with ice cream.

So many of the bad things I did as a kid were about ice cream.

5

As I say, the area we lived in during the first six years of my life was one of those parts of London that sits as a borderland between the smart and poor suburbs. To the east lay the grand white porticos of Chelsea and Belgravia. We meanwhile clung grimly to the very edge of the Royal Borough of Kensington and Chelsea, which was 'royal' in name only – it was an area you only drove through on the way to somewhere better.

To the west the cramped flats and council blocks full of Polish and Irish Catholics began. This was Fulham but also a part of London more specifically known as Walham Green. The area would later be renamed Fulham Broadway when its reputation for crime overwhelmed the place and the locals called for a fresh start.

World's End itself was far less notable. A thin freight line divided the Stamford Bridge football stadium from the Brompton Cemetery. We later found out that this was the route that nuclear waste trains would use as they regularly trundled through London.

*

We lived at 24 Fernshaw Road in a basement flat with a small, paved garden at the rear that you accessed by narrow steps. Most days I could be found sitting on those steps staring at the uneaten portion of my dinner. My mother was a stickler for finishing all your food. This was a time when recalcitrant children would be reminded of our starving counterparts in Biafra as a logically flawed way to try to guilt us into eating everything on our plates.

It was usually egg whites that did it. I just couldn't face them. There was something about their slipperiness that made them claw their way back up my throat when I tried to swallow them – my gullet in revolt. I'm not entirely sure whether it was that mucus-y layer on the top of the runny yolks of fried eggs that suggested my mother had a really bad head cold, or the first cold spring of the rubbery whites of hard-boiled eggs. Either way, they weren't for me.

I can't remember baulking at much else – other than perhaps stew made with cheap gristly meat, or Friday fish that smelt of three days 'maturing' in the back of a truck that had been driven from port to market to shop and back home. Possibly more than once.

It wasn't until years later when a friend opened his own fish-monger's down the road in Fulham that I discovered that fish was supposed to smell freshly of the surf and the briny sea, the flesh flaking like white petals, rather than announcing its imminent arrival with wafts of ammonia – a truly rank odour that recalled the Parisian pissoir at the end of a hot summer's day I'd been equal parts thrilled and appalled to go into as a child when peeing in the street seemed both strangely exotic and exposed. Of course, that was all to come. My revulsion towards bad fish was something much older and more primeval; a hardwired survival instinct.

My endless refusals to eat fish eventually wore my mother down; you can only sit a five-year-old for so long on the back steps. My resolve was strengthened by two things. Firstly, the arrival of younger siblings to ally with in the cause who were probably much better loved or, more likely, far smarter at arguing than me. And secondly, the fact that we soon moved into a house that didn't have any back steps at all.

After the battle had been won to ban grey, old fish from our lives, seafood was limited to battered cod from the local chippy, the smoky joy of my new dad's curried kedgeree, or slices of smoked salmon. My mother's silent protest, however, would be to boil large, satanic and bubbling pots of coley (a type of cod, otherwise known as saithe or pollock) for the cats' dinner. If you've never smelt over-boiled coley my congratulations to you on your good fortune, as it's the sort of stench that is three-dimensionally disgusting. A fug that drapes itself, hot, damp and pungent, over everything it touches; worming its way up stairs and under doors to wherever you are in the house. It's a stink that still makes me retch. In fact, any cat food will now do that to me. Thanks, Mum!

On the upside I can happily unblock a dunny with nary a backwards step. Perhaps I should thank my mother for this too, as without that 'it could be worse, it could be coley' experience, I wouldn't have the sort of resilience that would eventually win me the approval of the parents of the woman I love. This was, after all, an Australian couple who had hitherto viewed me as a fey layabout with no prospects and all the usual notorious soap-and-hard-work-dodging predilections of the English.

But once again I'm getting ahead of myself. Instead I should mention at this point that now that I live in Australia, fish is one of the greatest pleasures the continent has to offer. I'm always in the market for flathead or calamari plucked from the depths by friends with patience, skill and a tinny. And when I return to England I naturally yearn for the thick slabs of cod of my childhood, or the unsold sole that my friend fed us at the end of every Saturday's retail.

While Fernshaw Road certainly wasn't rich, there were a few smart people who lived across the street in a mansion block of apartments. These were the sort of folk who read big broadsheet newspapers and wore horn-rimmed glasses and knitted ties. Their hulking 1850s block of flats was all ornate red brickwork and grand black double doors with curly gold writing above it proclaiming the name of some long dead aristocrat after whom the building was named. Probably Lord Fernshaw, if he had existed anywhere other than the pages of bodice rippers, and wasn't a total cad.

It was in this mansion block that my first girlfriend lived. I say 'girlfriend' in the way that parents annoyingly used to try to pair off their child with the very first friend of the opposite sex they ever had. She was, needless to say, beautiful, with jet-black hair and a high German name that started with 'von'. I came from the bad side of the street. The side where kids assaulted each other with cricket bats. Still, we played happily together, never drifting into any uncomfortable role playing as would be a trend down the track. Six years later when I needed a date for a youngsters' Christmas ball, I asked her. I have a horrible memory of it being a terrible, terrible date – the nadir being when I asked her if she had bought her Christmas presents yet. Gosh, I still blush at the eye-bleeding tedium of that question.

The street that divided us was a place of play and of death. We'd play tag, football and cricket here between the rows of parked cars. A small child could be totally obscured between the drab Ford Anglias and then dart out, making them perfect for tag.

This was less ideal when the ice cream van would arrive and park over the road tinkling 'Greensleeves'.

As a youngster, I had a sort of Pavlovian reaction to that tune. The first notes would have me mesmerised with images of wafer cones of soft serve with two brown ears of crumbly milk chocolate sticking out of the high, groomed swoosh of heavily aerated slopes of sweet cool vanilla . . . Ah, those music-box tones were truly my siren's call. My mother could have lashed me to the railings and stuffed my ears with beeswax and still I would have broken free. Nothing else mattered but the lure of that sweetness . . . the promise of that tune . . . as the driver of the Austin Healey 3000 realised when I swooped out from between the parked cars and suddenly materialised in front of him!

I am fairly certain I saw the fast-approaching, smiling silver grille, silver bumper and the wild bugging eyes of the driver all at about the same time. I'm fairly certain I also heard my mother's scream blending in with the sound of the squealing brakes.

I froze as the bumper gently kissed my left thigh. I was still floating in that strange void in which you find yourself when death – or extremely painful, bone-crunching injury – is imminent. It's a void that I can still return to now – vivid the bugging eyes, my mother's scream, the smell of rubber . . .

Then *snap!* and the driver was shouting at me.

My mother was shouting at me.

And worst of all, I never got my ice cream!

The event was so jarring that even today, whenever I hear that blasted 'Greensleeves' song, I still involuntarily smell the burnt rubber the driver of that Austin Healey left on the road. Being deprived of a '99' does tend to scar a child like that.

Of course these days I always look left and right before taking off after the ice cream van with a nest of coins clasped in my sweaty right hand.

6

Like a lot of little kids, I was afraid of the dark. And of corridors. And of snakes. Particularly those snakes that lurk at the bottom of your bed, tucked away where the top sheet curls under the mattress.

When you're short, there's no danger that your feet will reach the end of the bed and find the serpents' sinuous, scaly backs, but as you grow taller the reality becomes ever more present until you have to bravely stretch out and explore, your toes expecting the sharp strike of double-puncturing fangs at any moment.

The fear of lurking snakes, I believe, is the main reason for the success for the doona or duvet over sheets and blankets in the last thirty years. With no hands to hang on with, the snakes drop out of the end of the bed . . . to be gobbled up by the monster living under it.

Such childhood fears are often – thankfully – balanced by similar irrationalities from those who care for us. Grandmother

Vivienne had grown up in a household with cooks and breakfast waiting in silver chafing dishes on the dining room sideboard. Breakfast 'cereal' was an alien concept but her logic around it was sound: 'If cereal with milk was what everyone else had then surely serving your Coco Pops with whipped cream would be the way it should be done in the better households of the land.'

I never disabused her of this notion.

Thus, Coco Pops with whipped cream is still my lazy response to the even lazier question of, 'What's your guilty pleasure?' They really are quite delicious in a rule-breaking, decadent sort of a way. Of course the preferred method of consumption is – in a manner not unlike those brutes who ate those pretty little Armagnac-sozzled ortolan songbirds – hidden under a velvet cloth, for fear of offending God and His angels.

It isn't merely a matter of gluttony. There's a culinary logic to it too. You see, the cool airy cream provides a soft bed for the crunchy chocolate puffs and, more importantly, it doesn't make them soggy. This means the bowl can be assembled in one procedure. Ordinarily, to correctly enjoy your Coco Pops without them turning to mush, you pour a little milk into your bowl and then sprinkle on only enough Coco Pops that can be eaten in five mouthfuls. This way they don't have a chance to break down. You then repeat the process with more cereal and milk until you are replete and there is just a little of that extra chocolatey, milky goodness left in the bowl as your sugar-laden breakfast full stop.

Later on, as a restaurant reviewer, whenever I'd go to a fancy gastro temple in which light, crunchy buckwheat groats or flavoured puff rice would be strewn on a creamy dessert,

I'd quietly doff my cap to my grandmother Vivienne's pioneering wisdom.

I don't remember much about school before the age of six, which is probably a blessing. It had been quite the thing for previous generations of my family to be packed off to boarding school as young as five. My mother quivered at the memory of being sent to a girls' boarding school while her parents were off digging up antiquities and fighting world wars. Blue was the school colour but she was packed off with a trunk full of red jumpers. Her parents were obviously not bothered with such details – Nubian pyramids and foiling Hitler were far more pressing concerns. For a child desperate not to stand out this must have been mortifying.

It makes me think that when, back then, they said kids should be 'seen but not heard', what the affluent and entitled *really* meant was that kids should be neither seen nor heard *for months on end*. Otherwise, they just got in the way of the adults' pursuits.

My first school, Falkner House, was notable mostly for the number of girls. And that we had to wear red jumpers. Of far greater interest, though, were the weeks spent with my grandparents. It is telling that holidays and fun occupy more of my amygdala than any school learning.

7

Vivienne and Boy lived in an Elizabethan farmhouse in the green folds of the Sussex countryside. The house was built in the late 1500s using carved timbers from wrecked Spanish Armada galleons which had been dragged back with horse and cart from the beaches by some enterprising farmer. A huge, ornately carved taffrail of Spanish design spanned the sitting room – a central beam of the house.

My bedroom's roof was fashioned from the timber ribs of a longboat and the leaded windows still held the original glass, complete with a scratchy message etched into one panel with a diamond by a bored girl trapped there with illness around 1655 . . . I'm thinking she was probably escaping the London plague. This may or may not be true but it's my theory and I'm sticking to it.

The farmhouse's front door had been designed by some Hobbit-sized architect, the front wall was covered in pink climbing roses, and three old stone cannon balls were piled by the redbrick path that led to the house. The entrance was framed by two deep herbaceous borders in which ranks of flowers and shrubs were sorted in order of ascending height. Tall plumes of clary sage and delphiniums in lilac, pink and white at the back, graduating down to lilies, Japanese anemone, penstemon and lupins, then the astilbes and the lobelias of the border. It was like someone had tipped out a seventy-six tin of Caran d'Ache pencils onto green velvet.

In spite of this picturesque approach, you always entered the house by the split stable door around the back. Here you were straight into the bright yellow kitchen that was cosy from the Aga in winter, and unbearably hot because of it in summer. I loved this room the best. The low kitchen table for three laid with the same threadbare napery I still use. The seemingly constant sound of the ancient whirring Kenwood CHEF. A wooden trug of home-grown vegetables – zucchini, asparagus, green beans, furry-lined pods of broad beans, almost always hothouse tomatoes – with the small bone-handled but wide-bladed paring knife that had severed their connection with the rich soil resting next to them.

Everywhere you looked was a still from a wanky 'rustic' interiors' magazine.

In the summer, when we weren't carting chairs, thermoses, milk, windbreaks and sandwiches to the beach in search of a patch of sand among the pebbles (and then I would probably have a gnashing tantrum about ice cream), I'd spend time with my grandfather in the kitchen garden with that trug. I'd cut the lettuces for lunch or venture into the sweltering greenhouse with its intoxicating smell of tomato leaf to pick the heavy red fruit. This greenhouse had central heating from a paraffin heater, meaning the tomatoes had more luxury than me in that house with no heating other than the open fires and the Aga.

Those tomatoes were best sliced thick with salt and too much pepper. You'd then layer them with acidic salad cream between heaving, buttered slabs of soft white bread. It's a weakness I still have to this day. The tomatoes are probably my second food memory. They're certainly a far more suitable first memory for a foodie than the branded merch nougat bar that I've hidden away out of embarrassment in a later chapter. Tomatoes are a perfect early food memory as it is a well-known fact that if you can't say that you first learnt to cook clasping your grandmother's or grandfather's apron, you really don't have the required clichéd beginnings of most chefs or cooks.

The knife I used to cut the lettuces had mythical properties and was sharpened on a mysterious slab of stone by the front door. It looked like a body-sized Iron Age altar where brutal sacrifices had once been made. At least this was the tale the locals told. The particular type of stone wasn't known in this part of the country – or anywhere else for that matter – so it must have been dragged there from afar. This helped confirm the altar theory. It was incredibly heavy for its size and took six brick columns to hold it up. Its most intriguing feature was a strange niche carved near one corner. Clearly, this was where blood from a sacrifice would drain.

The land that was originally attached to my grandparents' farmhouse was still being worked and the main barns were only a short walk from the back door and the kitchen garden.

Here Mr Ticehurst the farmer kept his prize bull Ferdie, a huge, placid black beast with a silver ring through his nose. As a little tacker I loved Ferdie with a passion.

But then one night my grandfather told me that the soup I was so enjoying for dinner was oxtail. This saw me have one of my more notable paddies, refusing to eat any more – or let anyone else eat any more – until we'd tramped down to Ferdie's stall to ensure that his tail was still intact. It wasn't . . .

. . . it wasn't damaged at all.

(See what I did there?)

In winter, besides soup, there was wood to chop and huge fires in the inglenook fireplace to warm against drafts so furious that the heavy velvet curtains over the doors would billow. That's the problem with old houses; nothing ever seems to fit together properly. Windows rattle (and sometimes leak) when there's driving rain, and doors creak and groan like the undead.

The Aga stove needed to be fed constantly as it heated the bath water as well as the kitchen. Sure, it also cooked the dinner, but best was the prospect on a frosty morning of getting up to warmed clean underdaks hung on the steel bar that ran across the front of the Aga. It was as delicious as a double malt choc-olate milkshake with extra sprinkles.

There was a downside though. All this combustion meant that someone had to drag buckets of cinders up to the kitchen garden to pour onto the paths, and drag coke back down to re-feed the Aga. Then there were the fires to be swept and laid, with more cinders for the path. I was a regular little Cinderfella when I stayed there.

My grandparents did eventually get an electric hot water heater and this meant that the Aga could be turned off over summer. Unfortunately, my grandfather found a contraption known as a Baby Belling to replace it. Grandmother Vivienne hated the little electric twin hot plate with the same sort of rancour many old chefs now spew at induction stoves.

For she had mastered cooking on the Aga – her famous beef and olives, braised chicken with an egg, cream and lemon sauce, and endless casseroles that gently bubbled away for hours in its warm heart when you were out. If time was short there were puffed and golden cheese frittatas or seared, shaved beef fillet tossed with garden chives and melted butter over mash from the top hot plates – yet the Baby Belling defeated her.

That meant during summer for lunch or after a show, it was toast with smoked salmon, escabeche of kippers (yeah, okay, she just called them 'marinated kippers with onions' but I have the recipe, I know what it is trying to be) or a croque monsieur. My grandfather preferred thinly scraped anchovy Patum Peperium Gentleman's Relish on his slices of white toast and used these moments to jokingly lament how meagre the meal was and how maybe he should break out the Baby Belling. Vivienne always rose to the bait and her response would drip with sarcasm. She called using it 'camping'. He'd think this all hilarious – the whole reason for the barb.

Avoidance of the dreaded Baby Belling meant my grandmother developed many cunning ways with no-cook fish mousses and pâtés. Flicking through her collection of handwritten recipes, how does a cod's roe pâté take your fancy? I was a bit of a fan of this on the summer roster. It was made with a quarter of a pound of cod's roe, a slice of crumbled bread, a clove of garlic, anchovy essence and the juice of half a lemon. You liquified the roe with the oil first and then added everything else. Looking back it makes me wonder whether the English actually invented taramasalata. After all, with such vast quantities of cod in their fish and chip shops there must have been an awful lot of leftover roe.

My grandmother also made a sardine mousse where rinsed tinned sardines were mixed with breadcrumbs, olives, pimentos, diced onion and hard-boiled eggs. This concoction was then 'moistened with mayonnaise' and set in a mould. Yum – not. Then there was the tuna fish pâté made by beating tinned tuna with an equal amount of butter, before adding chives, lemon and a little mayo for texture. Or, and we're ascending the staircase of the truly unacceptable here, a caviar pâté made by mixing cream cheese, lemon juice and tabasco then folding in a large jar of Danish lumpfish roe. The recipe says this was then supposed to sit in the fridge for two days. Undoubtedly because no one was brave enough to eat it.

I bet you're astonished none of these iconic recipes made it into any of my eight cookbooks. I'm just not that cruel. If I were, I'd be misleading you to 'must try' my grandmother's 'Curry Cream' where a tin of consommé was whisked with a block of cream cheese and a level teaspoon of curry powder . . .

She did however make a fine anchovy mousse which required no fish at all. You just pounded five hard-boiled eggs with two tablespoons of anchovy essence until it was as smooth as possible. You then blended in half a pint of whipped cream, stirred in some rehydrated aspic liquid and left it to set in a glass bowl for twenty-four hours. I'm interested to note here that this dish is remarkably close to one of those Escoffier recipes from the time back before emulsifying oil with raw egg yolks was a thing. I also remember this being, surprisingly, rather good. Her Patum Peperium–loving husband certainly approved.

When we weren't in the garden over summer we'd be in one of two other places – the local cinema because it was raining, or down at the beach because it wasn't. I am still grateful for those days. I'm also grateful for the times when my grandfather took over the breakfast duties for he was particular about his scrambled eggs and claimed in his matter-of-fact manner that his recipe was from President Kennedy. No cream, no butter, just a splash of water and a lot of time. I still make my eggs this way, scrambled very slowly, the softness of the curds against the crisp bite of the thin white, buttered toast the perfect contrast.

Grandmother Vivienne liked a leisurely start and so my grandfather would make her a breakfast tray of a pot of tea and marmalade toast while she read and planned. This was during the 'second phase' of their marriage. She didn't go shopping for groceries like my mother did back in town but would recline in bed in her salmon pink matinee jacket phoning in her weekly orders to the butcher, baker and candlestick maker.

That was almost as impressive as my grandmother Joan's Teasmade. What's that, you ask? Read on and all shall be revealed.

8

Grandmother Joan didn't have a devoted husband to bring her breakfast in bed each morning. Instead, she had her Teasmade. The Teasmade was genius from a future world to rival hoverboards and TV watches. Here was an alarm clock that boiled water and siphoned it into a teapot so you could wake with a ringing alarm and a steaming hot cuppa. Extraordinary!

While these clocks that made tea had been around since the end of the nineteenth century, the 1960s version that was powered by electricity rather than methylated spirits or gas was infinitely safer. I am sure this is where my obsession with strong, overly brewed tea comes from – compounded by time spent with the builders who converted my parents' first house from tenement apartments into a family home.

Holidays at Grandmother Joan's were rather different affairs to holidays at Grandmother Vivienne's. My mother's mother lived in Bell Meadow, a bright pink 1950s bungalow in Fittleworth. She loved amateur dramatics, enjoyed studying the form of the ponies, and worked as a nurse at the local point-to-point amateur country races and polo matches at Cowdray

Park, where the doors and windows of all the cottages in the town owned by the estate were painted mustard yellow.

She had a big black dog (Barty) and a big black cat (Simpkin), neither of whom seemed much interested in chasing the hordes of mice that came in from the woods and fields to launch a constant assault on the pantry. When you were offered chocolate mousse for dinner you always had to make sure the word was spelt with two 's'.

The assaults on the pantry at least allowed us to clean out those foodstuffs well past their use-by dates, sometimes by as much as a couple of years. My grandmother came from a wartime generation where nothing went to waste: you scraped the mould off the top of your homemade bramble jelly for your crumpets, trimmed the green and white fur off your cheese, and just got on with it.

Later Barty the dog became her defining signifier. In a life with two grandmothers, each had to have a nickname. Joan would be forever Barty Granny. A large black schnauzer, Barty would die of bum cancer, which seemed a particularly undignified way for a dog to go.

Summers with Grandmother Joan were far more sociable than those with Grandmother Vivienne. There always seemed to be a knot of kids around Fittleworth or Watersfield to go netting sticklebacks with, or to scour the hedgerows for blackberries among the brambles, returning home with mouths stained purple and fingers a mass of pricks and shallow scratches.

The food at Grandmother Joan's, however, was shall we say rudimentary. Whereas Grandmother Vivienne was all about thin toast spread with the anchovy bite of Gentleman's Relish and those strips of seared eye fillet with butter and chive mashed potatoes . . . at Bell Meadow it was mainly sausages and mash, or sandwiches made with a strange acidic gherkin relish called Sandwich Spread.

Dessert was seldom more than old buttered bread baked with sultanas and custard, chocolate or lemon mousse, baked rice pudding, or semolina, but then if you've never come in from the rain to a bowl of steaming, creamy semolina with a dollop of homemade plum jam then you haven't really lived.

That plum jam, incidentally, came from the fruit of the Victoria plum trees that lined Grandmother Joan's potted, puddled drive and flourished in the run-off from the septic tank. Still to this day my sister Katie will pick a few kilos each year to make the jam just as our mother did, and her mother did before her.

Of course, the other big difference at the pink bungalow Bell Meadow was that the pictures of the grandson – aka me – remained on display even when I wasn't there. Grandmother Vivienne constantly juggled swapping the photos of me with photos of her other grandchildren; it was only in her wallet where my photo stayed put.

Looking back on this I see it as more of an act of consideration rather than shame. Certainly, I was a little intrigued when I arrived one weekend to find photos of a strange man, his pretty blonde wife and their two children where the photos of me usually stood.

9

Chelsea Football Club is my team. It had to be, their ground was just an Ian Hutchinson–long throw away from that basement flat in Fernshaw Road that Mum and I grew up in. For those – unimaginably – who don't know who I'm talking about, Ian Hutchinson was a legendary Chelsea striker from the 1970s. He wore the number 10 shirt and had the most magnificent sideburns that curled under his jaw. Anyway, our street would be completely parked out every other Saturday, and you could tell how well the team was going by the muffled cheers and groans of 61,000 fans up the road.

That was back in the days when fans lived in the same part of the city, or at least the same city, as the club they barracked for. When Chelsea made the FA Cup Final in 1967, the houses in the area were festooned with blue and white streamers, the windows plastered with posters of Pensioner heroes like Tommy Baldwin and Bobby Tambling. Yes, Chelsea's original nickname, the Pensioners, is one of the least flattering out there. Slaidburn Street, a cul-de-sac around the corner, was tighter, the houses meaner and people reportedly far rougher, so they excelled at this parochial show of local pride, painting all their kerbstones in this dead-end street alternating blue and white, and festooning the street with matching bunting.

However, my first experience of the great game occurred the year before, when England miraculously won the World Cup. It was vindication for the country that had created the game that they could actually play it – something that had been in doubt in the previous decades. The history books celebrate the kings of that 1966 team, names like Hurst, Charlton and Moore, with Nobby Stiles the cavorting toothless jester, but for me 1966 was instead all about England's World Cup mascot, a lion with a Beatles mop top known as World Cup Willie.

Willie was the first ever World Cup mascot and set the tone both for future tournaments and other football clubs' mascots. After the win his image could be seen on everything from tea towels to kid's tracksuits – one of the first examples of cartoon-branded sports marketing. But World Cup Willie wasn't just found on posters, clothes and the black-and-white telly. No, he was also . . . a delicious nougat bar. How magical is that.

I became Gollum-like obsessed with those bars. I fantasised about the joy and satisfaction of ownership, the weight in my hand and the sweet smell of imminent pleasure that would gambol about my nostrils like fluffy newborn lambs made of spun sugar. But first, I would slowly peel away the waxed paper and spend a long, loving time just contemplating the naked nougat lion underneath . . . before taking the first tentative bite. Gratification both delayed and then prolonged.

World Cup Willie nougat bars can't have been cheap because I had to save up several weeks' pocket money to afford one. But when that marvellous Saturday morning finally came around, I dashed out the door, down the street, past the brewery, over the busy main road that ran from the north down to the river without getting knocked over (and you know by now my challenge crossing roads when there was something sweet beckoning me recklessly onwards) and up the three curved steps of the paper and sweet shop on the corner of Slaidburn Street and the King's Road.

I clearly remember standing on the top step outside after my long-awaited purchase, gazing at my World Cup Willie. I might have held it up to the June sun like a Saxon warrior raising his sword and saluting a famous victory – the sun catching the pale paper and the lure of the lurid cartoon lion . . .

This was for all of thirty milliseconds before I ripped off the paper and took a huge bite. No ceremony, no contemplation, just the sort of headlong tumble into pleasure that has become so much a part of my life.

Was it good? It was cloyingly sweet and suck-the-fillings-from-your-teeth chewy, but it was also the first of many examples when the marketed expectation is actually far sweeter than the event itself. Even the memory still makes my teeth ache.

10

There is no doubt that as a kid in the 1960s we had the best escapist television. Not just *Batman* and *Thunderbirds*, *Captain Scarlet* and the slightly annoying adopted boy spy *Joe 90*, but *Do Not Adjust Your Set*, *The Avengers* and, of course, *Doctor Who*. These last three series, all of which were British, had a huge influence on me for very, very different reasons.

I was equal parts obsessed and terrified by *Doctor Who*. The hairs on the back of my neck still stir when the first synth bars of that theme in E minor written by Queensland's Ron Grainer begin playing. As a kid, the music would start, the Tardis would pulse into view and I'd play it cool at first, but pretty soon I'd be behind the sofa, the big chair, the cat; whatever I could get between me and the screen.

When I look back at the two doctors from my pre-teen era, I can see more than a little inspiration for my later onscreen style – from the frock coat and checked pants of the second doctor played by Patrick Troughton to the flamboyance of the third doctor played by Jon Pertwee. Thanks to Jon Pertwee, I developed a slightly unnatural obsession with velvet. Even, later, red velvet. Pertwee, however, got about in rich jackets of burgundy, indigo and sage. It's a style I love to this day for its opulence and warm and decadent touch, whether you stroke with, or against, the pile. I was bought my first velvet suit when I was twelve to wear to dances. It was chocolate brown. I'd team it with a matching chocolate shirt and ridiculously fat cream tie. Understated I was not – even back then.

You may never have heard of *Do Not Adjust Your Set* but in 1967 it was about the funniest thing ever. Terry Jones, Eric Idle and Michael Palin were among its early creators, bringing their uniquely absurd, stupid and random brand of satire they would later go on to develop with such success with Monty Python. *Do Not Adjust Your Set* hit directly at a kid's funny bone and was the first show I ever fell off the sofa laughing to. Sadly, they only made two series.

My mum didn't understand it at all. I didn't understand it but I loved it with the sort of devotion I was unable to show early girlfriends. It was the show you rushed home from school to be ready to watch. And still it eclipses other great TV of my youth like wholesome *Blue Peter*, the pantomime humour of *Crackerjack* and even the similarly warped *Michael Bentine's Potty Time*.

The presence of David Jason (who went on to be Del Boy in *Only Fools and Horses* and Inspector Jack Frost) in *Do Not Adjust Your Set*, often playing the sort of underdog that my first comedy love Norman Wisdom had made famous, added an extra dimension. While Wisdom's antics now bore me, old episodes of *Do Not Adjust Your Set* still hold up well, especially Jason's lugubrious face and the Terry Gilliam animations that appeared in later episodes.

It's strange but writing this chapter I have a Pavlovian reaction. I find myself desperate for a crumpet. These TV shows were invariably on around teatime and therefore accompanied by butter-soaked crumpets with Marmite, or perhaps just a sprinkling of salt.

Another of the great TV shows of the era, *The Avengers*, was popular mainly because of the debonair male lead John Steed, but I watched it for his female co-stars. These were strong, clever women who could also kick arse. I slept with a signed photo of the first of these heroines, Cathy Gale (played by Honor Blackman), under my pillow for about six months. I even named our first cat, a beautiful, loving and silent Siamese, after Gale's successor Emma Peel (Diana Rigg). When we kept one of her kittens it logically became Tara, after Mrs Peel's replacement played by Toronto's Linda Thorson.

Now the wiser of you might suggest I had a thing for leather catsuits. I'd deny the infatuation but probably look away so you couldn't see the lie dying in my eyes. It clearly ran in the family as five years later my little brother William had such a thing for Joanna Lumley's character in the rebooted *New Avengers* that we had to call our new Siamese Purdey.

While Honor Blackman played Pussy Galore in the third Connery Bond movie, *Goldfinger*, she stayed under my pillow for her role in *The Avengers*. The clarity of this memory might also explain why my eldest son started sleeping with a Nigella Lawson biography under his pillow. Smart, sassy and always in control, Nigella could easily have made it as a modern culinary Emma Peel.

11

As a kid I was far too self-absorbed to ask about my parents' childhoods – or perhaps just too busy watching *The Avengers* or heading off to Chelsea FC matches. It's only now that my sisters, Katie and Eleanor, and I are able to piece together a snapshot of what they went through – and sadly the picture that emerges is far uglier than anything we ever experienced.

My mother Jennifer – an inconvenient only child – was packed off to a convent boarding school around the age of five or six before the war with the suitcase full of red clothes. One school holidays she was sent to stay with her journalist and book-reviewing aunt, Betty, who lived with her companion/ girlfriend in an apartment on the Rue Bonaparte on Paris's Left Bank. Aunt Betty and her friend hosted a sort of artistic expat salon of intellectuals; 'mostly single men or single women' was the polite description at the time. It may sound glamorous, but for a young English girl missing her parents it was probably quite boring and lonely. As Jennifer would later tell my sister Katie, 'I didn't like my aunt. We had nothing in common.'

Her days were spent at the Tuileries or the Luxembourg Gardens with a nanny. Which sounds pleasant enough, but evidently it wasn't. Even harmless diversions like the gift of a kitten went awry. When young Jennifer commanded the kitten to 'clean her room' and it just sat there miaowing, Jennifer lost her temper and dropped it out of the window of the fourth-floor apartment. Luckily it landed on a wide ledge a few feet below, though no one is sure if my mother knew it was there or not. The kitten was quickly rescued and removed. Katie always cleaned her room when she was told to after hearing that story.

In spite of them having little in common, I suspect Aunt Betty did her best. She taught my mother to cook, which was something, given the lack of parenting back home. During term time, Jennifer's father Larry would show up at the boarding school at weekends to take her out with his latest girlfriend in tow – even though he was still married to Joan. This would have scandalised the nuns, but Jennifer seemed to take it in her stride. Always the pragmatist, she quite enjoyed the outings as they'd invariably go shopping and she'd be bought a new dress.

As I've mentioned, Larry was undoubtedly cool, but I imagine he also sounds like one more uninvolved dud dad. That's what I always thought growing up, but after my mother's death I found a sheaf of correspondence between them that shed far more light on the complexity of their relationship. There was some warmth and humour there too. Larry's sister, Anne, played an important parental role. Aunt Anne was a society beauty who had gone to the Slade School of Art. She was tall, blonde and willowy, yet she described herself as a 'big galloping giraffe'. In 1951 she presented Jennifer as a debutante at court because, as a divorcée, Grandmother Joan was not allowed to. It must have meant a lot to Jennifer, as she kept the white ostrich-feather fan she carried that season and the professional photos of her that ran in *Tatler* magazine. Perhaps she felt her life was suddenly coming into sunny focus as she danced with a succession of eligible young aristocrats – that this was a golden moment of hope.

Aunt Anne would become like an extra grandmother to my siblings and me, taking us to see expensive theatre and panto-mimes each Christmas. My sister Eleanor remembers sitting in the best seats to see Yul Brynner and Virginia McKenna at the Palladium in *The King and I*. Anne was kind, lived happily with her husband Jocelyn a few villages from her ex-sister-in-law (Grandmother Joan) in West Sussex and was always beautifully turned out – even into her nineties when she was almost blind. She also had a wicked sense of humour, especially where her brother was concerned.

If my mother's upbringing taught her to make the best of a bad situation, her patrician roots had also instilled in her that manners were vitally important. One of the nicer tales she told about me is how I turned up to the first day at prep school, coolly walked over to the headmistress, stuck out my hand and formally introduced myself. Undoubtedly I was compensating for something . . . like that glass of wee or the fact that she might have heard that I would bite elderly people if I wasn't offered ice cream.

Like Jennifer's father Larry, both of my stepfather Antony's parents were Irish-born. And compared to Jennifer's patchy childhood, he was even less lucky. His parents weren't married and as a toddler he found himself swept up in a British government migration program known as 'Home Children' with other orphaned and fostered kids. It was a pernicious scheme that caused incalculable damage to generations.

The scheme had been running since the late 1800s and was phased out in the 1970s, but in the early twentieth-century, the number of kids sent to the colonies was staggering. After the First World War, Canadian farms were crying out for more labour, while newer countries like Australia and Rhodesia were keen for more white migration. Some 100,000 unwanted kids were sent to Canada alone, and between 1947 and 1967 around 10,000 to 20,000 children were sent to Australia, emptying British orphanages. They wound up at 'homes' or the various Christian Brothers missions and were set to building roads and scraping bricks. They were also often beaten or sexually abused. In essence, out of sight out of mind on the other side of the world.

Shipped off to South Africa around the age of three, Antony was settled with a dour Boer foster family outside Pretoria. His life there was close to slavery. His foster mother was possessive without ever being loving while his foster dad was weak. Letters from his birth mother were burnt. He was told she was dead. Back in the UK, no one could, or would, tell his real mother what had happened to the son she had given up. She had no idea he was not even in the UK.

A second foster family, far later in Antony's childhood, was more generous and enrolled him at King Edward VII School in Johannesburg. He then went to the University of Witwatersrand only to be asked to leave the country after a number of what he called 'pranks' but the authorities might have called 'acts of insurrection'. These included some shadowy form of involvement in blowing up the huge model of the bridge over the River Kwai that had been built in front of South Africa's most glamorous movie house for the film's launch.

After university, Antony returned to London thinking his mother was dead and not knowing his father. He didn't have much: a working knowledge of Afrikaans, a short career as a rally car navigator and a handful of childhood stories including one about a little green snake that he kept in his school locker and played with daily. It was only after it escaped that he discovered it was a deadly eastern green mamba.

One day, while sitting on a bench outside Earl's Court tube station, Antony was sure he saw his mother walking towards him. It was the sort of mystic Irish moment that W. B. Yeats and Lorna Byrne romanticise.

Yet incredibly, at a restaurant just a year later, he was approached by a man who turned out to be his godfather. The man had recognised Antony because of his striking likeness to his father, who had died in the Second World War. 'I knew your mother,' the man told him. 'I think she's alive.'

Antony's mother, later to be known to us kids as 'Granny Greenstamp' because of her generosity, grew up in a patrician Cork family with Fianna Fáil (the Irish Republican Party) leanings. She'd been the face of Pond's Cold Cream ads, a keen skier and studied at Trinity College in Dublin. She counted Brendan Behan among her friends, and had her own pioneering advertising agency.

Her unplanned pregnancy was so scandalous that she had to move to Salford near Manchester to have her son . . . When she and Antony's father went to register the birth – normally in these situations the man would cut and run, so his presence is unusual – he demanded that the registrar put down his name on the birth certificate or else he'd 'punch his lights out'.

Such unusual loyalty from a 'man of good family' who had much to lose is perhaps more understandable when I heard a rumour that he had in fact offered to 'do the right thing' by Granny Greenstamp – but she'd turned him down. Why she did this is open to conjecture. When my sister Eleanor asked Antony whether he bore any ill will towards his mum for abandoning him, he said he didn't, dismissing it as typical behaviour of this posh Irish set.

Antony started out working in insurance but ended up a journalist writing about his great love: warships. More of this shortly. He met his other great love, my mother Jennifer, at a party at his best friend Rupert's. She was lodging with a relative around the corner. Rupert's wife Anthea remembers that the chemistry between them was instant. Indeed, a photo of the occasion reveals the palpable sexual tension. She's laughing. He's looking wolfish and leaning forward. It's slightly uncomfortable to think about.

Soon they would marry because, as my sister often suggests, Jennifer was a Catholic and she wanted a family. Looking at the emotion in that photo, however, there was clearly more to it than religious obligation . . .

12

From memory, Jennifer and Antony's wedding was long, I wore a kilt, and the reception was held at Sir Thomas More's old house, where I spent most of the time navigating the adults' legs in pursuit of the canapes. It was also at this time that I was 'signed over' and my name legally changed to Preston.

I wasn't at all shocked at Antony's arrival. My mother seemed happy. I'd love to say that I resented him stealing her away or having to share her – or that I was excited to have a new name like a secret agent acquiring a new identity – but none of this registered. Either I was a very cruisy child or I repressed my feelings . . . or, and I fear this is actually the case, I was more likely to throw a temper tantrum over not getting my way in a game of Risk (as all good proto dictators do), or not getting an ice cream, than over anything more important.

The marriage meant that I did get to spend more time with my grandparents and they put a lot more effort into entertaining me during the holidays than my single mother ever did – and I really did like ice creams, and the movies, and being

out in the country when my mother and step-dad went away
for their honeymoon to Portugal.

The best thing to come back from the trip was a new family
cure for sunburn. Antony had milky patrician Irish skin which,
unprotected, quickly poached to an angry red. An old lady at the
pousada they were staying in suggested laying fat slabs of beef
tomato on the burnt flesh. This miraculously not only relieves the
heat and the burning sting of the sunburn but those raw tomato
slices also cook to an alluring softness perfect for spreading on
toast with a little salt. If you are so inclined. Yes, me neither.

Antony did make an effort with me but this invariably
meant me trailing along on assignments with him when he
moved from working at the National Maritime Museum in
Greenwich to becoming a naval journalist. I didn't resent this as
being allowed to scramble around an active US warship docked
opposite the Tower of London while your step-father was
being shown about by the captain was fun – especially when
the young officer charged with my care took me into the gun
turrets and introduced me to the mess room team, who had an
unfathomable amount of ice cream in their freezers.

There were trips to docks and to submarines, and while the
torpedo tubes and periscope in the conning tower were of great
interest to a pre-teenager growing up in a country still quietly
congratulating itself on winning a world war, an even more
thrilling pattern began to emerge. I realised with glee that when
confronted by a child they'd been lumbered with, most adults
resorted to . . . ice cream. I rewarded them by being happy and
pliant with this state of affairs – and I can sense I was locking
away the value of such a bribery culture.

*

Antony showed his love for my mother by teasing her, and by his nicknames for her. I suspect he was more devoted to his job than his family. Warships were his passion as a young boy and he transformed this passion into a career – something he passed on to all his children. The problem with doing what you love is that it can become all-consuming. He would disappear into his study for days on end.

He wrote over forty books, mainly on twentieth-century sea power, as well as editing numerous naval warfare magazines and journals. It came at a cost. We seldom saw him at sporting fixtures or school plays and this must have been a little lonely for our mother. Here he provided me with a fine role model because I never wanted to be like that when I had kids. I wanted to be present and at first I was.

At least that's what I've always told myself. There have been times when I selfishly pursued my career to the detriment of my family. The defence of being a 'good provider' doesn't cut it when your partner is looking after three children under the age of nine and you are off filming in Sydney . . .

Until I moved to Australia I felt I learnt little from Antony, but now I see how much, good and bad, I've taken from him. His biggest gift was understanding that to work at what you love is ultimately more of a joy than a curse.

His other flaws were also lessons. He was terrible with money and never made any, which put pressure on Mum. (Especially the morning there was a bailiff at the door demanding tens of thousands of pounds for an unpaid tax bill.) That was me early in my marriage but something that Emma and I largely sorted out. Antony was a little too slovenly in how he dressed professionally for my liking, but this too had an effect. When I was in the army he came to an end-of-course mess dinner at Sand-hurst, but all I can remember is being mortified in this bastion of spit and polish that he had a gravy stain on his dress shirt.

Antony's childhood had been far shitter than mine, but he gave me a love of Tom Lehrer records and singing at the dinner table. I also learnt to appreciate his obsessive love of history. I soaked up a lot of knowledge from his lectures on some historical moment or other, even if many of these were conducted when I was a teenager standing at the bottom of the stairs with a bladder full of beer after a big night out. I'd shift from foot to foot on the bottom tread, the bathroom tantalis-ingly close as he'd bless me with his insights on the Boer War, towed array sonar or whatever he was still up late researching. I fear that my children will read this and now know where I get such similar tendencies.

13

The new marriage also meant another big change: a move to a new house down the New King's Road to Fulham. Back then Fulham wasn't the posh suburb full of Eastern Bloc nannies, shiny German SUVs, and men with £2000 velvet-collared over-coats that it is today. It was a rough and tumble place teeming with those Irish and Polish migrant families. Gentrification was ten years away.

The River Thames holds Fulham in the crook of its elbow, a particularly languid meander of brown sluggishness that flows from Hammersmith down past Craven Cottage (home of my mother, youngest sister and nephew's favourite football team, Fulham FC) to Putney, where the river then bends in towards Chelsea. To take a ride over to the river at its closest point to us was to risk encountering all manner of street gangs who lurked in the shadows under the asbestos-leaching power station and rusting gasometers. It was an exercise in peer-pressured bravado to make it over there on our bikes. The only reward was the adrenaline rush of making it back intact.

Thankfully, the pocket in which our new home sat, between Parsons Green and the Eel Brook Common, was much safer. There were even three strips of green between us and the main road. One of these would be locked and full of daffodils and crocuses come spring, but another was the perfect shape and length for a fenced and impromptu neighbourhood soccer pitch.

Parsons Green would soon become a byword for yuppiedom but back then this triangle of grass and plane trees was anchored on each side by a dodgy pub. The Farmers Arms was the small, old man's watering hole, with an upright piano, frequented by low-level crooks and gangsters. The White Horse was a brick's throw away and full of slashed leather banquets and a faded picture of the 1965 Chelsea football team behind the bar. It would later become the clubhouse of young 'Trustafarians' and be colloquially renamed The Sloaney Pony. The Duke of Cumberland was the only place my parents might go which is somewhat weird because we all thought it was named after one of the prime suspects in the Jack the Ripper murders. Obviously at a young age this meant little to me but it would become of incredible importance down the track.

We later learnt it was in fact Queen Victoria's grandson and second in line to the British throne, Eddy, the Duke of Clarence, who was the suspect (even though he was in Scotland for three of the murders and was probably targeted out of homophobia). All the Duke of Cumberland did (that was Eddy's great uncle) was allegedly slit the throat of his valet in a fit of jealous rage. So, nothing really. (There should probably be a quizzical or bemused emoji here for clarity.) Still, it was pretty odd to go to a pub named after him.

*

At the far side of the Common at the other end of our street, there was a playground and a paddling pool, but to reach them was to venture into the bottleneck territory of the kids who lived in the exhaust-grimed tenements along the Wandsworth Bridge Road. They were trouble and seldom came in groups smaller than four. Yet it was worth braving them for the ancient sweetshop on the edge of the Common that juddered slightly when the Tube trains in the tunnel rattled beneath it. Even though it was en route to the Tube station, this corner store was far enough away from home to bring pilfered small change to spend on sherbet fountains, Wizz Fizz flying saucers and small white paper bags of pear drops, without fear of any questions being asked or stories being told. I should note that I have had to curb such thieving tendencies.

Those Wandsworth Bridge Road gangs only really became a worry once I started to take myself to school in a sweet blue cap and a natty matching blazer. I might as well have had a bullseye painted on my back. Going to school in the morning, short-panted with chubby thighs chapped and stinging from the bitter winter cold wasn't the worry. It was coming home when those thugs would hang on the stoops, all snot-nosed, grubby and threatening. The heavy black briefcase I carried became part weapon, part shield. At least until I had the life-changing realisation that I could take the Tube *one more stop* to Parsons Green and avoid them altogether. Genius! I fear that this cowardice (that I now – and then – dress up as pragmatism) is still very much part of who I am today. When in doubt, flee!

*

The tall, terraced house of three flats that my parents bought cost a princely £9500. Once converted, there would be space for five bedrooms, a study and a playroom. It all seemed a little excessive for just the three of us . . .

I should have seen the gathering storm clouds these extra and unnecessary bedrooms represented. My comfortable little life of being the centre of attention was about to change. First came the burping, farting, spewing apparition of my brother William. And then, soon after, two sisters – first Katie, then Eleanor – who were far less fun due to a distinct lack of explosive, end-of-the-pier bodily functions.

Growing up in Fulham was full of joys. Number one was having a Shell bakery at the end of the street. It became my job to grab a shilling from my mother's purse (plus possibly an extra one for the sweetshop later) and to amble down the street to buy the bread for tea. On a good day it would still be hot from the ovens. I'd run home, the brown paper bag held snugly, the homeliest of aromas wafting up every time I shifted it to redistribute its heat searing my arm. The expectation that the smell of hot bread prompts is something really quite special. Sometimes, it would all get too much for me and I'd need to pause outside number 37 to burrow through the golden crust and pluck at the hot cotton wool within. Torn, ragged and steaming like an open wound on a winter battlefield, it would make my mouth water – a transgression that wouldn't be ignored when I got home, but then I've rarely been one for delayed gratification no matter what the cost.

There is only one thing better than hot bread straight from the oven. And that's hot bread straight from the oven layered with cold butter and peanut butter! I would later graduate to adding salt and pepper, or apricot or raspberry jam, but I still love the purity of the 'original recipe'. Freshly baked bread and butter is also my nemesis in terms of recreating myself with the body of Channing Tatum. Well, that and a distinct lack of willpower and commitment.

It's better now but back then I had such a thing for peanut butter that when friends of the family came over from Holland or the school exchange students arrived from the US (two of the world's great peanut butter locations), they'd bring large jars of caramel-smooth Skippy or oilier Calvé Pindakaas, and I would love them forever. The only time I baulked was when somebody arrived with a huge jar of Smucker's Goober Grape. If you've never heard of this high-fat, high-sugar American spread, then consider yourself fortunate. Picture peanut butter rippled with thick seams of very-unlikely purple grape jelly. Got it? There's something about that Concord grape flavour that is still as off-puttingly fake as the colour, or even the original grapes.

But back to the wonderfully, steamy, airy white bread . . .

It was around 1967 that I first turned my back on sausage or bacon sandwiches with ketchup. This was all thanks to the mighty fish finger. The fish finger was a comparatively new thing. Apparently based on the US Gorton's Fish Sticks that were about in the early 1950s, the American food giant Birds Eye came along and launched the frozen fish finger at their sales conference in Brighton in 1955.

Now while these crumbed batons of cod and other white fish are quite acceptable grilled or baked with mash and peas, frying them and then placing them sizzling between slices of well-buttered white bread with a little lemon juice and salt takes things to an entirely new level. Later I would add mayonnaise after trips to Grandmother Joan's house (who as we know couldn't really cook but slathered bottled mayo on everything, so much so we reckoned she must have shares in Hellmann's). Later still I would simplify the recipe by cooking the fish fingers standing up on end in the toaster. No washing up, but the next couple of slices of marmalade toast would have a slightly fishy taste – but as they were unlikely to be mine, it was still a win.

Now, I won't say I invented the fish finger sandwich – that some might see as an overreach without evidence. But I look forward to hearing from you with proof of anyone else who made one before me. . . and don't try to pull the wool over my eyes by claiming it arrived with the Japanese Meiji Restoration and the katsu sando – the fish finger didn't exist back then even if crumbed pork fillet did.

I should note that as Antony was partial to Worcestershire sauce on his apricot jam toast and also championed the sausage and orange marmalade sandwich, the fish finger sando was never going to attract even a sideways glance in our house.

When you are a kid, danger – both real and imagined – is everywhere.

Before the Wandsworth Bridge Road tenement gangs became a problem (or when I later realised that out of uniform I was incognito, just another snot-nose in cheap frayed-hemmed Millets jeans) the playground on that side of the Common was truly a place of wonder. As a youngster of six or so moving into the area, the see-saw, the witch's hat, the swings and the round-about . . . were exhilaration all.

Constant was the prospect of doing yourself some really serious damage. Misusing the play equipment was a fine way of hastening the loss of baby teeth or grazing knees and elbows . . . for the pleasure of a few weeks of excellent scab-picking. Most adults fail to understand the fascination that scabs can hold to a curious pre-teen who has no grasp of the meaning of the word 'disgusting' (more on which later).

There was a skill in being able to bounce sitting on the see-saw so it jolted so brutally that it would see bitten tongues and bruised jaws, and there was even greater pleasure in cata-pulting the little kid off the other end. The best technique would involve putting mates on either end and then seeing who could stay on the longest . . . if you were small, and the last on, your angle of exit could be quite dramatic. You'd positively sail through the air.

Occasionally we heard horrific urban myths about the kid who lost his fingers in the crushing apex of the witch's hat. This contraption looked like a huge shuttlecock frame inverted on a 20-foot pole. It would spin around the apex in a range of ellipses that meant the base could flash inches above the tarmac or spin 3 feet in the air: the perfect height to brain an average six-year-old. Heightening the thrill was how you could throw your bodyweight inwards or outwards as it spun, causing the edges to oscillate wildly between this high and low. It was the first true white-knuckle ride as you had to hang on for dear life. It was safer the higher up you climbed, and the speed was calming, but that meant reaching up towards the grinding metal on metal of the cap of the hat that crushed its way around the top of the pole. That evil hat threatened to catch and crush any rashly stray pinky.

My favourite playground attraction, however, was the skeleton roundabout. This was a flat disc segmented by metal hurdles as handles that spoked out from the centre. There was also a wooden-panelled 'cake' roundabout which was strictly for 'little kids'. That flat dish, however, could be propelled up to the sort of rpm that saw the trees and back garden walls with their glinting icing of embedded broken glass turn to a watery blur. When the speed was deemed fast enough we'd all lie backwards, arching outwards, with our craniums skimming above the speeding concrete and the world whooshing past. Fun but the laughter really came when we hopped off and staggered drunkenly across the playground from the resulting dizziness.

Ah, the good clean fun of childhood. Well, apart from the time that kid spewed on the roundabout and splatter-painted the rest of us in acrylic yellow ochre spotted with carrot and corn. It was a bit like a Jackson Pollock.

Luckily, I never lost any fingers in that playground, nor cracked open my skull, but there was one Rosebud moment that is perhaps telling. It revolves not around revolving but comes from the textbook child's love of heading everywhere at high speed. Assuming of course that you'd class my twenty-two-second 100 metres as 'high speed'.

I had again been on the rob . . . possibly from the little black ceramic pig money box that doubled as my parents' change jar. After suspicion fell on me for my bread grift, the black pig was a far safer crime. Not only could you not see how much money was in there – or not – but its base was sealed in such a way that you couldn't open it without giving away the game. It was possible to shake the occasional coin out of the slot at the top of the pig but this took time and was as noisy as shaking a black ceramic pig full of coins could be.

Some claim cracking the Enigma code, Archimedes' moment of realisation in the bath and Alexander cutting the Gordian Knot as humankind's greatest problem-solving moments, but for me it was discovering that you could slide the blade of a bread and butter knife into the slot, tilt the pig carefully, and the coins would slide out down the blade noiselessly. Some might call this stealing, I'd just call it child tax on unwanted pocket change.

The more puritan of you might suggest that my biggest playground injury was divine punishment for this petty pilfering. You see, there I was speeding across the asphalt in pursuit of something unimportant as kids often do. Perhaps I was just excited that I had bought either a rocket-shaped ZOOM! or a FAB icy lolly with my illicit proceeds at the old rattling sweetshop.

Anyway, I caught a toe on a tree root at pace and ploughed a long furrow in the ground with my chin and my two tombstone front teeth. It could have been way less dramatic. All I had to do was extend a hand to break my fall, but there was no way that I was losing that ice cream.

Chin and knees bloodied, I picked myself up and coolly licked the ice cream, pretending that nothing had happened in spite of the chip on one corner of those pearly whites. If that tree root was trying to show me that crime didn't pay I'd outsmarted it. The dentist wouldn't see it that way.

*

This wasn't the first time my clumsiness had turned my knees into skin crayon drawings on the tarmac but it was the first time I'd had a scab on my chin and it was a doozy. Another plus.

No one but a bored child can understand the deep joy a scabbed wound can bring. It's a thing to be contemplated, picked at and teased, with the knowledge that going too far would mean it would sting and bleed – and leave you with yet more healing to be done. For me, however, it was worth it when the scab quietly slipped away leaving breathtakingly soft, pale pink, new skin underneath.

I'd love to tell you that I saw this as a potent metaphor for rebirth and reinvention but, well, I didn't. I was more interested in thinking about how best to dispose of that scab in some disgusting way.

Over the years the more dangerous, and therefore fun, apparatus was – or should that be apparati were? – removed from that playground. I always wondered if they did find any torn knuckles and fingerbones lodged in the industrially thick grease at the apex of the witch's hat and whether later generations regretted replacing the asphalt with springy, rubberised matting that would pose no such challenges when it came to holding on to your ill-gotten ice cream.

Now, sadly, the playground is a dour prison-yard triangle of London plane trees. It's still bordered by the train lines, those jagged-topped garden walls and some public toilets, but there are no gaudily painted spinning metal rides anymore. There are seldom children either. The little ones are now on the sunny pirate ship and the clamber zone of a bright grassy corner on the other, smarter, side of the Common, far away from where the gangs used to lurk. The older kids are of course inside playing COD or making TikTok videos.

The blue concrete paddling pool attached to the playground has been planted out as well. These days it's where the road sweepers in their bright safety overalls enjoy their mid-morning cigarettes, like large, orange-bellied parrots surrounded by the dense foliage and their corralled carts. This is less of a cause for melancholy than the loss of the paddling pool, which was locally known as the 'piddling pool' because it was filled with about 60 per cent toddler piss. On a hot summer's day it was so crowded; like a big, overflowing bowl of child soup.

Playgrounds were important when we moved to our new house in Fulham because they became part of the family Sunday ritual of tramping through suburban streets, invariably with a pram with a sibling in it. The playground was the honey trap that calmed my whingeing Prince. Among the most memorable was South Park, a manicured zone of 1950s corporate recreation space complete with rose gardens, 100-year-old London plane trees, tennis courts and football pitches across its 20-feet-high-Edwardian-walled acres.

Mostly, these Sunday walks were duller than a newsreel on the postwar Bulgarian farm collectivisation campaigns in the era of Valko Chervenkov, but South Park was different. South Park had the highest playground slide in the Western world.

It was a metal Meccano Everest. The steep, rail-sided steps towered into the sky towards a small wooden box that seemed to kiss the clouds. Here, once you'd ascended, you would ease yourself to the edge of the mirror-smooth steel. You'd hesitate.

It was, after all, a long, long way up and the slide itself had nothing but physics and a thin-lipped edge to keep you from tumbling to your cranium-cracking doom on the concrete far below. There'd be an impatient line of anoraks behind you so you couldn't wait for too long. So push off. Let go. There was no climbing back down those stairs even if you could, as the jeers and sniggers of derision would be too much. So, you'd push off, let go, and feel the salesman-slick metal race.

The first time, you'd think about breaking your rapid descent with hand or foot, but wiser next time, you'd avoid the smell of burning rubber or seared palm flesh and just surrender to gravity as you hurtled to the bottom. Then it felt like you were flying, the seat of your pants barely skimming across the steep shiny slope. I swear at one point it was like you were no longer in contact with the metal at all, and that just served to heighten the heady exaltation before the rude awakening of the on-rushing concrete and the need to ground your feet to wear off all that the momentum at the bottom, where the flat end was all too short . . .

I'd like to think that the slide was about three storeys high, and that seems far-fetched until I find a black-and-white photo of my little brother William and me sitting at the bottom of the slide in matching blue anoraks and matching toothless smiles – mine lost, his yet to come. The steep slope reaches up behind us like a stairway to heaven too smooth to climb.

That photo immediately gives me an unpleasant curdling of the stomach. I'm fairly certain I'd just taken my toddler brother up to the top so we could skim down together – much to his gurgling delight and the screams of my mother no doubt. What makes it worse is that my guess that it was three storeys high is no exaggeration. It's one heck of a high slide.

14

I know that English food used to be universally reviled for its overcooked veg and bowls of grey stodge that toned so beautifully with the overcooked meat and leaden skies. But at home it really wasn't that bad. My mother was a pretty good cook but didn't have time for it if she didn't have to feed anyone else. On her own, she preferred to have some cheese, an apple and a Magnum and call that dinner, or lunch, or anything in between.

With two sisters joining my brother and me, cooking was a relentless and never-ending chore. Which was a shock because in the adverts on the telly the mums always looked so happy with their lot. The evening meal was inevitably drawn from a small roster of dishes. It wasn't bad but it was very meat and carb focused. There was inspiration that ranged south through Italy and France, but more on that later.

Looking through my mother's recipe scrapbooks, most of the ones she clipped out and deemed worth trying were for dinner parties. None of our rostered family meals are featured. Unsurprisingly, the dinner party meals have dated far worse than anything she cooked regularly for us. These were recipes for fiddly food, often with self-consciously foreign names from travelogue menus. Perhaps twice-cooked cheese soufflés with chives, or choux puffs filled with tinned crab. There was also a terribly faux tandoori chicken and a Nyonya pork gulai. Or how about an unappetisingly named salmon and dill mould set with lots of gelatine; or baked chicken breast with fresh and preserved ginger? Yum! Chicken breasts, margarine, flour and gelatine are everywhere. Things are so much better now.

She once used us as guinea pigs when she served involtini di melanzane before unleashing it on guests whose opinions mattered. It was not a success. We were blunt. The rolled eggplant was leathery and both salty *and* bitter. The mozzarella, once melted, had congealed into something artificial and plasticky. We were saving her from herself and ensuring the dish never made it onto our roster. We tried the same approach with her heinous fish pie that *was* on the roster in our Catholic, fish-Friday family, but as that was made under instruction from God we had no such luck in turning her. Not even with requests for fish-finger sandwiches.

The only dinner party dish that we did lust after was a strange whipped and chilled combination of yoghurt and cream topped with brown sugar. I think this was brûléed under a hot grill. I say 'think' because I have never found, nor been able to come up with, a recipe that did justice to my memory of crunchy, toasted sugar topping and the chill airy cloud beneath. DM me if you know of one and your name will live on with it!

The only other good thing about my parents' dinner parties was sneaking down from our bedrooms to polish off the hors d'oeuvres – the ubiquitous devils on horseback, and smoked salmon mousse if we were lucky – and siphon off most of the remains of the aperitifs as the adults retired to the dining room. The rules were simple. Never drain every glass, or else it would look obvious. Pick carefully. You learnt quickly to avoid the whisky in favour of the Cuba Libre that was slowly going flat or the nutty Oloroso sherry. It was also important to see if anyone had left their evening bag or cigarettes behind – not so we could steal something, but because the guests' unexpected return could spoil our party.

The next morning if you were lucky, and assuming you could bear the smell of stale cigar smoke, there would also be wafer-thin mints to slip out of their sheer paper envelopes.

When it came to our dinner, my mother's roster of eight or so dishes was really only let down by one – other than that fish pie – her own mother's signature watery stuffed marrow or zucchini. Grandmother Joan grew marrows so large that these were unavoidable, but if we could I'd lobby for a golden tray of tomato and cheese baked cabbage rolls instead. Damn, these were good. They were filled with a herbed mix of sausage meat, mince and breadcrumbs, which was all salty and porky against the succulence of those leaves of white drumhead cabbage that had gone to satin baked in all those juices. Oh my! This, along with her roast chicken, is the dish I yearn for most these days.

So many of Mum's dishes are still nursery favourites, like tuna mornay (made with peas and corn but never with her mother's Yankee trick of topping with packet potato crisps, sadly), bangers and mash, shepherd's pie, and grilled lamb chops, which goes some way to confirming their universal appeal.

My mother had, however, lived in both Paris and Rome. She'd studied at the Sorbonne while living with a maiden aunt and her 'female companion' (as the family rather coyly put it) and then, from what I can tell, travelled to the Eternal City solely to date Aussie artists and the occasional carabinieri. I mean, how could she resist them with their long leather boots, midnight-blue jodhpurs, that dashing red stripe and glamorous bicorne hat with ostrich feather plume. She did seem to have a thing for ostrich feathers!

This all meant there was a faux resonance with dishes such as her memorable spaghetti bolognaise, cannelloni made painstakingly with crepes not pasta tubes, and ratatouille in the summer and autumn when the nightshades were cheap and in season. She'd turn this vegie stew of eggplant, capsicum and zucchini into a meal by poaching eggs in its tomatoey juices. And always with a good sprinkling of that cheap parmesan cheese that came in a cardboard tube and smelt of vomit. In spite, it was a delicious dinner.

These transitioning years from the 1960s to the 70s were obviously still a time of creaminess marked by dishes including Eggs Florentine (eggs baked on wilted spinach under a gratinated, bubbling and browned cheese sauce) and cheap salty ham rolled around leeks or fat spears of white asparagus and then baked in more cheese bechamel. Damn, the leeks were good in this – juicy and sweet relief against all that cheese. This I believe is originally a Belgian dish that's traditionally made with endive (aka witlof), and it really sings. Joan liked it. I tried it out, making it on my last trip to Brussels. The bitterness of the endive brings a lovely edge.

Eggs Florentine, ratatouille or my mother's dreaded fish pie would usually be served for our Friday night dinner. I'm not going to dwell on the grey, ammonia-scented fish and watery mash any more than I have to.

Most of these recipes have appeared in my cookbooks over the last decade or so. One of the few that didn't was a fat, round, churlishly pink gammon steak baked with either tinned peaches or a ring of pineapple on top. I love using pineapple in marinades for pork these days and even came up with a rather fine – if I say so myself – pineapple ketchup using tinned fruit, but there is something about those rings on ham steaks that bring on a twitch. Perhaps because, in the recipe books, the space at the centre of the pineapple ring would invariably be filled with a glacé cherry so the red would set off the green of the equally naff curly parsley garnish. Monstrous! Even worse when the pub served it with chips and a fried egg. Fried egg and pineapple is a stomach-curdling concept that is even worse in reality.

The other dish that wouldn't fly today was one of my mother's finest; her chicken liver risotto. After we'd outlawed the tubular, flapping, veiny hell of her liver and onions, this became her sole liver outlet. It was more like a dry rice pilaf than one of those oozy Milanese risottos but still quite delicious. As my mother always served it at a temperature only marginally below the melting point of steel, the only way to eat it was to flatten it out to the edges of the plate with the back of your fork. You'd then slowly run your fork around the circumference to trim away the cooled outer edges first, eating your way inwards. The liver would be grey sawdusty nuggets on the journey, contrasting with the sweet, succulent rags of red capsicum. Again, more cardboard parmesan would be put to good use to disguise the liver. Recently I was back in London, eating with one of my sisters, and I watched with a mix of melancholy and awe as Katie flattened out her risotto to eat it in this weird but functional way.

I should point out that in the 1980s liver would become a thing of beauty. I loved pub chicken livers seared in a rich sauce of madeira and cream when I started working. These would leave a delicious set tidemark crust around the outside of the small cast-iron pan they were cooked and served in. In restaurants there were veils of thin, pink calf's liver just seared and set and served with sticky, sweetened pan juices. 'Fegato', they call liver in Italian restaurants, from the ancient Romans' love of fig-fattened pig's liver, or ficatum porcinum. Oh, no wonder it tastes so good with figs.

It would be normal here for me to take off on a rant about the 'good old days' but actually all I wonder is, if we aren't eating liver anymore, and you seldom see them in the shops, what happens to all the livers from the cows and chooks we eat? Is there a secret liver stash somewhere . . . And how bad would it be if you opened the door to this liver warehouse and it avalanched out over you – all raw, red and slippery.

Lunch was the main meal on a Sunday in the Preston household. Roast chicken on heavy rotation with the occasional roast pork, roast leg of lamb or beef roast. Condiments and gravy were obligatory. I grew up believing that pork without apple sauce, lamb without mint jelly, beef without horseradish or chicken without a clove and bay leaf–scented bread sauce is like your favourite Hollywood actor turning up for lunch without their eyebrows.

If things were tight, or we needed some chastening, there'd be a stew of stringy, gristly beef only redeemed by soft sweet parsnips and swedes. Again, I could never understand why dumplings weren't obligatory here but I quickly learnt that 'as you ask so you shall be delegated'. The upside was that I worked out how to make dumplings both with and without the old-school presence of suet.

Following the main meal, Sunday night would ideally consist of packet chicken noodle soup. Again, there were strict rules about how the soup was to be eaten (rules set and, I fear, enforced by me). Always broth first and then the skinny, short noodles pushed to one side of the bowl for contemplation and the purpose of delaying the gratification. Otherwise, there was eggy bread.

Eggy bread is like French toast but with all the joy and sweetness wrung out of it. Think of a yellow kitchen sponge with aspirations way above its abilities and you have eggy bread. It could have been worse. In my mother's recipe scrap-book you will find sweet and sour sausages made with tinned pineapple, tomato chutney and hot dogs, so . . . bullet dodged!

There were occasional breaks from the routine. These came in three main forms and usually included Antony's involvement. This was a mixed blessing. Happily, he made a good chicken curry even if it was served with sliced banana and raisins, which I suspect was a South African thing. On the flipside, you'd never let him near the barbecue without informing the local hospital's poisons unit first.

Growing up, the barbecue was always over coals or charcoal. Getting the coals up to temperature either saw the chicken legs go on too early so they tasted horridly of the acrid chemical fumes that came off the briquettes as they heated, or they went on when the coals were red hot and the outsides of the chook would blister and burn to a charcoal mirror that contrasted beautifully with the cool raw flesh inside. It's a wonder none of us ever got salmonella poisoning but luckily Antony only broke out the barbecue occasionally. We'd pray for rain and the salvation of a cheese sandwich when he did.

He was far more effective when he took us out for burgers at the Great American Disaster – Maccas was some years away and these were proper chunky ground meat, lots of melted cheese and bacon, a little bit of lettuce and tomato that could be surreptitiously discarded – or for a flurry of curries at the local flock-wallpapered Indian restaurant. Then there was his favourite Sichuan place, which was a rarity back in those days when suburban Chinese was predominantly sweet and sour pork, special fried rice, or egg and chips for the less adventurous. These meals were all so different from what we ate at home. The crisp waiters. The aromas loaded with the fragrances of exotic worlds that I longed to explore. Ah, the memories – although they are almost undoubtedly false. I suspect it was more about getting my fair share of the pappadums or wondering how much crispy seaweed I could load onto a piece of prawn toast.

Antony's culinary adventurousness didn't end with naan and all forms of dried chillies. He was also fond of a Vesta ready meal, particularly the chow mien, which was all tinned bean shoots and too few crispy yellow puffed noodles on top. It was as far away from proper Chinese food as the Fulham Road was from the ancient Qin Zhi Dao highway that runs from Shaanxi to Gansu. For all that, I didn't know any better and it was a good thing when we heard the rattling of a couple of Vesta boxes in the shopping and knew that Mum's roster was getting a night off.

15

I may be going on too much about food but I do so largely to confirm your suspicions that I was a greedy child always contemplating the next meal. The weekly rotation of dishes was both reassuring and exciting, especially when that week meant fish pie and eggy bread were rostered off. You will of course have noted that there has thus far been no mention of desserts. The reason for this isn't because I do not have a sweet tooth but more that desserts require a chapter all of their own. Or possibly even two.

In our house today, if there is any dessert at all, it is too often some fruit or an ice cream from the freezer, but back in the 1960s and 70s your standing in suburbia was judged by the desserts your mother served. While Grandmother Joan was all about lemon mousse and warm semolina (plain with homemade plum jam or dark and mysterious from the addition of cocoa), at Grandmother Vivienne's home it was always 'sweet' – brown bread ice cream, bananas and cream with crystallised ginger, strawberries from the garden.

Simplest, and on reasonably high rotation, was treacle tart, a buttery combination of breadcrumbs tossed with golden syrup and a little lemon juice and baked in a pie case. I'd like to say my mother baked the case herself, but she bought it cheap in a cardboard box from the supermarket. The pastry was far sweeter and crumblier than hers. Utterly delicious, the treacle tart was, and as my Aussie girlfriend Ginger would later remark, unashamed 'povo food'. Heated in the oven so the filling shimmered like fresh lava, it was transcendental, especially when there was 'top of the milk' to pour over it in order to set the molten filling into something divinely chewy at the edges. My mother would always save a fresh, unopened bottle of milk especially for this purpose . . . and woe betide the man (we're looking at you, Antony) who accidentally spun or shook that bottle, recombining top with bottom. We'd howl at him if he brought in the milk – 'Don't you dare!' Antony didn't think much about those sort of things – in fact, most of what he thought of was painted battleship grey.

So, why the fervour over a bottle of milk? Well, 'top of the milk' was what doubled for cream. Back in the days when a milkman delivered your milk in bottles each morning, the cream – in other words, the gorgeous and ironically lightest part of the milk, the fat – would rise to the top. This happens whenever unhomogenised full-cream milk is left upright for a period of time. This 'top of the milk' was prized above everything else. Actually, it was prized *on* everything else, from rice pudding to cereal to porridge, jelly, tinned peaches, pears and, of course, that tart.

I'm not entirely sure why we never had a tub of proper cream. I suspect it was for financial reasons. The only times we got to taste the real deal was when on special occasions my mother sandwiched meringue between layers of over-whipped real cream, or dolloped it over tart English strawberries sprinkled with caster sugar in the summertime.

Bread and butter pudding was another flag-bearing example of povo food, where buttered stale bread was soaked in a simple sweet custard, then sprinkled with brown sugar and baked. The genius is when the sugar caramelises on the protruding edges, leaving the interior like the best bit of an escargot pastry – warm, pillowy and custardy. There have to be tea-soaked sultanas sprinkled through it as well, not least so some on the surface can blister and burn, bringing stinging bitterness against that unctuous custard-soaked bread. This is one of those everyday desserts from my childhood that today is lauded as an example of 'no waste' cooking. Back then, using everything from the dripping in the roasting tray to the stale bread was a necessity rather than any sort of political statement. We didn't have the money to buy avocadoes and marinated feta – and then throw away the avocadoes when they got brown.

Indeed, so many of my favourite desserts from this period were the sort a single mum could afford to cook if she could spare the time. How about brown bread ice cream, where stale breadcrumbs are tossed in melted butter and sugar and then baked until golden to stir through cheap vanilla ice cream? Or endless crumbles – gifted windfall apples (all bruised and occa-sionally wormy – 'What's worse than finding a worm in your apple? Finding half a worm' – boom-tish); blackberries picked from briar-choked hedgerows; and rhubarb grown in our small back garden where it was 'tended' by our first Siamese cat and all that followed – or so Antony's perennial joke would go each time we cropped the crown. He thought there was a link between cat's pee and the rhubarb's high oxalic acid sourness.

Above all else, though, was my mother's rice pudding – not made in a pan like a peasant but baked in the oven in a casserole dish so a good skin formed on the top. Better still, the next morning thick slabs could be sliced from the cooled bowl to fry in butter for breakfast. This would typically be served with poached plums. By the by, the other favourite breakfast treat was Swiss muesli (it was actually called Alpine muesli and the box featured lovely photos of Swiss chalets . . . then again, it was probably made in some grim industrial complex out by a roundabout in Slough).*

There was also a recipe for a nutmeggy pumpkin pie but this was controversial as Antony once let it slip that his ex used to make it . . . well, actually the term my mother used with teasing rancour was 'girlfriend' and it was unclear if that was long past or more recent. That the pie was talked about but seldom made implies the latter.

This was also an era when 'whipped' desserts were all the rage, like the family apricot syllabub, where 100 g of dried apricots were soaked with 300 ml of apple juice until plump, then blended with two egg yolks. Then whipped egg whites and 150 ml of whipped cream would be stirred in. 'Chocolate pots' were also popular in the late 1960s, for which 225 g of chocolate was melted with 14 g of butter and then beaten with three eggs and a couple of tablespoons of rum, coffee or

---

* Actually, the muesli came from the Weetabix factory in Kettering in Northamptonshire and from there it would spread across the world. But close enough. The story goes it was the Swiss au pair of the company's marketing director who suggested they make the stuff in 1971.

orange juice. This would be set in individual ramekins in the fridge and dusted with icing sugar. Whipped cream could be added for lightness. It always intrigued me that we had sufficient ramekins for twelve guests but never enough money for real cream other than on special occasions.

This milieu of whipped sweets can perhaps explain why I fell so hopelessly in love with butterscotch Angel Delight. In 1967 the first flavour had debuted – a very faux strawberries-and-cream mousse that was miraculously formed when a soup-packet-like powder was whisked with cold milk. The magic of the foamy liquid settling into a bubbly spoon-able dessert was there from the outset, but it wasn't until the arrival of the butterscotch flavour that I became hopelessly hooked.

I used to think I was alone in my obsession until I discovered it was shared by Heston Blumenthal. Then, in 2015, Angel Delight was named 'the favourite dessert of childhood' in a survey run by the Food Network UK, eclipsing other titans of my youth such as the Viennetta and the Arctic Roll. Needless to say, it required top of the milk to make it perfect.

Mind you, not all dessert was good dessert . . . some were marked by the devil. The bubbling spheres of gelatinous fish spawn swimming in milk that was sago and tapioca; the dry, cakey expanse of apple cake, where the freshness of the apple at least made the top 10 per cent edible; and, above all – and literally splattered with the snot of Beelzebub – the dreaded school spotted dick, made with suet (which is the hard fat around the kidneys and loins of cows, and was surely destined to occupy the same address in me).

It is a constant source of bemusement to my mate Manu Feildel that the English could have come up with a pudding called spotted dick. It would have caused smutty titters were it not for the prospect of actually having to eat this raisin-studded mound of stodge.

While the idea of plump sultanas, currants or raisins loaded in a light and fluffy steamed pudding sounds quite delightful, the reality called for adjectives more along the lines of 'leaden', 'dense' and 'wizened'. How different it was to arrive in Australia and be confronted with a sticky date pudding that delivered all the good stuff – and came with a butterscotch sauce that tasted like Angel Delight!

Of course, only an underpaid school cook with either a yen for taking out their frustrations on others (or a perverse sense of humour) would think of pairing a dessert called 'dick' with a ladle of warm white sweetness splashed over its cut face. Sadly, it was such a heinous combination of cornflour, sugar and water that the gag was lost on even a room full of puerile pubescents. Though we did gag . . .

Most of the desserts of my childhood – good or bad – were built around the unholy but celestial duo of fat and sugar. This is undoubtedly the reason why my waistband has been under strain for most of my life. A fact that was proven when my cholesterol dropped once I started reviewing restaurants, and 'povo desserts' and fast food largely vanished from my diet.

16

What your house laid out at teatime was almost as important as good dessert for supper if you wanted to be popular. There were the predictable carrot cakes, fruit cakes slumped in the middle from judicious undercooking, and glistening, cracked-topped but fudgy brownies thanks to the young women from Seattle who came to lodge with us while on exchange at the local state convent school.

It always seemed to me that the cake overwhelmed the icing; something that I have tried to redress with my recipes for bulging Victorian sponges filled with twice as much billowing cream and intense red jam as normal, or moist slabs of carrot cake collapsing under far more icing than would be morally and ethically advisable . . . You're welcome! (Oh, sorry, I thought I heard you say 'thank you!')

For birthdays there were chocolate and coffee cakes, but the best was a slice which, once cut, we called flapjacks. You cooked down 150 g of margarine with 100 g of demerara sugar and 1 tablespoon of golden syrup. Then when syrupy, 200 g of oats would be stirred in. It would set on the windowsill and shortly thereafter, all oaty and chewy, would just cry out for a cup of milky tea as an accompaniment.

I had already developed a taste for industrial-strength builder's tea when I was five years old and our first and only house was being renovated. If it wasn't a slab of flapjack with the tea, then maybe there'd be something fancy from the shops. The bright pastels of the Fondant Fancies, with their frilled patty-pan petticoats, would be ignored in favour of a Chocolate Royal.

Ah, the Chocolate Royal. Now, while I may have a terrible memory for names, I have an unrivalled memory for food. Like a chess grandmaster who can remember every move of every match against their great rivals, so is my memory for meals I have eaten. So, when Nigella Lawson told me I was mistaken (or possibly 'full of shit', but that doesn't sound very Nigella-like, does it) upon my mentioning there was a sweet blob of jam on the biscuit base of this dome of marshmallow, covered with the thinnest chocolate that would crack like ice on the surface of a puddle when pressed, I was incensed. It's hard to argue when you are fanboying as hard as I was, so I didn't. I just simmered until, while researching for this book, I uncovered Nigel Slater writing about these teatime treats. He confirmed the presence of jam, as well as stating that a Chocolate Royal is 'something I cheerfully would have killed for'. Maybe Nigella was posher than both Nigel and me and was given Tunnock's Tea Cakes instead, which look much the same but are inferior due to the absence of jam. These were invented by Sir Boyd Tunnock in 1956 and had not marshmallow but *la-di-da* whipped Italian meringue.

It should be noted that New Zealand's very similar Mallow-Puffs also lack jam.

Yes, it amazes me as well that something so trivial could occupy so much of my brain. It does somewhat explain why I might call you 'Kevin' or 'Mary' by mistake!

Of course, the Chocolate Royal and the Fondant Fancy are the sorts of things served by doting grandmothers, sitting somewhere between biscuit and cake, alongside the Wagon Wheel and, I would suggest, the Jaffa Cake. Everyday biscuits were a gingernut or possibly a chocolate digestive, but more likely a custard cream, a chocolate bourbon or a garibaldi. If we'd been good we might get fig rolls – their fat, sticky filling perfect when warmed and softened by dunking in the tea we were inevitably drinking.

Contrary to what modern marketeers would have you believe, biscuits were a bit rubbish back in the 1960s and 70s. This was the era before the chocolate Hobnob, while the Mint Slice – which didn't arrive until 1962 – was a luxury seldom seen or shared. On those plates of custard creams and chocolate bourbons would be the dullest of them all, the Rich Tea, officially the world's most boring biscuit (even eclipsing the Arrowroot).

'Softening with tea' – or 'dunking', as it is known among expert members of the ABAS (Australian Biscuit Appreciation Society, of which I am a founding member) – is one of the great culinary art forms, and vital when your biscuit is boring.

The most flamboyant and showy method of dunking is represented by the 'Tim Tam suck' or 'slam', where you bite a diagonally opposing corner off each end of the biscuit. You place one bitten corner into the tea and fiercely suck at the other corner to draw tea up through the chocolate-coated biscuit. The moment the warmth of the tea hits your lips, you slam the whole biscuit into your mouth, where it will explode, disintegrating as a riot of warmed and liquefied biscuit and filling. Don't tarry, however; suck too long and the biscuit will fall apart and become a soggy mess in your fingers – and . . . plop . . . in your tea.

There is a skill that all good dunkers know – an innate knowledge of how long a biscuit can be dunked before it does that splash into the cup of tea, only reappearing as a sad and accusatory residue at the bottom of the cup with each sip. A gingernut will resist the softening power of hot tea for longer than a digestive, especially if you are among those who dunk a chocolate digestive just long enough to soften the chocolate so it can be licked off. Traditionally, dunking a Club, Penguin, Tim Tam or other thickly coated chocolate biscuit is not advised, as I find the tea can get a little chocolatey. My advice is to reserve that dunking protocol for your mid-afternoon coffee, where the melted chocolate is a welcome addition.

The Jaffa Cake offers a similar attraction for the aficionado, as the spongey base soaks up more tea, which can then be sucked off to leave just the orange-jelly topping behind.

Like a slack housekeeper ticking off my shopping list, can I leave you with some observations about what I call 'invalid' food. Now, we need to start by acknowledging that food is medicine but also that food proffered to a sick child seemed designed *not* to excite one's stomach – or anything else for that matter – but rather to get you up to fend for yourself as quickly as possible.

At the first sign of an upset stomach, it was the blandest water biscuits with a thin scraping of yeast extract. When I was sick with tonsillitis (or after the op to remove the culprits) it was relieving ice cream and jelly, or, if I was lucky, butterscotch Angel Delight. Accordingly, certain illnesses were more welcome that others.

I should note that now I read labels I'm a little less enamoured of the chemical alchemy of butterscotch Angel Delight. Back then it made no sense how this innocuous, canvas-coloured cloud could taste like angels blowing sweet butterscotch kisses across your tongue, but it did. Today, reading the list of ingredients that includes disodium phosphates, diphosphates and propylene glycol esters leaves me concerned and no less bamboozled.

17

It started with drumming and then one of those jaunty military themes perfect for jackboots or hobnails to march across the prostrated backs of a subjugated nation. I suspect this was played over an old crackling PA, but at times there might have even been a real brass band. There were certainly an awful lot of red flags fluttering in the capitalist breeze of Notting Hill. Over the fence the Russian kids were marching for their school assembly.

I must have been about seven when I moved up to the 'big' boys–only part of Falkner House and discovered that next door was the Red Menace itself. We were at the height of the Cold War and it was a shock to see the children of the Russian embassy ranked like a battalion in training for the May Day Parade, or perhaps for marching down The Mall to accept the surrender at Buckingham Palace. The Cold War was supposed to be happening in Berlin, and yet here between maths and double geography the forces of the Communist Bloc were massing on the very border of our school.

Surely this was a chance for fostering détente and a deeper understanding that the children are our future – we could play football together or share our hopes and dreams – but instead we'd just stand on the fire escape and jeer, laughing at the red scarves tied jauntily around the necks of those steel-eyed boys and girls.

Or we did until the bell rang for lunch and the spectre of Scotch eggs or spotted dick presented a far more immediate threat to our freedom. The school canteen was in the basement – which I understand was often the pick for KGB interrogation cells – and here we were tortured with trays of gristly meat topped with dry cork-tile pastry, or maybe boiled potatoes and a cheap meat stew. I'd like to specify that this was beef or lamb or, well, anything, but all we knew – all we needed to know – was that it was grey, gristly and unedifying.

Still, it was better than the morning-break milk that had been left in the sun to develop some 'texture'. Warm 3D milk is about the worst thing to be confronted by in the morning – or any time. No one likes chunky milk.

That said, we were pretty happy. The playground at the rear of the school was made of proud-edged paving stones, perfect for tripping over when playing Off-Ground He, or skimming over beneath spread legs to free a mate in Stuck in the Mud.

Afternoons were even better, thanks to the chip shop opposite my bus stop home. When it's cold and wet and you're wearing tight grey shorts, there is something magnificent about how a bag of freshly fried chips can warm your lap. Dinner was a couple of hours of homework away (okay, ninety-eight minutes of bad TV and twenty-two minutes of homework away) so there was no guilt, but likewise there were no accusations in spite of the fact I must have smelt like

I'd been dunked in malt vinegar and cheap iodised salt when I walked in the front door.

After four years at Falkner House – when I was around ten years old – the school closed. It was sad news but boy did we make the most of the last term, playing ruler hockey on our hands and knees in the classroom, desks piled up against the walls, with one of those plum-sized polystyrene molecules from the chemistry class as the ball. It was a complex game with the sort of fully formed rule book of which Thomas Wentworth Wills or Harry Sewell would have been proud. The goalkeeper was allowed to hold a hardback book as well as a ruler. Fingerless mittens were permitted to protect knuckles from ruler-rapping but knee pads weren't.

In the midst of all this, the headmaster gave me a report that ended with 'Matthew is the sort of young man who has made the country what it is today'. As the country was spiralling into debt and the younger generation were discovering free love, long hair and drugs, I am not sure quite how complimentary this was. It did however impress my patrician Grandmother Vivienne, whose world view was still coloured Imperial red. It may have even affirmed the arrow-straightness of her bloodline or her decision not to disown me at birth.

The end of Falkner House meant a move to somewhere very, very different.

PRINCIPAL'S REPORT

VERY GOOD

Mathew has a heart as big as his frame. He is gay , tough and though the majority of boys here are so nice, the view is held that Mathew belongs to a very charming exclusive minority.

Signed_____

PRINCIPAL'S REPORT

Mathew is one of the very nicest boysiin a school where there are indeed many very nice boys. As his marked interest in football will indicate, he is also of appropriate athletic order, and so when adolescence takes its due course Mathew should indeed become a splendid example of man's estate.

Signed_____

18

It was also around this age that I started visiting Chelsea's home ground, Stamford Bridge, which was just a short walk over the Common from our house. Every second weekend throughout the season, I would head across with my bowl haircut, wrapped in my prized parka, to stand with my mates at the Shed End. We'd always go to the Shed End, entering through the cheaper 'Boys Only' turnstile; football supporters back then were almost all men. It was loud and surging but it was a lot safer than the North End, where there were the segregated visiting supporters and the hardest of the hard Chelsea fans.

You could wear your supporters' colours at the Shed End. Usually a satin, tasselled Chelsea scarf banded around your wrist and another knotted in a side belt loop of your impossibly wide-bottomed pants, hanging down. In the North Stand they'd wear nothing more than a small, enamelled Chelsea badge on the inside of their tank top that could be flashed as identification to fellow North Stand boys with malintent. This was years before the birth of the replica shirt (and shorts, and huggable, life-size player cushions. Sidebar: these are very weird, teddy bear–shaped pillows with stumpy arms and legs and a player's face printed on. Sometimes we felt my mother loved her Fulham FC Mitrovic cushion more than any of us – she certainly hugged him more). Going to the football – even to a posh club like Chelsea – was largely a working-class pursuit still. I quickly learnt to keep my mouth shut to stop the plums and silver spoons from falling out.

The Shed End swayed when the crowd sang, the noise barrelling around under the low corrugated iron roof that loomed over the back of the terrace. 'Osgood, Osgood, born is the king of Stamford Bridge!' This basic structure gave the Shed End – and the fans here – their name. Up the other end, the North Stand rattled and shook every time the Wimbledon District Line train rumbled below. In the packed terraces, whenever the opposition scored you'd see ripples then waves as mobs of hidden Chelsea hooligans swept like a rip current to reach the knot of opposition fans. As I said, the North Stand was where the really hard guys barracked; the guys with sharpened hatchets in their donkey jackets.

Of course, a day at the footy wasn't all terror and the reckless release when Chelsea scored. A trip to Stamford Bridge might also involve some of the worst food humans have ever conceived. The most dire were the grey Westlers hamburgers bobbing in buckets of warm brine. These would be wedged into buns with reconstituted dried and fried onions that tasted of stale sliminess and forgotten hope. There were also hotdogs that looked slightly less unusual slopping about in warm water. As such, you never ate at the football unless it was a Wagon Wheel. It's hard to spoil factory-wrapped, chocolate-coated biscuit sandwiches of marshmallow and some unidentifiable red jam.

My best childhood memories of the Bridge weren't actually from the games themselves but from the last Friday of each month, when a handful of interested local fans would wander up to watch the team have a friendly kickabout in the ground's car park. Here some of the giants – the Ronaldos and Messis of their generation – messed around in pick-up games on the asphalt. Afterwards, showered and smelling of Brut or Blue Stratos, they'd emerge to sign autographs. I had a blue autograph book filled from those Fridays, and the complete set of the team's football cards hard-bartered in the playground and changing rooms – swapping George Best or Franny Lee to get John Dempsey to complete my team or get a spare of my favourite player, the dashing number 10 and long throw aficionado Ian Hutchinson, pioneering playboy player Alan Hudson who'd grown up on the King's Road like me, or Chelsea's legendary number 9 and centre forward Peter Osgood. Osgood was our talisman. When he left Chelsea for Southampton in 1974, I cried. (Hudson went to Stoke City the same year. It was a sad time.)

My sulk over Osgood's departure lasted a solid twelve months. I will still argue with anyone who wants to that this bricklayer made good should have played more than four games for England. The fact that he'd turned down Arsenal because it was on the wrong side of London and preferred to stay on the building sites of Windsor than play for them – not to mention the fact that he scored *twelve goals in eight games* on Chelsea's tour of Australia in 1965 – was the sort of stuff that made him a proper legend.

19

My next school – it's probably best I don't mention its name – came as a rude shock after the supportive warmth of Falkner House. The fish rots from the head, and the school's head-master was, I felt, a pugnacious Little Englander racist. The kids weren't much better. I didn't make many friends and was bullied for my softness.

The school's prized sports offering was boxing, which was core to the winter program. I say 'boxing' but it was actually a matter of putting kids of a similar size in a ring and letting them pummel each other until one of them fell over or started to bleed. I think it's now referred to as 'milling'.

Not everyone dreaded this. The bully boys loved polishing their shiny, spiky menace as they waited to hear who they could legally pummel. They'd beat their thighs in a silent tattoo for the damage to come while we'd whisper up and down the benches that safety lay in the clinch. 'Get in close and don't let go' was the cowards' self-preservation motto. Then hang on for dear life, and always deny them the run up that supercharges their haymakers.

Like I said, this wasn't boxing. This was a reaping.

We wore a uniform of sorts. Oversized gym shorts and cheap, misshapen white vests that were too stretched and old to be worn any longer under your grey school shirt. A square or triangle of colour crudely sewn on the front marked each house – another sign of sensitivity lacking.

Name called, we'd be forced to clamber through the ropes into the makeshift ring. The grey-white of the vests showed the claret most clearly as it splashed from split lips or belted conk.

'How was your day at school, dear?'

'Read my sports vest, Mum.'

The school was also whiter than . . . well, I'm not sure there was anything much whiter than an English private prep school in the 1960s. My mother remembers going to the Open Day before I started and there were loads of parents and kids with South-East Asian, South American and African backgrounds, which she liked – broaden my outlook and all. When I began, however, their applications had either been white-washed or white-lost.

My greatest achievement was winning a history prize for a project on Lord Nelson and another on submarines. The fact that I'd stolen much from the proof of Antony's next book, I didn't view as cheating. And rather than being annoyed at me, Antony shared that famous truism that to steal from one source was plagiarism, to steal from two was research, and to steal from three was original research.

Next I was off to a boarding school run by Benedictine monks. Now, English boarding school is like prison but with marginally less buggery and isolation. Given the school's proximity to the international airport, deposed leaders or fragile despots and their henchmen often chose to send their children there. Besides the son of a recent president of the Philippines, there was the offspring of the bloke who fought the Nigerians in the Biafran Civil War and another kid whose father – or so the toilet stall gossip had it – had been eaten by Idi Amin.

If this makes the place sound a bit jet set, that's wrong because most of us arrived in old Saabs or Volvos free from the encumbrance of a security detail. Our parents surveyed the azalea-lined driveway and the dormitories that smelt of goat, and saw the ghosts of the money they'd scrimped or begged from grandparents that could have instead been spent on a Benz or a flash holiday to Cinque Terre or Cap Ferrat.

For all us kids swimming in oversized shorts and blazers and new to the quadrangle, we knew none of this. All we saw was the menace in men wearing black cassocks, ominously swinging rosary beads, and the dead-eyed stares of the older boys sniffing out contraband chocolate and weakness.

Bullying had been largely institutionalised. Dunny dumping and stabbings were rare so that, at least, was something. And working as a slave to the older boys with power came with the benefits of protection, access to their coffee supply and fresh toast come teatime. Huzzah!

Medieval princes granted bishoprics and titles, but our princes dispensed peanut butter and jam with equal pomp and circumstance. Harder to fathom were the cliques of your own year level. You were safe back in the dormitory but in the classroom you could be attacked with spit balls or find a turd in your pencil box come French lesson. I can tell you, it's very hard to write your French notes without a pencil.

There were certain rules for survival. Don't lisp. Don't love ducks. Don't have an unusual name that can be rhymed with a bodily function or genital slang. Ironically, as most of the bullying was psychological, all the real physical damage was usually self-inflicted as you played splits with a bowie knife, experimented with whether using your arse for a dartboard was possible, or tattooed your forearm with a compass and blue Quink fountain pen ink. Prison tatts, private-school style.

Given the fact the school was run by monks, religion was a big part of the curriculum. The school's abbey church was designed like a UFO and had the most beautiful acoustics. I loved the music but my reports show I was a fractious and difficult student . . . At least until I was placed in a class taught by Fra Andrew Bertie. He was a judo black belt and a friend of the Dalai Lama. He taught us comparative religion in among the rituals, smells and bells of Catholicism, a religion which I couldn't help being a wee bit cynical about after studying medieval history with my other favourite teacher, a rotund ranger of a monk.

Fra Bertie, not destroyed by having me in his class, went on to become a big wig in the Knights of Malta and is now being touted for sainthood. I'm not sure that putting up with me was part of the pitch put to the Vatican's Congregation of the Causes of Saints, the official canonisation tribunal, but it probably should have been.

Each Friday, lunch was nothing more than boiled butter beans. The money saved by this deprivation was sent to the monastery's mission in Peru. Those butter beans were an invitation to insurrection. Small camp stoves would be broken out in the dorms for lunch. Stolen bread from breakfast would be fried with pilfered pats of butter, then topped with canned baked beans in a combination that still thrills me. If not that, then it was packet soup or noodles made in a cup of water warmed by a 'boilette'. These were basically naked kettle elements. The fire risk was terrifying when the boilettes were forgotten and left to boil dry.

This all left me with an abiding love of instant cup-a-soup, and two-minute noodles as well. We would now call such a thing instant ramen. Plus instant coffee so strong, sweet and thick you could walk across it . . . if you could get your boot in the mug. All in all, far tastier that the stolen communion hosts taken in handfuls from that UFO-shaped church.

I had always thought I was quite smart at school, but finding twelve years of school reports among my mother's papers revealed otherwise. Comments range from, 'He suffers from the twin complaints of being both slow and an inaccurate worker,' and 'He has settled down but still suffers from an over-quick mind, a tendency to verbosity and an impatience with detail,' to such arch observations as, 'Matthew is so anxious to get good marks that he is not above helping himself to the answers of the other boys. This is a pity as sometimes he copies from the wrong boy and no benefit accrues.'

There are other insightful comments that I fear still resonate with me today. At five I was already being described as 'very silly and rather bossy'; 'too boisterous and wild'; and 'needs to talk less'. Here is advice I still struggle to heed.

There are also comments about me having quite a pronounced stammer back then. I'd forgotten about that, but the comments reminded me that this would frustrate my grandfather, Boy, and his pent-up frustration would in turn make the stammer worse. It seems I overcame this by talking nonstop. Practice makes perfect. Very occasionally, if my mind is running too fast, I catch moments where the bones of that stammer can return.

Another gem among the reports is a note that we had studied Australia in geography class. Apparently, I was most interested. Although there was a lot about sheep and Merino wool fleeces, nothing about land rights or massacres.

The arrival of punk opened up the city during the school holidays and saved me from the coffee-table tunes of old blokes with long hair and sideburns that almost caught up with their 'taches – dinosaurs like Manfred Mann, Ry Cooder and Caravan. Caravan's *In the Land of Grey and Pink* was one of those essential albums of my pre-punk years at school, along with Genesis, Deep Purple, Pink Floyd and pompous prog rock 'masterpieces' by Rick Wakeman and Mike Oldfield, which only really made sense when you were toasted – and we weren't. Around this time, I'd bought Ry Cooder tickets to try to impress a girl. I'm not sure how sitting in a theatre full of forty-year-olds who liked zydeco was going to do this but it was at least a little more impressive than taking my first girlfriend to see an old print of Charlton Heston in *El Cid*. We'd sat in the front row of an empty cinema. I physically cringe remembering it. So many schoolboy dating errors, and, yes, these all went down as badly as conversational gambits such as, 'Have you bought your Christmas presents yet?'

Who knows what my mother thought I was doing up in my room listening to David Bowie and Pink Floyd albums with one or another of the convent girls, but our activities up there made Sunday night train journeys back to school not quite so bleak, even if the bulb-traced wedding cake of Albert Bridge shivered and beckoned down the river in reflection towards me mournfully as we crossed the Thames, heading out of town and back towards lockdown.

I think the moment punk started for me was going to a sticky basement of a pub round the corner from Malcolm McLaren's boutique Seditionaries and the BOY store in the King's Road. Here we saw a band called Chelsea play loud, fast three-chord numbers like 'Right to Work', 'Urban Kids' and 'I'm on Fire'. These you can still find online in corners of the web. Gene October was the singer. He'd been instrumental in setting up London's first punk club, The Roxy. Originally William Broad was on guitar and Tony James played bass, but they left to form Generation X, where William Broad of the Bromley Contingent became Billy Idol.

Nights in those years were spent listening to sessions on John Peel's radio show and gigs at the Marquee Club or somewhere up north. The former Wardour Street club in Soho was a crammed fire hazard of a place where most memorably we saw a band called Ultravox – before they started wearing kilts, reading Descartes and singing about Vienna. They still had their original lead singer, a striking angular bloke called John Foxx. They played 'Young Savage' and we lost our minds. We threw ourselves around and left with body and hair sweat-slicked and steaming in the cold night air, to sit, later, in the hard light of the local Maccas suckin' the ice from a leftover root beer and wringing our T-shirts into the paper cup until it over-flowed – all a mess of running eyeliner and wet flesh sticking to the cold plastic chairs. I don't remember the night bus ride home but once in bed I know I fell into a happy sleep.

In my final year at the school, I bombed out at pure maths and had to switch at the last moment to English literature, which I never really got a handle on. I would eventually do well in economics and early medieval history, but I had already started to spend a lot of my time spending my money on pubs, drugs and women. The rest I wasted. (Thank you, George Best!)

I was made head of sixth form, which meant I got to host the sixth form dinner at the end of the school year. The thriller author Frederick Forsyth – he wrote *The Day of the Jackal* and *The Odessa File*, and could be called the Dan Brown of his generation – was the guest speaker. We talked solidly for two hours and he gave me a terrific piece of advice, which still echoes today: 'You never know where the next great idea, insight or story will come from. So, listen to everyone equally and intently.' I also was elected to the Vintners Society, where we drank wine, loosely disguised as 'tastings'.

My punk awakening was when my 'style' was starting to crack its way through the thick shell of my conservative upbringing. It was a long way from the uniform of flared sky-blue jeans and white shirts tightly printed with line drawings of biplanes.

Punk was a huge catalyst for wearing what you wanted. At least initially, before the rules of bondage, zips and $50 T-shirts of well-endowed naked cowboys came into place. Vivienne Westwood and Malcolm McLaren's boutique SEX, 'where punk was born', was just round the corner from home but Seditionaries (as SEX became) was *way* beyond my finances. So old school shirts were hand-painted with the riot scenes on the cover of The Clash's first album, and bootleg jeans had their legs roughly stitched together to return them to their old drainpipe glory. I'd then safety pin whatever I could find to them, covering them in bottle tops, old chains, bits of broken key-ring, anything.

Look, it was unashamedly shite, but worth it when, sitting in the railway station waiting for the train back to school after seeing The Stranglers at the Roundhouse, a couple of real punks, their hair spiked with sugar syrup and accents thick with East London sneer, invited me to join them on an adventure to Croydon to see some band called The Jam.

Living near the King's Road did eventually have its impact. When I'd had enough of dressing from op shops, I decided that I'd save for the items worth saving for. I started cycling everywhere and doing odd jobs.

Eventually, some lusted-after clothing was mine. Bright-blue suede Chelsea boots, bottles of hair dye that turned my hair the blue-black of a raven's wing, and a fearsomely expensive rockabilly shirt from Route 66 round the corner from BOY. I could have been a rockabilly. After all, I had a leather-backed donkey jacket from digging trenches for the local council, but I couldn't bring myself to craft my quiff with a handful of rancid beef dripping from the earthenware tub by the stove.

Less successful was my obsession of buying leather pants in a sad effort to be somewhere between Jim Morrison and Billy Idol. Instead, I found a pair of brown vinyl ones that replaced the cherry-red cords with a lace-up crutch (when the zipper failed). Sure, they were sweaty but they had swagger ... or they did until I leapt off a speeding bus to hear the sound of ripping. It was a disaster that couldn't be sewn back together with a blanket stitch, so the legs were saved to be relegated to becoming brown vinyl legwarmers. These could be pulled up like thigh-highs or pushed down like collapsed funnel-topped pirate boots ... or ... um ... legwarmers. Yes, people stared, but I've always had a bizarre ability to be oblivious to the stares of others.

Now, I don't want to claim that walking down the King's Road in ripped jeans with brown vinyl leggings ruched down around the calves inspired David Lee and Trisha Kate when they opened the first dancer's shop selling woollen legwarmers in the early 1980s, but next time you have a nostalgia rush watching *Fame*, *Xanadu* or *Flashdance*, remember that a couple of years earlier they were being worn by me in cracking brown vinyl.

Around this time, my relationship with Grandmother Vivienne started to wobble. It began with issues about the length of my hair and me subsequently being forced to walk to the local barber 10 kilometres away for a short back and sides. My choice of clothes and music was another concern, as was her casual racism. I still strolled the Downs with my grandfather and split wood for their fire but I was less talkative when my grandmother and I smoked, played cards and drank Americanos. It would take a beard and the looseness of my post-school life to fracture our relationship completely.

Oh, my last year at the school was also notable for a report card which ended with some very ominous words. 'Wait 'til the army get hold of him.'

Name PRESTON, M		Subject R.I.

		Marks	Place
Form or Set UIVB	Term		
No. of Boys in Class 9	Exam.		

Progress: —   Industry: —

General Remarks: *Matt. though he tends to 'show-off' slightly (and irrelevantly) is a keen though "fidgetty" listener and participant (occasionally precipitate) in the group's discussion his faith is sincere but the witness is sometimes lost by the 'fidgets'*

Signed *Br John.*

Name Matthew Preston		Subject History

		Marks	Place
Form or Set L VI	Term	44.4	9
No. of Boys in Class 9	Exam.		

Progress: C/B   Industry: C

General Remarks:

To speak in cliches, he can be good when he wants to be. But when he doesn't, he can be awful. I do hope that he will make up his mind to do justice to himself.

Signed *Stephen Othen*

20

There was no money to send me to university so if I wanted to go I'd have to get someone else to pay. Enter the British Army's scholarship program, which paid you big dollars even for a bursary. I attended the interview at the Woolwich Arsenal barracks and felt happy that I'd done enough to get a bursary. But as every other kid there seemed to have been in the army cadets at school, I was sure my ignorance of marching, shining shoes and handling an ArmaLite rifle would ensure I wouldn't get a scholarship that required actual army service.

A week later, with smug anticipation, I opened a letter only to learn I *had* indeed won a scholarship and was required to report for basic officer training in twelve months' time.

I was utterly out of my depth at the Royal Military Academy Sandhurst. I must have been some sort of experiment, or a cruel joke being played on the long-suffering company commander. I couldn't march. I didn't know what they meant when they said 'dress the line'. I couldn't iron a shirt to the exact army specs. And then there were the boots. Huge heavy clodhoppers in which we'd wade chest-deep through a cold lake so they became sodden and would dry to the shape of your foot. If that weren't bad enough, the toe caps had to then be coaxed back into a shine last seen on a Steinway concert grand piano.

In the British Army there is a distinct class hierarchy – the kids from the poshest private schools were already destined for the guards (ideally Coldstream) or a swank cavalry regiment with tight pants, long boots and lots of braid on their dress uniform. Kids like me got courted by the Transport Corps or obscure regiments like the Royal Irish Rangers. I spent a few days with them in Belfast – lovely people – and I really liked their caubeens, a green bonnet worn with a jaunty green feather hackle. But the most memorable thing about the short posting to Northern Ireland – and one of the few times in my life when I've been truly terrified – was the bus trip back to the airport when the twelve-seater broke down in the Catholic stronghold of the Falls Road.

We were already on edge as this was loyalist marching season. The previous night, the sounds of the fife and drums of local Protestant Orange bands practising for the 12th of July parade had clattered over the barbed wire–crowned walls of the base. These annual celebrations of the victory of Protestant King William III at the Battle of the Boyne were often cause for an increase in sectarian violence and bombs, as both sides had their hackles up.

Luckily the bus was unmarked, we reassured ourselves, and the bold anti-British graffiti on the walls gave us something to read while we waited. No one knew we were 'the enemy' – or they didn't until the officer with the plummy English accent driving the bus felt it was a good idea to hop out and ask around for a phone box. His outfit of brogues, cavalry twill pants and a tweed jacket made him stand out like a red bullseye on a shooting range.

Back at Sandhurst, basic training culminated in exercises against a company of Gurkhas playing the enemy. There were ambushes, and mock attacks, and cold nights on watch warming your hands with a cupped cigarette and trying to ensure that the glow didn't seep between your fingers and alert the men with their wickedly curved kukris and even more wicked senses of humour.

We ate US-style 'C-rations' out of tins because there was never enough time to heat anything other than water for a brew, and quickly learnt the best things to eat were condensed milk and marmalade sucked straight from the tube and that a little Tabasco made anything in those tins almost edible . . . even the steamed pudding.

At the end of basic training, there was a mess dinner and a passing out parade. But I'd never fulfil my scholarship. I'd never go and spend the Easter holidays with the artillery regiment that I signed up for. It was obvious that in joining the army you had to be prepared to kill people. Unlike the recruitment adverts, it wasn't all army ski team and drinking daquiris on some exotic posting. It wasn't that I didn't think I could kill people. I was frightened that I might discover I could.

Once, when we were pushing through, clearing an occupied enemy trench on an exercise, a dark Gurkha shape had loomed up through the yellow smoke that swirled around us. I'd raised my rifle instinctively and squeezed off three quick shots – blanks – into the centre of the bulk without even thinking. This unnerved me.

Still, that was a long-term conundrum, and I was purely thinking short term. They were going to pay for me to go to university and they'd given me a tremendous wardrobe of camouflage clothing. Perfect attire in which to enjoy emerging bands like Teardrop Explodes and Echo and the Bunnymen. But that was all to be under a very different killing moon.

21

I think I had been at the University of Kent for precisely twelve hours before I met someone with a bag of grass they were keen to share. I was officially there to study politics and economics. In my first economics lecture the professor in his tweed jacket with leather elbow patches turned a J curve upside down. The rest of the auditorium nodded their heads but I just scratched mine. I quickly dropped that part of my degree to concentrate on the politics.

My family had bought a cheap and tiny two-up, two-down fisherman's cottage by the beach in Whitstable, a spot that is now a trendy weekend prosecco location for DFLs. (DFL = a disparaging term for people 'down from London'.) For my three years of uni, I called it home. There was a small open fire in the front room that only partially compensated for the room's ill-fitting sash window, which rattled when the horizontal rain lashed it most winter nights. The wind comes in off the sea there something savage, bringing both sea spray and rain. You'd wake up to find your jeans damp and cold. Some mornings there was ice on the inside of the window where your night-breath condensation had frozen like crystals. Some mornings it just wasn't worth getting up until the weak winter sun had melted them. Other mornings the sound of the Sea Scout band marching past with their bugles, each one ever so slightly out of tune, would make it impossible to stay in bed.

I say 'by the beach' but this was one of those nasty, lumpy English beaches covered in stones and devoid of any pristine white sand. There was no Summer Bay surf either; when the tide went out it left sucking mudflats behind.

There was a little corner store down by the telephone box where I'd reverse charges to my mother once a term. I wasn't a good son back then. Too self-absorbed. The corner store sold a rainbow of different lollies from big jars, fireworks come October, and custard creams. We were convinced that the bloke with the long hair and beard running it was actually Jim Morrison of The Doors, his death in a Paris bathtub a ruse. Someone said they'd seen him wandering around in the backyard in leather trousers. I mean, where better to hide out than an old beachside suburb that was part commuter belt, part faded fishing town and once world famous for its oysters?

The place did have a lot of pubs. Pretty much each terraced street had its own boozer with names like The Fountain Inn, The Rising Sun or The Dredgerman Arms. An incomplete list of licensed premises at the time runs to over ninety-four establishments for a town of about 6000 people. Simply put, we had over twenty pubs within less than ten minutes' walk.

The rickety old Neptune on the wrong side of the sea wall was our preference – and it was the closest. In the dark of a stormy winter's night, the place glowed like a welcoming smile. You arrived cheeks rosy from the short walk in the stinging winter rain that slashed in from the sea. Damp coats were piled on hooks by the door. Locals to the right on the way to the metal-trough toilets; students to the left. The floor sloped, it was tiny, packed, and they served Stella by the pint. Occasionally there were bands even though that meant – especially if they had a drum kit – there wasn't much space for the audience.

Three minutes in the other direction was The Guinea Inn. It was named after Armada galleon treasure found in the waters off Scotland by the deep-sea diver owner who used it to fund the pub's construction in the 1830s. Here, on a good night, as many as half a dozen people thronged the bar to see the piano player and his old mate on the lagerphone. Also known as the zob stick, mendoza or Murrumbidgee river rattler, this was a broom handle with loads of rattling bottle tops nailed loosely to it and an old hobnailed boot tied to the base so it could beat time against the scratched and pitted floorboards of the ale house. I rather fancied getting myself one and had already started to obsess about random musical instruments like this – the miniature Casio VL-1 keyboard with built-in drum machine had been the first. As well as the Casio, I'd picked up a tenor sax in some dodgy deal and would practise it out on the mudflats. Echoing across the grey, cold sludge, it sounded quiet extemporary and, perhaps, even a little bit cool.

I had one of my three great regrets over a sax. The local music shop where you could go and try out bucket-list guitars and basses had a hulking, honking bass saxophone which was the most honey-toned thing I'd ever heard. I lusted after it, but this was after I'd walked away from the army scholarship and was now living on £15 a week and didn't have the £1000 to buy it. I didn't even have the £1 for my next pack of No. 6 or a pint.

While the first year at uni had been cruisy with that army money, after I resigned my commission, the sponsorship cash dried up. Having so little cash now required some hard decisions and reliance on the generosity of others. The choice was usually whether to spend the last dollar of my weekly £15 allowance on cigarettes, beer or tea, milk and biscuits. The latter usually won. Having next to no money for my last two years left me feeling nervous. Even today in these tap-and-go days, I still feel a little twitchy when I don't have any cash in my pocket. Being skint is, to be honest, pretty shit.

I quickly worked out that inviting my benefactors over for tea rather than dinner was much cheaper. Milk, tea and custard creams in front of the open fire were about where my budget sat. Custard creams also kept my flatmate happy because he was one of those rare, and somewhat challenged vegetarians who didn't eat vegetables. This meant he lived off chips, baked beans and fried eggs . . . and custard creams. And thanks to his generosity, so did I.

This was also where I started to cook – pasta, risotto and shepherd's pie became signatures. My brave and innovative experiments with dyed food were less successful. If you only take one thing away from this book, it should be to never serve blue mashed potatoes.

*

At first, my friends were in the sailing club and played rugby. Before long, I found another tribe, people into music who were happy to share their eyeliner with me. We formed a band. The theory was simple . . . five people who could play and five who wanted to learn. This was all very egalitarian and democratic but didn't make for the greatest music. We called ourselves the Volcanic Rabbits and gave away sweets to our audience (which seemed to quell any thoughts of rioting at our trite ditties and ponderous dance numbers). We supported far better bands and enjoyed a certain cult following for our untalented exuberance.

Now, I went to university in a cathedral town so there were no nightclubs and little open after 11 pm. This did push the focus onto house parties in the winter and beach parties in the summer and drugs pretty much all of the time – self-propagation and foraging were common. Oh, there was also playing music and slot-car racing – you get the gist.

In my second year of uni, I joined a couple of societies as well as the alternative university paper, which was looking for someone to run and lay out the music pages. It was a way of getting free entry to see bands and if you interviewed them after they played you could raid their booze and food riders. I wanted to learn Italian but stopped going to the Italian club when the lecturer who ran it gave my pretty friend an A+ for work she'd copied off me. I got a B.

Joining the rugby club was more successful. My lack of interest in giving up nights out for training saw me happily ensconced in the university seconds with my friend Doody. Doody had a trick shoulder that he could pop out at will, which used to freak out other student teams we played. I stopped playing in my second year but still went to the end-of-season ball. It's a conundrum knowing what to wear when dreaded jeans and a polo shirt seem to be every rugby player's uniform. The solution was found in the reject bin of the haberdashers in the town's high street. So cheap. Who would think you could buy black negligees for the price of a couple of packets of custard creams?

Wearing negligees to the ball was more rebellion than self-expression for me and my mate Richard. We had the late teen militancy – don't tell me what to say, don't tell me what to wear – and that pedantic questioning of why wearing a satin negligee was any different from the kilt I'd worn as a preschooler or the sarong I wore down the beach. Admittedly, we also liked the reaction we got from some – Richard's legs were better than mine, so it was likely his shoulder that was tapped for a dance first. The moment he turned around and some boof, buff and drunk rugby lad saw Richard's bushy Freddie Mercury moustache for the first time was priceless.

When we arrived, however, neither of us received any hate for what we were wearing – nor were many people particularly surprised. No one really cared, but we still felt politically powerful. What young fools we were.

The Prestonian::

Rights for students is an old cry that is resurrected by most campaigners in student elections searching for a slogan to chant at the ballot boxes. It's a catchy phrase but the form of these rights revolves around anything from the right of a student to go to bed at whatever time he wants, to the rights of all students, male or female, to have the right to bear children. But enough of this banal rambling.

WHY I SHOULD BE PRESIDENT:

1. I can lie better than most.
2. I am so pompous I can stonewall most opposition.
3. I can bullshit better than most.
4. I am moral, upstanding and honest (see what I mean about the lying)
5. I am not a political animal, (political parties are mostly full of gesticulating windbags too wound up in their own self-importance and that of their cause).

   I do, however, have views on political subjects, but feel that these should not influence Presidential decisions. The President is your Representative! (another corny catch-phrase).
6. I use "I" a lot which proves I really am pretty egocentric.

WHAT I WOULD DO

The students' union should be responsible for the welfare of the students, which involves making sure life is as pleasant as possible during their stay here.

Here is a cross-section of the vast array of areas I would aim to improve:

1. Free beer and spirits (by organising brewery and distillery promotions).
2. Late night and all night movies (to go on after the bars close and bands finish).
3. Full use of bar extensions and late night discos.
4. An organised system of roll bars so every night it is possible to get cheap food.
5. To provide a fuller use of video equipment (i.e. showing old movies/T.V. programmes for students).
6. To make all my speeches in poetry to liven up UGM's.
7. I will represent all students not just select factions. (To me it seems strange that political groups get free coaches to demos where sporting societies must pay for travel.)
8. I will continue campaigns against high rents and an unjust catering system.

Manifesto...vote...matt

it's the Presto manifesto....

WHY I SHOULDN'T BE PRESIDENT

1. I've had little experience on the plethora of committees that fill the campus.
2. I am scruffy and wear silly clothes.
3. I am degenerate. I like drink and other vices.
4. I don't take life very seriously.
5. I'm pretty lazy (I prefer bed to work, I've already missed several seminars this term) naughty, naughty, slap wrists.
7. I can't count.
8. I believe in compulsory nose rings for all students with blue serge army jackets.
9. I feel that people with died hair have something to contribute to society.

To elect me would really be a radical change and a way forward to a bright new future.

It might also be an act of gross political negligence, a fatal mistake from which the university may never recover - now there's an idea.

Voting: Monday 1st March - 1-2, 6.30 - 7.30 p.m.
In your own college

matt `president´ preston

22

While year one of university was all army camouflage, later I promoted myself when I found a naval commander's dress jacket at an op shop. It was a fine discovery until it was replaced by the most gorgeous double-breasted white dinner jacket with huge, angular flyaway lapels. It was made of a fabric known as 'shark skin', which was a heavy blend of wool and silk. It was satin-smooth, never creased and was a pleasure to stroke because it always felt cool. Damn, I loved that jacket. I used to wear it with my first cravat – a length of turquoise and red African fabric stolen off my friend Myles.

At this time I had an Irish girlfriend, Karen, who had magnificent plum-coloured hair. I met her driving up to the Navaratri Festival on Streatham Common with some Indian friends. She was hitching with a mate into town and we picked them up and persuaded them to come with us. I remember falling for her when she opened her huge handbag and there were two chilled cans of strong lager in there. We bonded in a huge marquee the size of a footy oval as the only non-Indians among the two thousand or so dancers clashing sticks in traditional Dandiya Raas dances. Think Indian Morris dancing but far cooler, and more painful when you get rapped on the knuckles.

Together we'd spend hours, before going out, crimping and then backcombing each other's hair to magnificent heights and applying layer after layer of eyeliner and blush. I'd found a pair of brown jodhpurs at an op shop as well as a belted, wet-look leatherette pea coat, but I had to send them both back when I realised I looked like Ernst Röhm in his Sturmabteilung (SA) days. I was horrified . . . that was never, ever my intention.

Then there was the rubbery black vinyl duster coat worn with what would eventually be known as 'jeggings' but back then were just thick woolly tights. That was when I had an extremely long Phil-Oakey-from-Human-League fringe that I'd mostly dyed raven black apart from some white-blond at the roots. It was supposed to make me look like I was a blond with the black-dyed hair growing out. From a distance it looked like I was going seriously bald along my part line as the blond hair just looked like scalp. I was told it appeared as if I had a comb-over that was permanently flopped forward rather than combed across the bald patch.

It was also about this time that I bought my first pair of white jeans, a fashion item that would become a fixture in the early years of *MasterChef*. They were Wranglers and looked the business when teamed with my French blue suede Chelsea boots. When these boots died I 'borrowed' a pair of long black motorcycle boots from a fine redheaded fellow known as Edinburgh Richard. My friend Doody and I had a badly behaved Hogmanay up in the festival town with him. I'm still sorry for some of the things we did. If this chapter were about 'acting like an entitled little shit', I'd reveal all, but sadly it's about my burgeoning sense of style so it's just not the right place to bring that up.

I can see now that my love for those long tailored coats was echoing Robert Mitchum as the snake-eyed preacher in *The Night of the Hunter* and Clint Eastwood in *The Good, The Bad and The Ugly*. Sure, these gents never wore white polka-dot pants with a long heavily waisted cream coat that hung to the top of their (motorcycle) boots but perhaps they didn't have the chance. The look was certainly a foreshadowing of my obsession with frock coats and velvet-collared and cuffed Teddy Boy drapes to come in the latter years of *MasterChef*.

23

After university, I managed to avoid an army career that probably would have seen me on garrison duty in the Falklands. It was all thanks to Grandmother Joan, but more on that later. For the moment, there was a living to be earnt and so a succession of casual jobs ensued.

I found myself selling cameras, TVs and clock radios in a high street chemist, as well as looking after their photo printing counter. In those days, before digital cameras, at least one of the rolls of 35 mm film handed in would be grainy shots of old people having sex. These would be passed around the store before they were collected ... the whole place stalling when the red-faced owner of the film would come to collect them. The trick was to *pretend* to be looking for their envelope of prints rather than grabbing them too quickly because you knew exactly where they were filed.

I worked for the local council next in a small park between Queens Park Rangers' football stadium and a West London council estate of fearsome repute where all the pubs were named after Boer War heroes, and where a good fight could be had most Saturday nights.

I started at the park so early I often hadn't gotten home from my night out yet. As I joined the strange underworld of people on the first bus of the morning, I realised I was a long, long way from my leafy private boarding school. We swept leaves, dug ditches and picked up litter. I spent tea breaks helping colleagues decipher labyrinthine forms from social services – it helped that I could read (rather than I had a degree which helped nothing) – and arguing over the merits of the current Chelsea FC and Rangers squads. This park was a rough old place of drunks on benches and brown beer-bottle glass smashed on the cyclone-fenced exercise yard and basketball courts where the rings were so bent they hung their heads as if lined up to sign on.

There were, though, two really good things about the council job. The first was a total surprise. At the back of the park on a small rise someone had planted a Japanese garden complete with a stream dancing across pebbles, rocks covered in moss so green it glowed and bobbing branches of Japanese maple. Working here was a delight, bringing calm and order to a place that most people just walked quickly through, eyes down to avoid drawing attention.

The other benefit was that on Fridays and Saturdays I had sole responsibility for a couple of football pitches over the train line from the old bluestone prison at Wormwood Scrubs. My tasks were simple: open and sweep out the dressing rooms and put up the nets on the goals. I even had use of a shed with a large window so I could see everything that was going on. There was an electric frying pan to cook breakfast – eggs, bacon, mushroom, bread fried in butter, beans, of course – and to warm the place. And an old kettle for brews of industrial-strength builder's tea with plenty of milk. In pride of place was a supremely comfy broken-down old armchair that sagged joyfully as you sank into it.

If I got too warm, too comfy or didn't want another snooze, I'd wrap up in my council donkey jacket and bobble hat and wander out to watch the game or talk to the locals walking their dogs. I also had to make sure no one rifled through the clothes hanging in the dressing rooms. The looming hulk of the prison seemed to be deterrent enough, but I still locked the dressing rooms while the teams were playing and checked the high, narrow bathroom windows round the back.

Even then I knew this was as perfect a job as you could wish for. I don't know, then, why I applied for a gig at a magazine that was a notorious hotbed of communism and about as woke as woke could get. And there wasn't an electric frying pan or comfy old armchair in sight.

24

I felt I had the perfect skills to sell ad space in a cranky, clunky listing magazine called *City Limits*. It had been set up by the former staff of *Time Out* after they'd gone on strike and all been sacked. It was a worker's co-op where the editor got paid the same as the receptionist and all the staff had a say in the running of the place. You really felt as though you were in the middle of things at a time when Thatcher's Tory policies were squeezing the city and the country so hard the pips, and the people, squeaked. *City Limits* was almost the definition of 'alternative' at a time when being alternative had become the cooler version of 'radical'.

I'm not sure why the world-weary manager who interviewed me, Andrew Ryan, and the charming Ms Fi Ferguson gave me the job. Maybe I was the only candidate. Maybe I was the only candidate who didn't turn up in a Guatemalan peasant smock or a black leather biker jacket with a messy anarchist 'A' painted on the back. Certainly, the pay of £3900 a year wouldn't have attracted many ad sales professionals to work in the only capitalist bit of this radical organisation.

They trained me up and I sold ads to endless futon bed companies, wholefoods stores, bike shops and to people who made handmade felt shoes. I'd also go see major ad agencies, which was far more punishing. They'd leave me waiting in reception for hours, and then attack me for daring to even come to them when the magazine was so obviously socialist and anti-capitalist. The number of cups of tea I had to drink with a teaspoon of salt in it rather than sugar are too many to mention but that inside back cover had to be sold.

Doing this taught me that when things have to be done, they just have to be done any way or any how. You cajole. You beg. You bribe. You seduce. You argue. You stand up for whoever you're representing with the knowledge that if I don't get you this time, I'll get you the next. In essence, you do whatever you can to ensure that there's enough money in the bank account at the end of each month so the rest of the staff can get paid. Simple.

Another big lesson I learnt while at *City Limits* (and I've tried not to forget) is to shut my mouth and listen when the big guns are talking. For example, when titans of the left like Beatrix Campbell, Melissa Benn and Australia's own Di Simmonds were discussing whether the word 'black' should be capitalised or not, and if so when. At the time it did seem a little crazy but it slowly dawned on me that it is only civilised, if something really matters to someone else, that you should have the good manners to listen to find out why.

Those meetings also taught me that too often the left would tear itself apart rather than unite against the real enemy. The right were the ones who were killing jobs and industries.

They allowed interest rates to rise to a whopping 15 per cent and break families. They were introducing the Poll Tax, which would excessively penalise the poor over the rich, and they supported the homophobic Section 28 legislation. They even allowed their air bases, sorry, our airbases, to be used by American F-111s to bomb Libya when the French and Spanish denied the planes access to their air space. And don't get me started on Greenham Common and the cruise missiles stationed there.

Sitting in some ad agency's billion-dollar glass-and-steel temple to Mammon in my dead grandfather's immaculate Savile Row suit and his handmade black brogues from John Lobb, when the magazine was railing against all these excesses, enraged my ad agency friends. Why? Was it because I was better – or, even worse, seemingly more expensively – dressed than them? Was it because they couldn't work out what was going on . . . why wasn't I wearing a black leather jacket with an anarchist's 'A' painted on the back or some Guatemalan peasant smock? Was it because, as now, the status quo is always threatened by anyone who asks why? Who queries whether there is a fairer way?

This was a time that was the start of great change. A time before Mandela was free, before love was love, and before the idea of equal pay and opportunity regardless of gender . . . oh wait a second, we still haven't fixed that last one yet, have we. Shame on us.

My Marxist mate Marcus told a story of how huge the gap was back then between those who believed and those who didn't. He'd gone into an East End greengrocer to buy oranges and, mindful that he didn't want to support apartheid, asked whether the fruit was from South Africa.

The greengrocer nodded slowly and said, 'Nah, mate, they're not but I know why you're concerned . . .' He paused, then added, 'I mean, I wouldn't want to eat anything touched by a black man either.'

Words fail.

Certainly, the power of a good suit to enrage as well as impress was firmly imprinted on me and is something that, even today, I still care deeply about.

I did have some luck with the big brands repped by the big agencies but mainly this was from female buyers who weren't Neanderthally threatened by the conundrum I or the magazine posed. As one told me, they also liked the fact that I'd take them to tea at glamorous five-star hotels where the decor complemented their mood. They could then tell the story of the well-dressed commie and the finger sandwiches, which intrigued their colleagues so much they'd now all take my calls.

Tea, as I had learnt, was a far cheaper option for the cash-strapped magazine than lunch. Those pot-less days at university had taught me something.

After a year or so selling ads at *City Limits*, I shifted over into the marketing department. This was far more to my liking. We didn't have much money, but we did have distressed space that we could trade . . . glamorous covers on gorgeous shiny paper. As I knew we weren't getting much for them, I went out to see how we could take the magazine deeper into the heart of our community through partnering up with events that shared our cultural and political ethos.

It was this that saw us partner with small concert promoters to do everything from Nina Simone's comeback tour and Nirvana's first UK show, and to champion a roster of world music acts like Baaba Maal, Fela Kuti and Manu Dibango as well as sell-out music weeks at The Greyhound. These had some of the coolest hardcore acts on the bill, from Skinny Puppy, The Shamen, Adrian Sherwood, and The Young Gods, to The Sundays and Runrig. If you know, you know. There had never been stickier carpet. The venue was so packed and so hot that you'd walk in from the cold street and before you could sweat, others' sweat would condense on you.

We also – with Billy Bragg's manager – ran the first non-Japanese karaoke club in the UK, hosted by Frank Chickens, and arranged shows with comedians such as Robbie Coltrane and Lenny Henry.

I'd always loved music, from my time writing fanzines or DJ'ing with Myles when we were teenagers. Well, at least, he'd DJ, and I'd just look moody and pretty in the booth. Going out to see music was always central to who I was, whether it was The Stranglers at the Roundhouse, the Ramones at the Rainbow or tiny venues for Sham 69, U2 on the Boy Tour, or The Pogues. Then there were stadium shows like Live Aid, or The Clash at a park in Brixton. Forty years later, music is still a passion of mine – while food is largely a solitary pleasure, music is something you can celebrate en masse.

Soon after my new role, my mate Jonathan and I received the shattering news that the block of flats we were living in off High Street Kensington was being developed. We were being thrown out. We packed what we wanted and punted the rest out of the back window into the courtyard far, far below. It was the easiest way to empty the apartment and was a whole lot of fun . . . There goes the couch, look how those shelves fly, there goes that rickety cupboard that I hate in the kitchen. Smash, crash, boom, echoing up the walls.

Happily, the owner of the block had another couple of rundown flats he asked us to mind until he decided what to do with them. House sitting? Score! Even better, we'd be house sitting in one of the best addresses in London, Eaton Place.

Sure, the pubs were like something out of the East End because the only people actually living in the area were the security and the cleaners, only two burners on the pre-war stove worked, the carpet was an angry fluoro mustard, and it was a twenty-minute walk to get milk because Belgravia didn't do corner shops. And you couldn't stop for a pee in an alley on the late-night stagger home because every other doorway had an armed diplomatic services policeman lurking in its shadows. Other than that, it was a terrific win.

The first-floor flat had a flat roof out back for sunbathing and another above the portico above the front door that was the perfect size for a TV and double mattress. We watched the 1986 Mexico World Cup from there, shouting down the football scores to the coppers on duty opposite through the night.

We also had the key to the lower flat where we set up a Scalextric slot car track and band practice room in the basement, and used the huge, bay-windowed front room on the ground floor for a dining room, having found a giant mahogany table and chairs. We filled the place with sprays of discarded flowers from a florist's dumpster that dried artistically. It looked like something the late Dutch film production designer Ben van Os might have styled. Or where Miss Haversham could have lived.

Of course it couldn't last and it was a comedown moving from Eaton Place to a basement flat in Shepherd's Bush. We held parties round the same huge dining room table that now looked like a stranded ocean liner in the small front room – even with the middle leaves taken out – and we burnt stuff in the back garden with petrol as the trains loaded with nuclear waste rumbled by on a long-forgotten branch line. That's how I nearly lost a hand, the flames dancing up the plume of fuel I was pouring on the fire one night. The paw tingled for a week after like a reverse phantom sensation.

We ate bowls of bigos in the Polish cafe round the corner but avoided Shepherd's Bush after 2 am as twitchy locals would take on one carload after another of outer suburbanites heading back east who'd foolishly rolled the dice to stop for a kebab and a 'chon. That's 'chon as in 'punch-on'.

Parking was a lottery but it wasn't too far to walk back from Notting Hill, and now I had money I'd started to eat out. Expense-account meals at a French place in Fitzrovia that did the best chateaubriand – perfectly pink with an endless bearnaise sauce that was all twang of aniseed-y vinegar against all the butter. And Peter Ilic's cheap bistros with the bargain set-price menus that usually included crumbed camembert with red currant jelly. Daggy, but still something I struggle to go past.

On one very special occasion we had lunch at La Tante Claire.

Pierre Koffmann's three-Michelin-star in the heart of Chelsea was an epiphany. I'd eaten at a couple of two-stars and the snootiness of the floor staff had put me off. I'd rather be in my local Indian with a smile, a lager and a rogan josh. But this was different. It was as if the maître d' knew that we weren't big hair Sloane Avenue matrons who were here for status rather than excitement and that it was a very special treat. Maybe the frayed shirt collars gave us away. The sommelier even downsold us on the wine. 'Try this. I've taken a liberty, but this is better and twenty pounds cheaper.' The maître d' slipped in a little bonus course 'from the chef' even though we were on the cheapest set-price lunch menu. We left with a double box of petit fours and an understanding of the true hospitality behind a truly great restaurant. The difference between two stars and three wasn't really the champagne chariot, more crisply starched aprons or a broader choice of petit fours, it was the care and concern. I was well and truly bitten.

Bitten and smitten . . .

25

City Limits was a place built on the very Aussie principle of giving you a go – often because there were never enough people to do everything that needed to be done. Sports editor Steve Pinder let me write previews of lower division soccer games. For a while I was the magazine's Formula 1 correspondent, which resulted in a memorable summer's afternoon at the 1986 British Grand Prix at Brands Hatch, standing inside the track with a photographer's pass as the cars whipped past, braking so terrifyingly close you could see the whites of Nigel Mansell's eyes. And when someone foolishly gave me my very own column, co-editors John Fordham and Nigel Fountain were gentle with my gibberish.

The column was supposed to draw readers past the classifieds at the back of the magazine so they'd see the advert that I'd once sold on the inside back cover. We gave stuff away and sometimes the prizes were conventional – tickets to see an advance film screening, a complete collection of Blue Note albums, tickets to see U2 – and sometimes not . . . for example, a vial of Elvis's sweat.

Entry to the competitions was never something as bland as 'in twenty-five words or less . . .' but rather, 'send us something green, or draw us a picture of your cat'. We once had a three-piece jazz band come in when entry required sending in 'something musical'. I loved it. And the punters seemed to love it too.

Over the years, the column evolved into an exploration of everything that was wrong with the world but seen from the perspective of someone who was benefiting from all that was wrong with the world. It was very wrong, written by a fictional character that was part Robert Maxwell, part Keith Moon, but our alternative audience thought it amusing enough and voted it as one of the '200 best things' about living in London. They also voted the fictional character who wrote the column, Barry Backhander, as one of the two sexiest men in the world. Admittedly I tied with Sir Les Patterson.

City Limits did have a restaurant review section run by a woman (who also covered the theatre) called Lyn Gardner, but I never wrote for her. She was smart and I think she saw me as a bit of a shallow idiot. She wasn't wrong. She also wasn't alone in thinking that.

I'd witnessed first-hand a restaurateur's anger after one of Lyn's bad reviews. That was always hard, especially if they advertised in the magazine, but it also meant I didn't care in the future if my own bad reviews stung. Even if you've paid money for ad space, that shouldn't compromise independence because the reader has also paid money for the magazine or newspaper – and your loyalty is to them.

In an ideal world you should get the review you deserve rather than the one you think you are due.

So, work at *City Limits* was going well, and for a chap in his twenties in London, I was loving larking about. The family were all fine and my relationship with my maternal grandmother, Joan, was in a particularly good place. In a beautiful and completely unprompted act of generosity, she paid back the army the cost of my scholarship. It lifted a huge weight off my shoulders. I think she felt I'd been railroaded into taking the scholarship by my other grandparents, who were very pro army. The truth is, I really didn't have a choice if I wanted to go to university.

Things were now rather less tense with Vivienne – there had been a rapprochement of sorts – but we soon had something far worse to deal with.

26

Growing up, there were really only three ways people I knew died. First up were car or motorbike smashes. And with a number of my friends jobbing as couriers, a rule was established: you'd have an accident in your first year, and a serious accident in the second. You gave up the job before the third. Couriers aside, the road toll took an ex-girlfriend and the fastest bowler at school. They were both gone before we were twenty.

AIDS was another big killer. This took kids I'd grown up with and men I'd worked with. It was a brutal scourge that did not discriminate between my most sexually promiscuous mates who loved a bit of bath-house action, and a dear friend who'd had sex once, on a school trip to France.

Most prominent in my world, however, were deaths from drugs. Doing heroin morphed from shooting up on a dirty mattress in the corner of a squat to users chasing the melted drug across a folded sheet of silver foil – chasing the dragon – less confronting but no less damaging. This combination deadened the kids.

I lost two of my good childhood friends to heroin. First figuratively as we dropped out of each others' lives, and then literally as the drug finally dug its sharp claws into them. Then there was Stevie from the pub. He passed out in his squat and fell forward onto his electric two-bar heater. The smell of char eventually alerted the neighbours.

It was around this time that a friend's brother was murdered on holiday in Turkey. It wasn't a good death. Violent. Ugly. I tried to support my friend but felt whatever I could do was as good as nothing. It was devastating for her family. We must have all been in our mid-twenties. She tells me now that she felt seen and held, which goes to show that doing something, anything, can be enough. With what was coming, perhaps I should have leant on her more.

In November 1988 I was staying with Vivienne at Upper Cowden when the phone rang. My grandmother answered, then held out the receiver with a look on her face like someone had died. Someone had. I assumed it was my other grand-mother Joan. She was old.

I took the receiver. It *was* Grandmother Joan. 'William's dead.' Just two words. My brother. Dead. He was twenty-two.

I felt numb. Still am. Numb and distant. Part of the family but also for the first time strangely not. I loved him as my brother but William was Antony's only son. He was Joan's favourite, which seemed fair enough as I also had Vivienne. Joan would be keening.

In an act of what at the time seemed like stunning insensitivity, Vivienne suggested I stay with her, as it would be a shame to waste the tickets we had to see the Kirov Ballet that night. We drove there in silence. The ballet was *Les Sylphides*. I'd never seen it before. I watched through misty eyes.

Then I started laughing. Across the stage were tombstones. A cemetery. And from the graves spirits in white arose to dance with a young man. I have tried and failed over the years to think of a more inappropriate place that I could have been so soon after my brother's death. And in the dirty black hole that I was in, nothing could have been so awfully, bleakly wrong. So utterly and completely terrible. I really could do nothing else but laugh.

'Sorry, darling,' Vivienne said on the way home. At least she acknowledged that that hadn't been easy.

And it wouldn't get any easier. A chill ran through the entire family after William's death. Katie was twenty and Eleanor seventeen. It made no sense to any of us. How could he just die . . . Dead in his sleep in the bedroom that the two of us had shared as kids.

Sudden unexplained death in epilepsy (SUDEP) seldom made it onto death certificates in those days. Its causes are still not that well understood, but slowly we are learning more. It can affect one in a thousand adults with epilepsy. The numbers are smaller for children but it seems that young adults – especially males – are particularly at risk.

William had epilepsy. We found that out when he had been hospitalised with a seizure four years earlier. He'd never had seizures before and they weren't common after. He had completed his degree at Wadham College, Oxford, and was now studying to be an English teacher. He wrote comedy, loved *Doctor Who* and played complex correspondence board games with friends around the globe. He was 'the brain', knowledgeable to the point of obsession, the kid who'd career down the stairs with me in sleeping bag bobsleighs.

No one knew that he was at risk.

Soon after William's death my mother wrote the following letter.

Saturday 12 November should have been a Saturday like any other. It was not.

At 9.30 am I knocked on my son's door. No answer, so I knocked again because he likes to adjust the duvet since he sleeps without pyjamas.

Still no answer so I went in.

The bed was empty. William was asleep on the floor. I was not that surprised. Sometimes he would have a minor epileptic fit in the night and end up on the floor.

I bent down and shook him gently. No response. I tried again, harder. Still no response.

Then I realised he was unconscious. Panic.

I rushed upstairs when the telephone was downstairs. I finally got through on 999. I tried to explain coherently what had happened.

I went back upstairs to check William's position, that he had not been sick and could breathe. Then I cleared odd bits of furniture from the stairs so that they could get the stretcher down. Ran down to front door. No sign of an ambulance.

Ultra calm friend who saw me asked me if I had checked position and breathing and talked to me until it finally arrived ten, perhaps fifteen minutes later but it seemed like thirty.

One ambulance man climbed slowly down, wandered into the house and up to William's room, half-closing the door behind him. A few minutes later the second ambulance man followed carrying a fold-up stretcher, and was asked by the first to go and fetch the defibrillator. Now I watch Casualty every week so I know what that is. In Casualty, though, when they are trying to revive someone there is a great deal of rushing around, orders and noise. I just stood on the landing saying to my daughters, 'There isn't enough noise. It's too quiet. It doesn't sound right.'

Eventually number two ambulance man came out and asked me to carry two heavy boxes down to the ambulance for him. I heard what he said but did not understand. Anyway I couldn't lift them so got my daughter to take one. As we went downstairs I realised, subconsciously, that they were trying to distract me. I asked if I could go in the ambulance with William but was told no they were going to have to 'work on him some more' and could I get myself to the hospital. I really did not feel I should drive so the calm friend offered to give me a lift. Just then my husband returned from shopping but decided to stay with the girls. [My] calm friend drove beautifully and talked soothingly to me at the same time – both of us conscious of her six-year-old in the back of the car.

Got to the hospital and was met by ambulance man two who led me through the general waiting area and into a coffin-shaped room. The smell of old cigarette ends was overpowering.

Apart from the enormous floor-standing ashtray there [were] three chairs and a wash basin. No window, no table, no carpet, no pictures. He shut the door and I was left alone.

A few minutes later a nurse came in and offered me a cup of tea. I don't drink tea so asked for water. She left, again closing the door, and came back later with a cup of warm water. Alone again – feeling frozen, inside and out.

At last the door opened and two nurses came in, one, a sister or staff nurse, carrying a sheaf of papers. Admission papers, I thought, until I noticed the blue label on the back which said 'REFRIGERATION'. Then I knew my son was dead.

'He's dead, isn't he?' I asked and they said he was and sat down. Then they just sat and stared at me, waiting, I suppose to see how I would react. Not one word of sympathy, no arm around the shoulder, no hand to hold – nothing.

The younger nurse found me a corrugated paper towel to dry my eyes on. As soon as they thought I could speak they apologised and said, 'I'm afraid we have to fill in these forms . . . Name . . . address . . . date of birth . . . name of doctor . . . doctor's telephone number . . . name of specialist . . . name of medications . . .' I can't remember these things under normal circumstances.

One then asked if there was anyone with me. Silly question, really, since there were only three chairs in the room. Would I like to phone someone? And tell my husband on the phone that his best loved son had died? How was I going to get home? I said I would walk.

They thought this was very odd, offered me another cup of tea and then let me walk out of the hospital, alone, onto a busy road. I was just relieved to get away from their stares and be in the fresh air.

I went into the church opposite and prayed for strength and comfort and then walked carefully home, saying to myself all the way, 'I must not get run over.'

Later that morning two policemen came to the house and very politely and very gently broke it to us that our son had been brought to the hospital, dead on arrival. But we know, we said. They had been advised that William had been 'unaccompanied'. It is always going to be terrible to hear that one's son of twenty-two had died but surely it doesn't have to be that bad? I want to try and see that other people are not put through that ordeal. I was lucky. I had a husband and three other children to go home to, and best of all a Faith that believes firmly in heaven. Others may have none of these.

Afterwards I wondered what could have made it more bearable. First of all, that hellish room. Surely, they could find one which was more comforting? A window, a carpet, some pictures and a box of Kleenex would have helped. I realise that some people will have to smoke but is it not possible for the ashtray to be emptied occasionally? If you had a room with a window of course you could open it and let in some comparatively clean fresh air. Surely I shouldn't have been left alone for so long? Would it not be possible for the Friends of the Hospital to find a sympathetic volunteer who could come and sit with you, or hold your hand or whatever?

Then, if you had come in alone, she could escort you home and get in touch with whoever you wanted. The trouble about being newly bereaved is that you cannot trust your voice, particularly on the telephone.

All you can do is cry.

27

At first, the tragedy closed me down and shut me off. Then I needed to get away. I kept seeing William in the street. Walking on the other side of the bridge or ducking into the Tube a few carriages up. It was unnerving but strangely reassuring. I didn't want to forget him. To lose him forever.

I wasn't as supportive to my sisters and mother as I could have been, but I was struggling with this notion of family and how I fitted in. I'd never questioned my relationship with William. We were brothers in every sense of the word. But I was Antony's stepson and William was his first born, and that, as I said before, made me feel set apart. It would have been too selfish – unhelpful, even – to unpack it all back then. So, I went on just doing my own thing.

If my way of dealing with all this was to run, to bury myself in the loving new family I had found in my friends, then my mother's was altruistic. She wanted to fix things. To make things better. That letter she wrote shortly after William's death was an early sign of this.

She was shocked by how the bereaved were (or more accurately weren't) supported and how the news of the death of a loved one could be delivered with such insensitivity. She was bemused that there was so little information suitable for kids about epilepsy. Something that was apparent after William's first seizure. She was also shocked at how little was known about SUDEP.

So, she started. She raised funds to publish a free booklet, *Epilepsy and the Young Adult*. It featured a cartoon of William in front of a Tardis on the inside front cover and was full of no-nonsense, practical advice. Within a couple of years, working with the family of Antony's best man, who had also lost a daughter to epilepsy, they printed and distributed more than 10,000 copies and raised so much money that they were making five-figure donations to researchers such as Dr Stephen Brown.

Everybody wanted to help. William's old headmaster initiated a sponsored general knowledge competition that raised £5000. My friend Myles did the design of the booklet for free. My sister Katie was the secretary of the charity behind it.

Mentions of SUDEP before 1992 were still extremely rare, whether you were reading a pathology report or just trying to find out more about epilepsy.

After gaining quite a bit of media attention, my mother and four other women who had lost children or partners (all aged between twenty-one and twenty-seven) set up Epilepsy Bereaved. In 2013 Epilepsy Bereaved become SUDEP Action – a body designed to ensure everyone from the media to clinicians, and the broader medical community, understood that SUDEP was real. And that more was needed to be done to lessen the effects on those who suffered from it.

These incredible women spoke at meetings big and small. They held hands and offered tissues. And they got on the panels of conferences around the world to shine a light on SUDEP. Always the teacher with boundless energy and positivity, my mother ended up helping school a whole generation of medicos, specialists and professors. We'd remind her of this anytime the story would come up about how her father had told her it was a waste to spend money on a university education for her because she wasn't bright enough.

As I say, my reaction to the tragedy was more primal. Caroline, the wonderfully supportive Aussie girlfriend I was living with at the time, suggested that we take time off and travel. *City Limits* were supportive too and gave me four months' compassionate leave. After almost thirty years in London, we set sail on a cut-price, backpack, grand tour of India, Singapore, Australia, South-East Asia, the South Pacific, the US and back via Europe.

When we got home everything was different. Football had become everyone's favourite sport and drinking on the terraces had moved on to taking E's and whizz. Everything was going a little bit sideways. Bizarre inflatables floated above the hooligans. At Cardiff City, a club not known for its Shi'ite leanings, they were slapping their chests, their foreheads and then the air, chanting 'do the Ayatollah'.

Back at Stamford Bridge, meanwhile, they were throwing around bunches of celery. It was the brave new world of MDMA-fuelled fans on the terraces. At least it seemed to calm the in-ground violence. Nice one, geezer!

28

City Limits had changed. The founders had moved on and the new recruits had better haircuts and clothes, and less of a 'peace and love' outlook. After five years, it was time for me to move on too. I had a plan, but I couldn't have been going to anywhere more polar opposite. *TVTimes* was the establishment TV listings magazine for the UK's twelve commercial regional channels and Channel 4. And I was the new assistant marketing manager.

From punk music and militant rallies, I had moved into the faux-glamour world of *Coronation Street* soap stars and ex-Goon Harry Secombe singing *Songs of Praise* on a Sunday night. There was no politics in those pages unless it was selling soma, the bread and circuses, that was being broadcast. And as the second biggest magazine in the UK, it was shifting almost 3 million copies a week. A mere *hundred times more* that *City Limits*.

It was also distinctly uncool.

But I was getting paid properly and had a company car and a car spot under the offices in Tottenham Court Road in the West End. I'd go for sushi for lunch with my boss Jane, who was smart and inclusive. That was when I wasn't invited to join the MD, the head of advertising and the head of finance, for lunch in the boardroom as my office was next door. I'm not sure why these two kept inviting me but it was good to have the ear of power. I know, they were probably bemused by me . . . and I did laugh at their jokes.

My job was simple. Arrange the competitions. 'Get me Colombo's raincoat!' the editor would demand. I'd call our 'fixer' in LA. Sort out any promotional 'tip-ons'. There was a woman in Leeds who would help with that. I also had to oversee the making of the weekly TV ads because, as we were owned by the twelve commercial broadcasting companies, we received seven minutes' free advertising each week on each of their stations. Few other brands could afford that amount of airtime. This deal persisted even after *TVTimes* was bought by the massive IPC Magazines. It was a powerful platform to play with. Bizarrely, the guys who wrote and made these stupidly cheap ads would go on to make the initial series of UK *Master-Chef* with Lloyd Grossman.

IPC was known as the 'ministry of magazines' and had a very different work culture. They'd already tried to rein in the way of life at *TVTimes* that saw the journos get alternate Fridays off and the execs all have extensive drinks cabinets. These had been wheeled out by the trolley load to much wailing and gnashing of teeth. It had however created a wonderful us versus them attitude which suited me perfectly.

The real power at *TVTimes* resided with the editor, Bridget Rowe, and her deputy, Terry Pavey. Rowe went on to become one of the most powerful Fleet Street editors. Bridget was brash, opinionated and terrifying, but I always rather liked her.

Terry was her attack dog. Everyone told me to be wary of him but he was accommodating with me. However, I could never understand why he always moved behind his desk whenever I went to see him in his office.

This mystery was solved when my Irish assistant told me that she'd put it about that I was an ex-army heavyweight boxing champion with a hair-trigger temper. Her lie was like my cloak of invincibility.

Terry was a worrier, too, but this could be used to one's advantage. We were having terrible trouble getting the page layout right for some African safari holidays we were giving away. He liked the picture of the elephants but hated the headline. Finally, we were almost there, 'but try the header in red'. This had been going on all day. I was over it. The harassed designer was on the verge of tears and wanted to go home to his kids.

'But doesn't red remind you of the blood shed by the elephants shot by poachers?' I asked.

Terry looked nervous. 'Blimey. Better keep it green then.'

Done. And it was sent.

As well as competitions, we offered merch for sale off the page: holidays, coats, lovely summer blouses for all sizes up to twenty-two. I can't remember why I ended up pitching these in editorial meetings but I quickly learnt that if Bridget loved the item it would die when it came to sales off the page. She was like a reverse weathervane of our readers' tastes. 'I fucking hate it, darl,' she'd drawl. 'Well, it'll fucking sell like crazy then,' I'd reply.

Even when she got stuff wrong – and this was seldom – she got stuff right. She had a true journo's gut feeling for the right story but she was also brave. I remember the features editor Doretta Sarris and I persuading her to put the first person of colour on the cover. I think it was *Coronation Street* star Lisa Lewis, who played Shirley Armitage. That wasn't done back then for fear of some whispery racist backlash. The resistance from the old guard in the editorial meeting was fierce. When sales only dipped marginally, a point was made and that barrier was broken. There are other ways to bring about change than capitalising the letter 'B'.

Later, I had to arrange and oversee the making of our weekly ads for Capital Radio after we did a big contra deal with their head honcho David Briggs. This led to us hatching a plan together to do the UK's first ever £1 million giveaway with a unique number printed on each magazine and the draw done live as part of the national chart show. A national in-show radio and TV promo campaign like this was unprecedented. It was a nervy deal to put together until we managed to insure the jackpot. It only cost us a very reasonable £35,000 to sleep soundly at night. David Briggs at Capital went on to grow the idea into *Who Wants to be a Millionaire?* Nice work by him!

The promo did sail quite close to the wind, but we had a marvellous and somewhat cavalier in-house lawyer whose attitude to such deals was, 'First they'll write you a letter, then they'll threaten you with a fine, and only then will they look at prosecuting you. Keep going until you receive the second letter and you'll be fine.' Some would call it brinksmanship, but he pointed out that profit often lay in the grey areas between legality and illegality. You have to love an entrepreneurial lawyer.

Of all the things I did in my job of marketing manager, the 'tip-ons' were the worst. These were the little gifts that were stuck on promotional editions of our magazines. They were a minefield of choking hazards, sharp edges and cheap and toxic lipsticks that melted. There was also danger in how you mounted your gift and your chosen cover line. You'd think that the words 'THIS PEN IS FREE' were quite safe on the cover of kids magazine *Look-In*, and they are, until you stick the pen between the words 'pen' and 'is'. As a result we got a number of shirty letters about what looked like a 'THIS **PENIS** FREE!' coverline on a kids' mag.

Far more popular was a beer 'tip-on' that saw us offer a free can with every issue. Again, something at the time that we believed no one else had done. I mean what is the point of a job like that if you aren't striving to be bigger, better, brighter?

If this is all starting to sound a little too much like bragging, let me tell you about the time I nearly died . . .

29

I was lying prone below the level of the dashboard. My seat had collapsed on impact. We'd been driving round a curve on a drizzling, grey morning and had somehow flipped off the road and into the trees. My heavy waxed cotton jacket looked like a Swiss Christmas, glistening and embedded with thousands of tiny pieces of glass. My left hand was bleeding but otherwise the jacket had pretty much saved me.

The driver was fine but shaken. My left arm wasn't. Flying upwards I'd hit something and snapped a bone up by the shoulder. My arm was just sitting across my lap like a Sunday joint for eight waiting to be roasted.

I had been down visiting Grandmother Vivienne for the weekend and her carer had kindly agreed to drive me to the station. I had tickets to the League Cup Final. Looked like I wasn't going to get to see Sheffield Wednesday beat Manchester United in one of the great games now.

*

Thanking my waxed cotton jacket again, I picked up the cuff to sling my arm, managed to kick open the door of the now crumpled white saloon, got out and sat down to wait for the ambulance. I wasn't yet twenty-eight. At the hospital they thought they might have to operate so they wouldn't give me any painkillers. This wasn't good news and became worse when they decided that they needed to put a loose cast on my broken arm.

They lay me on a gurney and told me they'd need to re-separate the two ends of the bone which my spasming muscles had incorrectly re-knitted. The doctor called over three nurses; one to pinion my shoulder against the gurney and the other two to hang on my dangling broken arm. Together they tried to pull apart the shattered bone so it could then re-knit.

Saying it hurt quite a bit is a bit like saying Mozart wasn't too bad on the piano.

Of course, I was a Greek god back in those days, my arms as strong as steel hawsers. (This is my memoir. I'll remember it how I like, thank you!) For all the nurses' grunting and groaning, the arm refused to budge so the doctor helpfully told me to relax and then added his 100 kilograms of extra down-force. If you can imagine trying to drag a heavy fridge across the kitchen with a broken arm, you'll get a mild sense of what it felt like. Not fun but it wasn't childbirth.

With a sort of wet cracking sound that a chicken wing makes when you twist the drumette from the wingette and snap carti-lage, the two halves of my bone separated and re-knitted. The pain turned to an intense white flash at this stage.

They wouldn't operate or properly cast it at the country hospital so they sent me back to London – a two-hour drive with my friend Michelle who had come to rescue me. Every seam on the road and pothole sent an electric jolt of green nauseous pain through my body as the broken bone bounced like it was doing a bungee jump.

It took three days to get into the hospital back in London. These were not the best three days of my life. By way of exposition, I will share just one thing. There are few things weirder than waking up in the morning, sitting up in bed and realising that you've left your arm still lying there on the futon. (As if sleeping on a futon wasn't punishment enough.)

Having only one working arm for three months caused no little problem in the kitchen. In particular, the cold butter in the unheated basement flat was a nightmare to spread. And as we all know, hot toast needs cold butter like chips need chicken salt. I will blame my injury for the fact that to this day I like to slice cold butter into tiles to lay on the toast so it is, as the Swedish and Nigella say, 'tandsmør' or 'tooth butter'. That's my excuse and I'm sticking to it.

At the six-month mark, I returned to the hospital for a checkup. I had pretty much full movement in my arm, thanks to the 20-centimetre steel pin bolting the bone together, and the fat gash of a scar that looked like it had been sewn up with bailing twine. The doctor told me the operation had been tricky. Those muscles, my magnificent guns (see above), had fought all the way to resist the insertion of the pin. 'I had to call in three nurses to help me,' he happily shared. I've never been more thankful for a general anaesthetic in my life. Apparently playing first base for the softball team that played in the Regent Park league helped the rehabilitation of my left (-mitted) arm magnificently.

30

The car crash wasn't the only shock that I had to deal with in 1991. The other came when Grandmother Joan asked me to stay with her when a stranger came to visit our Fulham home. It was all very mysterious until I opened the door and standing there was a woman who looked exactly like Joan had done in her youth. It was the child she had adopted out some forty years earlier when she had fallen pregnant to an émigré White Russian aristocrat while staying with her lesbian sister in Paris. Boom! Overload.

It had been a family secret for decades, even from my mother. Suddenly Jennifer had a half-sister and we had cousins. It certainly put a very different light on those conversations Joan would have had with my mother about keeping me or fostering me out. Had my quiet grandmother, whose nickname was 'Mouse', been as wild as Grandmother Vivienne back in the day?

*

Around this time, I'd begun dating another Aussie by the name of Ginger. In case you didn't know, Aussie girls are grouse to date.

We'd hit it off the first time we met at her birthday party, when I was taken as a 'gift' by my friend (previously my girl-friend) Irish Karen, she of the plum-coloured hair and beer in her handbag, but our first real date was at the famous Battle of Britain exhibition AFL game at the Oval in 1987. This was the match when North Melbourne hard man (and current coach) Alastair Clarkson broke Carlton's Ian Aitken's jaw. I was bug-eyed at the passions for such a non-event of an exhibition game.

Ginger would go to work on Saturday mornings leaving the TV switched on to Stephen Quartermain's AFL highlights show. This is how I fell in love with Peter Daicos and the Collingwood Football Club. It was the longest lasting love of our relationship. Thirty-five years and still going strong.

Ginger and I had moved into a basement flat on a main road in World's End, just 50 metres from the maisonette where I'd grown up. A fledgling INXS were living upstairs when we arrived, but I'd have to wait another thirty years or so to meet the force of nature that is Kirk Pengilly, when he became a contestant on *Celebrity MasterChef*.

Ginger worked on a TV variety show that I had once auditioned for called *01-For London*. It had been my first attempt at getting into telly as a presenter, but the audition had been a fiasco to rival Albert Brooks's character's anchoring debut in *Broadcast News*. I was wooden. Sweating heavily from nerves. My eyes were darting from left to right. I looked shifty and the worse it got, the nicer the producer got. This made me worse. Shinier. Like the black ball on a pool table. It was one of the most horrible things I've ever done and over the years I've been horrible at so much.

At least I left knowing I had no chance. An up and coming Canadian comedian called Mike Myers got the job. Wonder what happened to him?

There was a penance to be paid in my relationship with Ginger. I was always late. She was always later. Much, much later. I had to learn patience and to be canny with the plans I made.

She eventually went on to work on a kids' show that won an Emmy. We fought a lot. The usual clichéd stuff. I was a shit. My actions made her act like she was mad. We got on because friends told us we were so alike. That's as good as it is bad. She was also loving and warm.

Ginger enjoyed eating out at nice places, and as she didn't cook that fell on me in our little basement kitchen with its rattling oven and low wooden table.

The flat was tiny but we could still cram ten in for dinner so I'd rustle up huge chillies and bolognaises from recipes raided from my mother's cookbooks. Or I'd just load all manner of good stuff on the table. Stuff that I'd found on deli expeditions around town. A big bowl of nettle pasta. A salad of witlof, aged parmesan and balsamic. A warm salad of grilled radicchio, blood orange and black olives. Focaccia, grilled and topped with slices of avocado and melted dolcelatte cheese. It sounds dated now but it tasted good then. I was also learning that cooking was about entertaining and good food didn't have to be fancy. So long as there was wine to drink and something to eat, people would leave happy.

31

After we were swallowed by IPC Magazines, the staff at *TVTimes* were moved into IPC's huge skyscraper, King's Reach Tower, on the Thames near Blackfriars. I was given a corner office on the nineteenth floor and was put in charge of a 'team'. I was a terrible boss. In fact, looking back, I was barely a boss at all.

King's Reach Tower was a strange place. The pressure to conform never quite managed to infiltrate the huge suite of mags that ranged from *Horse and Hound*, whose editor mythically rode his horse into his office, to music titles like *NME* and *Melody Maker*, as well as the country's biggest women's magazines, *Woman* and *Woman's Own*.

The move to Blackfriars spelt other changes. Lunch was either egg, chips and beans at the Doggett's Coat and Badge or, at another pub, a legendary chilli that folklore said had been made in the same endlessly refilled pot since 1983. It had a certain complexity and was pretty darn good.

The ugliest moment was when my old rivals at *Time Out* challenged our long-held right to the copyright of our listings – and won. Suddenly anyone could print the week's TV shows rather than just us and *Radio Times*. That lovely situation (for the publishers only!) where you had to buy two magazines to see what was on in advance was now gone. As was the huge cash cow of Christmas double issues where we'd sell 13 million copies each and make enough money to cover our costs for the year.

We launched a new title to bolster and protect the lower end of the *TVTimes*'s market backed by the theory that market share drove profitability. This magazine, *What's on TV*, immediately found itself in a price war with *TVQuick*, which had been launched by one of the new German mag publishers who'd entered the market. *TVQuick* was winning, but editor Peter Genower and publishing director Linda Lancaster Gaye held their nerve longer, keeping the price down. Almost overnight after *TVQuick* put their price up, *What's on TV* became the biggest magazine in the UK. *TVTimes* held on to third spot. That was 4 million magazines sold each week! It was a beast and magazines were, back then, a habit that stuck.

One of the big positives of being with IPC was their commitment to staff training. Some training experiences were good, some were bad and some were amazing. Bad was being taught with the rest of the managers to edit and design pages in case of a strike. This sat uncomfortably with me in spite of my lapsed union membership.

Good were the residential courses on time management and advanced sales techniques. One tip I picked up was to always keep a pile of papers on the chair on the other side of my desk to discourage lingerers from taking a seat. Another was to shut the door and take the phone off the hook for two hours twice a week to allow for thinking time.

Amazing was being sent away for a week with the management A team, who were seen as the next generation of MDs. (I think I got in on a technicality when someone dropped out sick.) We were taken to some very interesting places of truth and honesty by an opera director who had recently worked with famed American soprano Jessye Norman. Much was said about how to read people, spot threats and allies by how someone held their eyes, and how our minutest actions can alter how we are perceived. It was all quite weird and wicker. We also learnt how to accept compliments, which was challenging for some.

Most importantly, we were forced to think about what we actually wanted to do with our lives. That crew of a dozen or so participants from across all parts of the business became a close-knit unit back at King's Reach Tower. We'd meet up regularly as mutual sounding boards, as friends, as lovers. In the end almost all of us left to chase very different dreams rather than grinding up the wage bands in the ministry of magazines.

32

My quietly capable, chain-smoking, punting and much-loved Grandmother Joan was the first grandmother to die. It happened in her sleep in Brittany after an excellent lobster dinner with her two best friends. I felt this was a good way to go. We decided to keep her house in the country near Fittleworth in Sussex where we'd spent so many summers running wild through the woods and fields.

Bell Meadow was a snapshot of all our childhoods and still held strong memories of William. His first strokes in the plastic pool. His fierce underbite as he tried to master his toy bow and arrows. Endless, enthralling games of Kingmaker, Cabbie and Escape from Colditz. He always wanted to be the commandant. He always had the shoot-to-kill card.

Bell Meadow also became a regular weekend trip for my friends and me, drawn by ale off the wood at The Black Dog and Duck, or in the beer garden at The Swan.

*

On these trips to the country, I'd be the one who had to cook. My girlfriend, Ginger, maintained throughout the five years of our relationship that she couldn't. It was only much later that she admitted that all that time she in fact could cook – it was just that she was lazy and I was better.

The trouble with the food I cooked for her was that it came from my family's cookbooks. Honest, homely stuff from my mum's limited and low-budget repertoire like shepherd's pie, her bolognaise (spelt the French way because we'd once been posh), or stew with dumplings. Not the fancy fare Ginger was used to in Melbourne restaurants. 'Oh no, not more *peasant* food,' she said one weekend when I was discussing the shopping list for the ten of us who were down at Bell Meadow. She'd never said that when we were eating the cheap pastas at Pollo, Centrale or Bar Italia in Soho, so I was quite hurt.

Ironically, when I published my first cookbook some fifteen years later, these would be the recipes that people loved the most. So there!

I suppose it's just the way most relationships go. They start with weekends in bed, tightly entwined, breaking only to drink pots of tea and occasionally play games of Scrabble to decide who would get up for more papers and milk. Then next thing you know, you're fighting a trench war over the toothpaste lid or a stir-fry.

We'd already been through the process of getting Ginger de facto status, which basically and rather depressingly had involved turning up to an outer suburban office with a few letters and bills and an immigration official looking to see how white you were. Ginger's pale colouring earnt a pretty immediate rubber stamp, even as far more deserving and desperate families from Rwanda and Mali jumped through ever more tortuous hoops.

But a few years after that (and in spite of the 'povo food' comments), there was a sense that we should be moving towards something more permanent. That basically meant marriage or having a crack at living together in Australia. Fair go's, and all that.

Having never lived anywhere other than London, Australia was an attractive proposition. I was also reaching the end of the road at IPC. I couldn't go anywhere bigger in magazines and still do the job I loved. My old editor had moved to the *Sunday Mirror*, so I chatted to them about joining, but it just sounded like more of the same but with Robert Maxwell in charge. I don't know whether the third bottle of wine was part of the interview process but it seemed a wee bit unprofessional.

Ginger's career on the other hand was flourishing. She'd been asked to direct on the Saturday morning kids' show on which she'd been a researcher. Wanting to hone her craft, she'd applied and got a place at the prestigious directing course at the Victorian College of the Arts in Melbourne. She was going home, with or without me.

So, I started the nine-month process of proving to the Australian authorities that our de facto status wasn't a sham and that I wasn't headed to their shores riddled with infectious diseases like some kind of Typhoid Mary.

33

During what would be my last few months living in London, one weekend Ginger and I headed down to the family's cottage by the beach in Whitstable without my mother knowing and let ourselves in with the spare key. Not much about the place had changed since my uni days. There I was, lying on sun-warmed pebbles on the beach with a pint of Stella from The Neptune cradled in my palm and a beatific smile on my face when an old mate, a local, rushed up to say there were 'coppers in your house'.

Sure enough, I found a couple of squad cars and the promised policemen standing in the front room. Easy to deal with. The scowling woman next to them less so. A neighbour, who had never liked us because we called out his con-man boyfriend, had rung my mother to tell her that squatters had moved in. Vindictive or what?

My mother picked up an empty but very heavy-bottomed Paul Masson wine carafe and cracked me round the back of the head with it. The coppers panicked, said it was 'a domestic matter' and left, which really wasn't what I wanted. Couldn't they charge me and put me in a cell with at least six inches of steel between me and my irate mother? Please, officer, do a bloke a solid.

I saw stars like a cartoon cat but the blow must have hit a particularly bony bit of my skull because the impact resulted in shock rather than concussion. Always the joker, when I got engaged to my future wife, my mother gave her that very same carafe. She'd squirrelled it away until that moment. This might be the most telling of all insights into my mother. Unpack as you will.

After the shock of Joan's death, Vivienne would be next.

34

My grandmother Vivienne and I had fallen out. My hair was too long. And of course I hadn't joined the army. The stuttering path to our reconciliation had started when my grandfather Boy died had a sudden heart attack. His death brought Vivienne and me closer together for a while but there was still tension. We clashed when I forgot that I'd arranged to spend a weekend with her down at Upper Cowden. My apology was too offhand, too late and left on her answering machine. It wasn't my best work.

She sent me a letter: I was wasting my life with a second-rate university and a second-rate job. I was turning into a second-rate person. She wished they hadn't wasted their money on paying my school fees.

All that I could accept. I'd heard her say similar things about her son, and his only crime had been to go into a food manufacturing business rather than insurance or banking like her grandfather. That judgement seemed far more unfair but my grandmother Vivienne was a woman who was adept at burning bridges when she was wronged. When she started in on about how disappointed my grandfather would have been with me, it really bit. It was a vicious letter designed to hurt but reading it back now I can see how much she was hurting too.

I suspect there were also older tensions that ran under our relationship; about her estranged son and me being the replacement who wasn't living up to expectations. It was as if she'd backed the wrong horse.

I didn't see her for a couple of years after that. Eventually I softened. A birthday card here. A postcard there. No acknowledgement of the smouldering piles and trusses left of that old burnt bridge.

When all is said and done, I was being a selfish dick with someone with whom I'd had a close relationship most of my life. Now she was alone and obviously suffering. I'm not sure that 'but I was in my early twenties' is any excuse. There was duty there too. I just had no understanding of the grieving process and how it was affecting her or had affected me.

When we eventually met up again I'd cut my hair to remove at least one of the thorns on the path. It was good. I still loved her as family, as she did me.

She was obviously lonely. So I'd go and stay. We'd go to the opera or the theatre. Smoke cigarettes and drink from crystal-cut tumblers in front of the fire like the old days, listen to her stories. But slowly the years started to get the better of her mind. At times she would mistake me for her son. She'd share deep secrets that were best left unsaid over the smoked salmon mousse spread on thin brown toast. She called my mother a slut, and said that she'd trapped her son and ruined his life. It was as if she'd regressed twenty-five years to the months before I was born, and the conversations she must have had back then.

The fury I felt was ice cold. I pointed out that this was my mother she was talking about and she crumbled with the realisation of her delusion. It made it hard to hate her.

In time, she needed a live-in carer and then there was an old people's home that she went to and hated. When I visited her there she was catatonic and so, with help from her extraordinary solicitor, we moved her back home and she rallied. She wouldn't have been an easy charge; she was always particular – right down to having to have her breakfast tray set exactly the same way every morning. And there was that ferocious temper too. Few carers lasted long.

Closer to the end, dementia took most of her faculties and physically she just shrank away. She had to go back to that dreaded home. It was a sad turn of events for my proud and posh grandmother Vivienne, but the memories of long summer days in her garden, of her smoking and drinking Americanos, were a salve for the sting of seeing her demise.

35

Vivienne's death meant a funeral and the prospect of meeting my biological father, Michael, for the first time. I'd obviously seen pictures of him and his offspring when my grandmother hadn't done a good enough job of changing over our photos, but I wasn't prepared for how much his daughter looked like Vivienne when she was young. Michael's wife seemed to me to be the most distressed person at the funeral, which is more a mark of how 'civilised' everyone else was being.

Now, I know this should probably be a big moment in the book, like when the kid in *Lion* finds his way home . . . or maybe, more accurately, the end of *Milo and Otis* (with me playing both title roles). But it wasn't.

From the age of five up until that point, Antony Preston had been the only father I'd known. I had no pent-up emotions about not knowing my biological father. He seemed like a nice enough bloke, there was a family resemblance, and he gave me my late grandfather Boy's gold watch, which was a lovely gesture.

My reaction was also tempered by my mother's presence and not wanting to appear disloyal. I didn't leave with any desire to pursue a relationship with Michael. The family complications were part of this, although I did find out that he and my mother would talk in the years to come over issues regarding Grandmother Vivienne's estate and also tabloid journalists who came snooping around their story when I was on *MasterChef*.

I search my emotions today and still there is nothing. It's as if when I first realised as a little kid that I had no father any pain started and finished. If someone doesn't want to be part of your life, that's their loss. When I was young I remember burying my head in the cushion of an armchair and wailing, I remember that feeling of loss and apartness. But this feeling was as fleeting as my tears. I mean, what are you going to do? And it wasn't as if I wasn't surrounded by other family who showed their love for me.

And I had a father soon enough when Antony adopted me after marrying my mother. I had someone to argue with at the dinner table about rugby versus football. I had someone to roll my eyes at over long boring stories about 'back in my day' and being too busy with work to come and see me play sport.

With both grandmothers gone – those two women who had played such different yet vital roles in my formative years – it was the end of an era. In a way, there was no better time for me to forge ahead somewhere new. My time in the UK was coming to an end. The lures of London, like the music and the late, late nightlife were waning for me.

Before we leave London, I should say something about ligging, which was an artform back then. The aim was to pay for as little as possible because there was always some rich

My maternal grandfather, Larry.   My maternal grandmother, Joan.

At a dinner in a club in Jamaica, my grandfather Boy, at the near end of the table, flirts with my grandmother Vivienne in a time before children.

My mother, Jennifer.

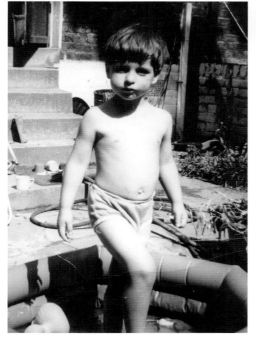

Top left: On the beach with Jennifer before my worrying seaside habit of bad behaviour over ice cream. Judging by those stones, this is taken at either Whitstable in Kent, or Rustington or Climping in West Sussex.

Top right: Style was a constant aim, even when I was a small child. I loved this red duffle coat and my grandfather Boy's battered old trilby. I fear the red was so I could be spotted if I ranged too far into the snow at Upper Cowden.

Left: Even in the backyard paddling pool of Fernshaw Road I already had my signature cocked hip stance.

Me and my Siamese cat Emma (named after *The Avengers'* Emma Peel) in the Lake District. Feeling a little guilty now that she didn't have matching rubberised raincoat and sou'wester.

Antony and Jennifer at their wedding. (I wore a rather cute kilt.)

Me and baby brother William. The playground was a place of terror. Here is the giant slide at South Park that we braved together, and some of the other exciting rides such as the witch's hat and the seesaw. The slide still looks terrifyingly big!

Horsing around on the beach with William and sister Katie.

I'm not sure if this photo is here for my epic matching floral tie and shirt combo or because it was my sister Eleanor's christening. I'll say the latter but Eleanor will still suspect it's the former.

Ridiculously over-excited but just keeping it together to meet the first man on the moon, Neil Armstrong, at the Royal Geographical Society. My grandfather Larry is looking on.

Rare proof that I did actually play sport. Me, centre back (like you need to be told) in the school U16 1st XV.

Even rarer proof of my misstep into the army. I'm back right. Mine was a very short soujourn at Sandhurst.

PRE-UNIVERSITY COURSE No. 9 AMIENS COMPANY — SEPTEMBER 1980

Rear Rank — 2Lt's W. H. Daniell, G. R. Pinney, A. R. Boliton, J. Southworth, A. P. Sharpe, W. J. F. Kingdon, G. H. L. Baxter, T. H. Emck, S. P. Hunt, P. W. Walker, G. R. Smith, W. T. Taylor, M. P. Preston, K. E. Hughes

Centre Rank — 2Lt's R. B. Hannam, M. J. Stratton-Christensen, G. R. W. MacGinnis, C. J. Reynolds, I. N. Potts, R. P. Jeyton, T. C. Foster, R. L. Kimbrenne, J. B. W. Stratton, V. E. Acheson, I. M. Thompson, R. Bokerman, M. J. S. Kenney, R. R. Smith

Front Rank — 2Lt's J. D. S. Moir, H. W. Blacket, T. P. Evans, Capt R. M. Rundle, S/Sgt C. Robertson, Capt R. A. Stewart, CSM B. Smith, Maj C. N. B. Wellwood, C/Sgt I. Davidson, Capt J. D. Fuller, 2Lt's H. D. J. Pickard, J. B. Lay, M. S. Watson

Posing.

Posing in my first cravat and favourite white sharkskin dinner jacket while at uni.

Posing again in an early cravat, Zazou-style white sunglasses and army fatigue pants, with one of my cooler best men.

Posing on an unconnected telephone at university. Yes, a scarf, ascot or cravat was a feature even back then, though some columnists dismissed it as a TV-created affectation when I started on the small screen.

Breakfast with my Dutch friend Manon and kitten Starcrush in Vathi on Sifnos. That is an army shirt – customised. Just out of shot is Manon's boyfriend at the time, Stephan. I reconnected with them years later thanks to the success of my cookbooks in the Netherlands. A beautiful thing!

Left: My wedding to the woman I love in a little Anglican church in Benalla, Victoria. You may be able to see that I had been crying. It was a beautifully emotional moment of my life.

Above: My amazing sisters Katie and Eleanor at the wedding. Such impressive women and the best MCs ever . . . period.

My mother Jennifer was a regular visitor during the Australian summer. This is a calmer moment – most photos from her trips are of her ticking things off her bucket list such as going gliding, learning to fly or diving on the Great Barrier Reef.

Below, clockwise from top right: Jennifer, Katie, Eleanor, William and Antony. (I have no idea who the other person is. Sorry!)

Jennifer with Katie, William and Eleanor on a picnic.

It's been a conscious decision to keep my family out of the media as they didn't sign up for public life, but photographer Julian Kingma (who shot the cover of this book) did a beautiful job on this rare family shoot. Jonathan, Sadie, William and Emma sitting round an upright piano with my favourite 1970s paisley wallpaper, which came with the house.

My daughter Sadie being unbearably cute. Strange to think our kids are all adults now and range in height from 178 to 196 cm. Frankly I think it's a wee bit disrespectful when sons get taller than their fathers!

Above: I'm not sure why I bought these onesies on tour in South Africa – but they seem to capture something about us!
Left: Me, Sarah Wilson and a Logie.

It's not true awards are irrelevant, especially when you win one. This AACTA was won by the talented *MasterChef* production team and we were so happy for them.

Such a huge part of my adventure: my food guru Marnie Rowe and my manager Henrietta Stride – the women who made food happen for me. Some R n R after a South African food festival.

My third 'sister', great friend and manager Henrie Stride – we've worked and played together for nearly fifteen years now.

Above: Just a little off the top, please!

Left: I'm 190 cm – the other boys, not so much.

Fossils and some ruins. LOL.

Trying to look moody in the back streets of Rome. Gary took the shot, and a macabre pleasure in telling me we were on the Via dei Coronari.

I've worked with some amazing people over the years, from the world's top chefs to the Dalai Lama, but filming with HRH Prince Charles – now King Charles – was a heady highlight.

Another highlight – the three unlikeliest people ever to be seen in the General Assembly of the UN.

I came to Australia to write about Aussie soaps so to appear in the thirtieth-anniversary week of *Neighbours* with heroes like Alan Fletcher, Colette Mann and the rest of the cast made my mum (and me) very happy.

Meeting food lovers of all ages around the world has been a highlight of my life in food. This is just one such moment at Brisbane's Regional Flavours event.

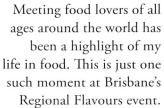

Always a delight – hanging with Nigella Lawson when she's in town. This time she was here for the Melbourne Food and Wine Festival. She's taught me so much.

Massimo Bottura is one of the great food thinkers as well as an inspiration to me, both in person and at his restaurant, Osteria Francescana. Here, we are outside the old Noma in Copenhagen.

The man who taught me how to cook pasta and make perfect risotto. Antonio Carluccio, the last time we met. One of the great entertainers and a very generous human.

Gaggan Anand is a true pioneer. This was taken outside his old Bangkok restaurant.

Love this photo of Warren Mendes and Emma Warren eating crab on the shoot for my cookbook *World of Flavours*. These two make everything better.

René Redzepi is a truly unique culinary thinker and great company. Always good to catch up with him.

I first met Heston Blumenthal in Milan. A beautiful human whose approach to flavour, theatre and creativity has been hugely important. Here we are standing on a dazzling pink salt pan near Mildura.

Left: On stage with Carluccio at Gourmet Escape in Margaret River. I love doing demos, and having a master on stage with you always makes life easier, if a little more stressful!

Right: With Elena Arzak at her amazing restaurant in San Sebastian. Elena taught me more in an afternoon about writing recipes than almost anyone else.

Left: The top half of the swan at a food festival in Abu Dhabi. Warren and Emma were the frantically paddling feet down in the kitchens.

Right: With Jamie Oliver, Tobie Puttock and Matt Skinner. Good times!

I've always loved dress-ups so it was a no-brainer when the News Corp team asked to make me over as a pirate (I'd written a column on a pirate dish called *salmagundi*). The Statue of Liberty shot took a long time in the make-up chair but was worth it to promote a *MasterChef* trip to New York. I love a bit of silliness.

George being very brave beside the camel I terrorised him with in Dubai.

DISGUSTINGLY GOOD

Seriously, I've been to some amazing places but on a doof stick at a music festival must be the most surprising.

Catching up with young *MasterChef* fans in Bangladesh.

At Film City, Mumbai (officially called Dadasaheb Phalke Chitranagari), the home of Bollywood, where I hung out with some of the world's most skilled crew.

World on a Plate in Bangalore was keen to dress us up as maharajahs, so with significant misgivings I agreed.

I've always loved my time in India, so I was honoured to help the team at *MasterChef India* judge a challenge for their show in Sydney. Zorawar Kalra, Kunal Kapur and Vikas Khanna were amazing hosts.

Just a few of the many chefs from the Cinnamon Grand Hotel in Colombo, Sri Lanka, who gave me a surprise welcome when I was a guest. A bit overwhelming and I was seriously underdressed for the occasion. I was so saddened by the tragic attack there in Easter 2019.

More dress-ups. I had a gnome I was very fond of at school, so dressing up as a giant 4-metre version on *The Masked Singer* was a no-brainer.

With Manu Feildel and Gary on the set of *Plate of Origin*. We had so much fun together and I loved finally working with (and teasing) the big Frenchman.

Doing things that scare me and chasing new experiences saw me spending a couple of days filming with the team at ABC Comedy's *Aftertaste* in Adelaide. Such a privilege to watch Erik Thomson work.

My new broadcast family: the ABC weekends team across Victoria. My sports co-host Catherine Murphy, *Breakfast* host Alice Zaslavsky, our GP-in-residence Dr Vyom Sharma and *Sundays* presenter Lisa Leong. Gee, I love this gig and these people!

My mum would have laughed, but I loved the intense, cathartic and elating experience of working with Jess Raffa on *Dancing with the Stars*.

corporate with a marketing budget to splash out on keeping our coterie of designers, editors, journos, musos, model agents and PRs entertained.

It had all started when I was thirteen and I went to a record company to ask for badges and stickers and free albums and whatever else they had ... and magically walked away with loads of stuff. Like Siberian wolves that have learnt the sleighs scooting across the ice will thrown them elk steaks to lose some weight, so I came to associate PRs with free stuff ... nay, expected it.

Before the end of work in London we'd compare what we'd been invited to and then pick where we'd have most fun – which had the full bar, which was the best band, which venue guaranteed mayhem – and get each other on the list. Going to these sorts of events and functions for work gets pretty old pretty fast but going with all your mates is like having your lifestyle sponsored. None of us was well paid but we lived the social life of the rich.

My blagging career reached its zenith when we landed the front row of gilt chairs in the royal box at Wembley Stadium to see Pink Floyd. In those days Wembley was building a reputation for some of the greatest moments in music history. I was sitting on the pitch for Freddie Mercury's amazing performance at Live Aid in 1989. We scoffed because Queen was distinctly uncool then with all those dodgy 'fat bottomed naked girls on bicycles' album themes. Filing out of the stadium the crowd baa'ed like lambs and sung 'In the name of love', marking U2's performance as the pinnacle of the day.

Similarly, I was there when Nelson Mandela walked out on the stage at the Wembley Tribute for a Free South Africa in 1990, his first global appearance since his release from jail two months before. If Live Aid felt warm and worthy, this was an extremely emotional moment. The standing ovation for Mandiba lasted for five minutes from the crowd of almost 80,000. His first message in an inspiring speech: 'Thank you for choosing to care.'

It felt, at that moment, that music (in support of the far harder, long political straggle of the ANC in South Africa) had helped achieved a major political change in the face of a British government that had been tacitly supportive of the apartheid regime. I would argue that the anti-apartheid movement was back then a similar cause (in terms of its importance to the left and others) to societies demanding action on climate change now. It had a similar long history – emerging from the Boycott South Africa movement after the Sharpeville Massacre in 1960. It was a musical campaign that helped break the dam world-wide, starting with the anthemic protest song Jerry Dammers wrote for The Specials AKA in 1984. 'Free Nelson Mandela' became a hit in the UK and across sub-Saharan Africa and was played at ANC rallies. The Mandela movement was powerful, and a cause of hope that it was possible for a soft, popularist campaign to help achieve real change eventually.

As I grew older, concerts and festivals increasingly became a part of my life, whether that was endless visits to Reading's or The Big Day Out in Melbourne.

These marvellous events paled behind Glastonbury. The first time I went we stayed in a local pub and got tangled with some Morris dancers. Later we were better organised, mainly thanks to the fact one of our group was now working in A&R and had some serious clout. Love the music and all that but festivals are usually a horror show of over-flowing toilets, bad food and an endless crush getting from stage to stage missing the one band you really wanted to see. Getting backstage with the bands, however, meant the greatest of your problems was avoiding Snoop Dogg smoking all your stash. The area had its own bar, toilets that were mostly flushed and empty, and sat between the main stage and the second stage so you could rush across it after seeing the Chemical Brothers or The Offspring and still catch the end of the Oasis.

In terms of musical moments, Radiohead playing 'Creep' under the stars for 50,000, Pulp's blistering version of 'Common People' with a rabid crowd singalong and dancing to Chic with the greatest friends were the sweetest times.

There would be other festivals when I arrived in Australia as I love the magical atmosphere of togetherness that a great one promotes among the attendees, and I'd still return for the occasional Glastonbury: in later times we slept in hired record company teepees and stood among the other old folk watching the Rolling Stones, Portishead or some hot-but-unknown-in-the-UK Australian act I'd dragged everyone to on a back stage. We might return to that later. I certainly will.

So, with my visa secured, a clean bill of health, and no regrets other than leaving the three big 'Fs' – friends, family and football – behind, I packed my bags to join Ginger for a year or two in Australia.

TWO

The Land
of Sun,
Surf and
Small Screen
Opportunities

36

'I'm not sure this is a good idea after all.'

These are *not* the words you want to hear from your Aussie girlfriend when your bags are packed and you're about to fly off to your new life on the other side of the world.

Was it cold feet or something else? It's sort of irrelevant. I'd already cancelled the lease on my flat. Quit my job. There was work waiting for me in Australia. I'd paid for the airline ticket, the insurance, the visa. I was, as they say in the poker classics, 'pot committed'.

Hearing those words made me feel as if I was running to the edge of a huge cliff and just as you leap over the edge someone shouts, 'Wait a mo!'

No matter how fast you flail your arms, you're going over the edge.

Thirty-eight hours later, I pushed through customs in Melbourne. Cold feet were understandable. Ginger and I had been apart, on and off, for six months. But she wasn't there to meet me. She was always late so it wasn't a shock but it certainly was a shit way to start.

For a moment I considered flying home, tail between my legs, but I'd cast my bread on the water. So I took a taxi to the little house her father had bought her in Middle Park. I needed to see what was going on. I needed to embrace the unfamiliar and not be afraid.

I finally realised our relationship was dead that Christmas when she gave me a towel. Just a cheap yellow beach towel.

At least the job worked out. Those two blokes who'd invited me to lunch in the boardroom back when I started on *TVTimes* wound up running Reed Business Publishing, which owned loads of trade magazines in Australia. They found out I was moving and organised a computer and a desk for me in their Port Melbourne offices for as long as I wanted. I would act as a stringer covering the Aussie soaps for my old magazines and *Woman's Own*. Thank you, John. Thank you, Jeffrey.

Soon after, the young CEO of the company, Murray Hamilton, asked me if I wanted to write for some of their other titles. This explains how I ended up in a zoo laboratory interviewing a 'bloke who wanks rhinos for a living' for *The Veterinarian*. It was a genomic storage story, but I liked my headline better.

Trade publishing is a long way from celebrity TV magazines, and Australia was a long way from Blackfriars. I wrote for *Plantline* and *Food Processor*. I took on the role of Melbourne journo for *Counterpoint*, writing about air conditioning and kitchen appliances. This was at a time when retailers were still characters, more likely sales people than dry accountants.

Gerry Harvey would always take your call, even if it was from a minnow like me. He always gave great quotes. And from John Radonich, who'd started the Betta Electrical chain (worth millions) with just £600 and allegedly couldn't 'read or write so good', I received Yoda-like retail philosophy: 'Always make sure you get paid for what you give, and get given what you paid for,' and this gem, 'Play the long game.' John had learnt this lesson with his very first customer. He'd pushed John hard on price that first time but then became a regular. John loved that he was now selling stuff to the bloke's grandchildren. He understood just how much that first sale had really been worth to him over the years.

While Aussies have a reputation in the UK as being fearsome workers, in Melbourne it seemed like my colleagues defined themselves by the sport they played after work rather than anything they did during the day. I ended up joining a softball team and reprising my UK role of first base with the big mitt. I also played volleyball. I found a cheap gym under the police headquarters; I was only working two days a week but could afford the fees thanks to the fact I was getting paid London wages in pounds. I had money for luxuries that would have been unfathomable back home, where each month's pay cheque just seemed to pay off the current account overdraft.

And how easy is this: I was getting paid to watch TV.

From late 1993 until 1998 I was the world's number-one expert on Australian soaps. This is no idle boast but fact, born of five years of carefully watching and annotating every single episode. I'm talking more than 2350 episodes and 51,700 minutes of soap.

We were past the golden era of Kylie and Jason, but *Neighbours* and *Home and Away* were still massive in the UK, regularly drawing over 15 million viewers an episode. There was, therefore, a huge competitive advantage in knowing the storylines months before the rest of the UK media. So, each week I'd watch both shows – five hours of Aussie soaps in total . . . every week . . . forty-seven weeks a year . . . and write copious notes on what happened and what might make juicy stories for our magazines.

I learnt that nothing good ever comes from weddings or picnics out in the country. I learnt about Archie Roach and Hunters & Collectors from the soundtracks. I also learnt about the joy of breaking directing conventions when my director friend Sally-Anne Kerr decided to feature extreme closeups of Toadie's mouth in one of the greatest ever food-eating scenes to be seen on Australian TV . . . Toadie eating peas with tomato sauce. I also learnt about the extraordinary debt our current crop of young stars owes the older actors who schooled them on set. I learnt about how quickly drama could be forged, and how from a cheap backlot in an outer Australian suburb you could make a show that resonated around the world.

Then after six years I just stopped. I realised I needed to be wasted to watch the soaps. It was the only way I could face them. I also needed the time, as I'd landed a couple of gigs at *The Age*. One of the last things I did was to research a potential 'This Is Your Life' episode for Anne Haddy (Ramsay Street matriarch Helen Daniels). It was a fitting finish.

Writing about *Neighbours* and *Home and Away* helped connect me to my mother. She was a huge fan of both – so much so that in 2010 she told me she voted for *Home and Away*'s dishy Luke Mitchell for the Best New Talent Logie rather than for her own son (I was up for *MasterChef*). Frankly, I found that a little hurtful.

When she first started coming out to Australia to visit, she'd insist on trips up to Pin Oak Court in Melbourne (*Neighbours*' Ramsay Street) and to Palm Beach north of Sydney (where *Home and Away* is shot). I still have blurry photos of her with characters Pippa and Michael at his boatshed. After that visit she kept a small jar of hand-harvested 'Summer Bay Sand' on her mantelpiece. Much later, when I was shooting publicity at the Seven Network's Sydney studios for *Plate of Origin*, she rather enjoyed the shots of me polishing glasses behind the counter at *Home and Away*'s surf club and cafe. It was the closest I got to a cameo on that show but, as you will see, I was luckier with *Neighbours*.

37

Of course once I left London, Chelsea FC started to play well. It was a good thing I'd bought an open return airline ticket – it got a lot of use for two FA Cup finals and the last ever Cup Winners' Cup Final in an empty Stockholm in 1998. All the locals seemed to have evaporated with the influx of 20,000 football yobs from London. I wonder why. The police would later remark that the city's crime rate actually went down as even the crims stayed home. One of my favourite players ever, Gianfranco Zola, came off the bench to score the winning goal against Stuttgart. It's always been club before country in my book. The photo I have of Chelsea player, and future manager, Roberto di Matteo, in the swanky Opera Bar that night after the game is among my favourite possessions, even if I have a stupid, slack 3 am grin on my face.

I was only working a few days a week as a freelancer in Melbourne, which meant I could linger on the way in or out of the UK. In the first few years I also tried to spend about a month a year in New York, transiting. At first, I'd sleep on the floor of my friend Fran's apartment in Alphabet City, which was a rat's nest of crack dens, street crime and bodies found in Tompkins Square Park most nights. Screeching brakes and occasional gunfire were our bedtime lullaby.

Over the years I'd return to stay with two other great friends, Bonnie and Stevan, who had relocated from London to edit magazines like *TV Guide* and *Wired*. Stevan's still there. We'd go for cocktails in the Monkey Bar and drink Sazeracs at the new wave of speakeasies like Employees Only; have steaks in a booth at the Minetta Tavern or at Balthazar; or eat plates of incredible corn and ham or those now famous sweet, steamed buns filled with melty pork belly, lightly pickled cucumber slices and hoisin sauce at David Chang's original low-fi Momofuku Noodle Bar. I lingered in New York because I relished the edge and intensity that I felt Australian cities sometimes lacked. New York is still one of my favourite places, even if at times it's unrecognisably gentrified, and I feel unrecognisably old there.

Another favourite waypoint, if the flights were cheaper, was to go to the UK via Manila to eat vinegary pork adobo and ride jitneys. Manila back then was poor. It was only a few years after Ferdinand Marcos had been ousted and behind the advertising hoardings that lined the main roads you'd see slums stretching off into the distance. There was an intense, suffocating atmosphere with armed guards outside even the shittiest, cheapest hotels where you'd share the bar with out-of-shape business-men waiting to meet their mail-order brides. So depressing. It also didn't help that brownouts could kick in unexpectedly and all the street lighting suddenly went off so you had to feel your way home in the dark. Still, the wreck-diving in Palawan was next level and worth the detour.

The only place I've felt more unnerved was Auckland. One mad, bad Saturday there was a pitched battle between gangs of huge blokes. It was bad, but not as bad as the lunch of mutton bird, cabbage palm and local fiddlehead ferns we ate the next day. The mutton bird tasted like old grey and hairy anchovies. It became my least favourite ingredient for a decade until Tetsuya Wakuda roasted a couple at an impromptu supper during a Noosa Food and Wine Festival afterparty. In his hands, the fishiness was more like the umami hit of dashi and the skin was bronzed and superbly crispy.

Soon after, one of my new Aussie friends, Caroline Roessler, rang to offer me a job reviewing restaurants for a new glossy free mag she was editing called *Inside Melbourne*. Caroline had interviewed me for a job on *Who Weekly* and we'd become friends when she'd moved to Melbourne. It was her partner Donna who had suggested me as when we played FIFA together I'd talk food and restaurants. Naturally I jumped at it. Getting paid to eat out seemed an even better lark than getting paid to watch telly.

Looking back, I was pretty raw. I was scared about getting stuff wrong, and about getting sued. I wanted every review to do two things – tell you what sort of experience you might have, and be enjoyable to read. It wasn't my place to berate an Italian restaurant for using dried pasta instead of fresh (unless that wasn't what was on the menu), or to deduct a point for paper napkins.

Restaurant reviews should be fun and occasionally funny. They should capture the joy of eating out. And as I've said before, they should be written for the reader, not the restaurant. You want to know if it's worth spending your hard-earned cash there. The advice, freedom and support Caroline and her partner, the Walkley Award-winning Donna Reeves, gave me shaped me and started me off on a career in food that I never would have had otherwise. I dedicated my third cookbook to them and asked them to be godmothers to my daughter, such was the debt I felt – and still feel.

In time I learnt how to tell if a restaurant suspected what my job was (my piece of fish or pork would be much larger than next door's). I learnt to go back and re-review a restaurant if a meal was unexpectedly good or unexpectedly bad. I learnt to take the calls when the chef rang to rant, and to keep back a couple of negatives to point out that I wasn't being vindictive in the review.

It soon became apparent that just as everyone thinks their baby is beautiful (even when it isn't), every restaurateur thinks their place is perfect (even when it isn't). Some would threaten, some would phone my editor, but the bitter truth is that it's never in the reviewer's interest to write a bad review. You get hate. You stress about making an error for which you'll be pilloried. It's far easier to write something faintly positive that denies the truth. But that, of course, is dudding the readers, and they are what matter. To the restaurant and the chef you only owe honesty.

Melbourne's highly engaged foodie audience largely made reviewing a joy. I was once told Melbourne was a city of 3 million food critics and the rest were chefs, and that wasn't far from the truth. This also means there are few other places where writing about restaurants, and reading about them, is taken so seriously – Singapore and New York have a similar obsession and adventurousness. It was a privilege to review in Melbourne.

Most of the chefs whose noses I put out of joint in those early days – Jeremy Strode, Gary Mehigan, Shannon Bennett, Alla Wolf-Tasker – I made up with afterwards and most became friends. I even ended up working with a couple of them. And I was always happy to discuss what I'd written. I'll never forget the 1000-word email I received from Alla Wolf-Tasker about a review of her Daylesford baby, the Lake House, and my 2000-word response where I accepted the good points she had made and I stood my ground on others. I think Alla's original gripe was about a single sentence, some eight words, but when you love food like we do there is always so much more to unpack. I view her as a sister these days.

There were a few who never forgave me, like the restaurant owner who fifteen years after the event pulled a faded review from his wallet when I bumped into him at a function. These things can fester. Over time, I decided to only run a bad review if it was of a restaurant where people were going to spend good money – you know, the flash new opening with a suite of PR people – rather than a place that was already dying in the outer suburbs that no one was likely to visit. Far better to use the review space to tell you about a great little joint that no one had heard of, and that had probably never been reviewed.

This is the attitude that I took to *The Age* when they offered me Matthew Evans's old review slot in the 'Epicure' food section. I'd come to their attention because I'd raved about a restaurant so much that their *Good Food Guide* reviewers couldn't get a table for eight weeks – and that meant it would miss their deadline. It was a family run French place called Le Petit Bourgeois, not flashy, I think BYO, and from memory the duck and the soufflé were delicious.

I spent ten years writing the 'Unexplored Territory' review column for 'Epicure'. I wrote cover stories too – the first was a simple recipe story about my five favourite country kitchen biscuits. As you have already been made well aware, I'm a sucker for a good biscuit!

Awards are meaningless unless you win one and I was lucky enough to pick up a few at the glam Australian Food Media Awards early on. Getting Best New Writer and Best Food Article for a piece on a devotional lunch at a Sikh temple were lovely, but I was blindsided when, later, I won the award for the year's Best Recipe Feature for an epic piece on jam making, beating the biggest names in recipe writing, some true icons.

I was so convinced that I had no chance given the huge names I was up against that by the time of the announcement I was happily toasted. I was also wearing the bright red frock coat I'd bought in Harlem and about which I'd sworn to the woman I love I would never ever wear out. As I stumbled to the stage, all I could think of was how much trouble I'd be in when she saw the photos in the papers the next morning.

I also landed nominations in the World Food Awards for reviewing and food writing. In 2009, I was shocked to be named the World's Best Food Writer. This was another gong I was so certain I wasn't worthy of, I was in India doing a publicity tour when I heard the news. Winning the world's Best Food Section in a newspaper or magazine the year before with the rest of the team at 'Epicure' was even sweeter.

In 2002, I was invited to write for a new food magazine called *delicious*. I loved it immediately. It was intelligent, the food was attainable and tasty, and I'd already marked it down as something special when a mate who never cooked presented chocolate pots he'd made from the first issue of the mag for dessert one night.

The principles I absorbed from the late food director Valli Little and editor Trudi Jenkins are core to how I write recipes today. The recipe must be approachable. It mustn't be alienating and require fancy equipment, and if you can't find the ingredients in Coles Toowoomba or Wagga Wagga, then you must supply a readily available alternative, or make these optional (assuming you can do so without destroying the flavour). Far better, though, to achieve deliciousness through more prosaic ingredients. This is why I find recipe inspiration as much in the aisles of the supermarket as on trips overseas.

I also learnt from these two women that you should write recipes – and this echoes the first rule of restaurant criticism – for the reader, not to impress your peers. If you can teach people how to make no-fail poached eggs, an easier mayonnaise or even a faster mayonnaise that doesn't use eggs at all but still doesn't compromise on texture or flavour, it's of far more use than a recipe for spherifying peas or smoking reindeer heart.

It also helped that, initially, part of the job at *delicious.* was sourcing recipes from chefs for features. This taught me a lot about the pitfalls of a professional cook writing for the home kitchen. You just can't pro rata down the ingredients to make something for four when the original recipe was for forty. And few people want to read a recipe that begins, 'Start preparing two days before . . .'

Going to photo shoots taught me about photographing food for print. We only shot with natural light because the food looks better and we dismissed many of the tricks that commercial food stylists employed in the past, like using cold mash to stand in for ice cream, or glossing roast chicken with motor oil. If a dish started to look tired and we still hadn't got the shot we'd just make another one – although that was seldom necessary when working with quick and accurate pro shooters like Mark Roper or William Meppem.

I learnt that a minuscule movement of a fork or a napkin could be the difference between a humdrum shot or a shot so tasty you want to lick the page. Food director Sophia Young at *Vogue Entertaining + Travel* was the master of this. She also ate double cream and jam off the palm of her hand as a snack which impressed me just about as much as her collection of antique cutlery.

And I learnt that cold food never looks quite right on the page. It seems dead, almost. You have to heat it up or make it from scratch again. These are all rules that I've subsequently lived by – although, if you find yourself flicking through my fifth cookbook, see if you can spot the one shoot where the food is cold. It's surprisingly easy!

*

Along with writing for *delicious.* magazine, which 21 years on is still one of my favourite things to do, came the job of writing for the luxe *Vogue Entertaining + Travel*. Both required me to file travel stories. Well, travelling on assignment was like charging my culinary batteries. Cities such as Madrid, Buenos Aires, Cape Town, Mumbai, San Francisco, Seoul, Copenhagen and Istanbul were among my favourites. Not so much for the fancy places, which were often revelatory, and the people who we met, who were a treat and so generous with their knowledge, but for the holes in the wall and shacks, whether that was a kaymakeria in Besiktas (which sold plates of clotted cream with honey), or a bloke with a bubbling pot of cow jigsaw pieces sliced into tacos.

My regular shooting partner Catherine Sutherland is as big a food nerd as me and it drove us to longer and longer days, visiting more places than is really necessary or normal. It also meant it was only fair that I helped her with her gear in pursuit of the shot, whether that meant navigating the surely cobra-infested grass along the banks of the Musi River in Hyderabad, or helping her to get a shot of San Francisco's Golden Gate Bridge from beneath so the upper stanchions or towers were wreathed in cloud (or fog maybe) and the rest of the orange bridge was wreathed in sunlight.

That second shot didn't go as planned. We clambered down onto Marshall Beach blissfully ignorant that it was for nudists only and had been nicknamed 'Nasty Boy Beach'. Once we were set up, a succession of elderly blokes placed themselves between the camera and the bridge to do their callisthenics, touching their toes or doing star-jumps. Every Christmas since, the dead turkey heads lolling upside down in the butcher shop have had an even uglier significance.

We had a similar challenge taking a photo of the sunrise in the fishing village of Colaba, which has survived in the centre of old Mumbai. Catherine lined up what seemed like a beautiful shot – until we realised that the blokes squatting along the shoreline weren't squatting to take in the stunning view. That was a photoshopping job no one wanted.

On another occasion, Mark Roper and I found ourselves in Port Lincoln in South Australia shooting a story on the area's touchy tuna ranchers. We were in a small boat on the way out to the pen when the skipper began regaling us with stories of the huge white pointers that cruised the surrounding waters between the massive, filled tuna-fattening nets.

'How big are they?' I asked.

'Easily over four metres,' he replied.

'How big is this boat?' asked Mark.

'Just *under* four metres.'

'There's a line in *Jaws* that covers this predicament perfectly,' was Mark's droll response as he slipped down from sitting on the gunwale, his bum hanging over the water, and placed it firmly on the deck.

It wasn't fear but it would have been rude not to join him.

38

Working for *delicious.* magazine and *Vogue Entertaining + Travel* became a staff position when Neale Whitaker, yes, the same bloke who is the stylish judge on *The Block*, turned my contract role into a part-time job. He was all about the food back then. When everyone else was shifting to contracting out, this was a big win. It also meant that I had two and a half days for another little project.

I'd been on the board of the Melbourne Food and Wine Festival for a year and when the job of part-time creative director came up, I jumped at it. There seemed so much potential. Even though they were looking for a 'self-motivated ideas person experienced in events and communication' – I still have the crinkled and yellowing ad and that's what it says – I got the job.

For the next few years or so, working with CEO Natalie O'Brien, Chair John Haddad, and especially event managers Ann Houlihan and Ute Biefang, who did so much – if not all – of the heavy lifting, we took what was a beautiful, if low-key, event and made it into one of the biggest and best food extravaganzas in the world.

No idea was too crazy, and I was constantly arguing for bigger and pushing for more. Let's build the world's smallest restaurant! How about suspending a dining table 100 feet in the air above Fed Square and selling tickets for lunch! Let's paint the stanchions of the Bolte Bridge with a giant knife and a fork so it looks like Melbourne is plated up when you fly into the city, or drive into town over the Westgate Bridge! Or how about serving sushi on an ice rink as though you were in the world's biggest iced seafood buffet?

Imagine working with a particularly demanding toddler and you'll get the picture of what I was like. Natalie's and Ann's eyes were constantly rolling. Ute would just snort her derision!

One of our first changes was to tear up a model where big international chefs did dinners in hotels. Instead, we co-funded their visit and partnered them with local restaurants. This was better for all concerned and built some great international alliances. It also largely meant better food. Working with the Langham Hotel and their marvellous executive chef Anthony Ross, we also resurrected our MasterClass concept and had tastings along with the demonstrations. In a logistical nightmare, the Langham kitchens had to accommodate up to twenty-four top chefs and their culinary needs. At the end of each series I am sure the Langham was cursing us, but Ross made it all happen.

Along with the MasterClass, we implemented a new 'Theatre of Ideas' concept for those more cerebral chefs who wanted to talk about their craft. Pretty much every major chef in the world turned up to the festival in those years . . . René Redzepi, Elena Arzak, Andoni Aduriz, Alex Atala, David Chang,

Roy Choi, Atul Kochhar, Michel Roux, Magnus Nilsson, Fergus Henderson, Sat Bains, Jun Yukimura, Rose Gray, Iñaki Aizpitarte, Christoforos Peskias, Nobu Matsuhisa, Gabrielle Hamilton, Vimal Dhar, Phil Howard, Jonathan Waxman, Carlo Cracco, Samuel and Samantha Clark, Angela Hartnett, and the great Antonio Carluccio several times. Heston Blumenthal and Thomas Keller came as guests of Neil Perry, and Walter Wagner at Crown was a huge supporter, bringing many as well as turning the Festival dinner – whether held among the cornucopia of the loaded stalls of Prahran Market, at an old meat market dramatically lit blood red, or in a huge, deserted Docklands warehouse – into a signature event.

Persuading the world's top chefs to fly to the other side of the world for a puny honorarium and a fair amount of labour took leg work, bare-faced cheek and boundless enthusiasm. Gabrielle Hamilton, author and chef from Prune in New York, summed it up best when asked why she came. 'This bloke in an ascot bowled up to the pass after service with a huge smile and just asked me to come to Melbourne. I couldn't think of a reason not to go.'

I was just convinced that she wouldn't say no and that she'd have a good time when here, which seemed to make a compelling case. Without these chefs' sense of adventure and their generosity with their time, the Festival, Melbourne and my life would have been infinitely poorer.

With so many more festivals around the world these days all chasing the same small pool of top talent, it's much harder for the current incumbents who are running the shows. Especially as some of these are so heavily bankrolled by government. When I joined the Festival we received $180,000. By the time I left it was dramatically more but still insufficient for an event with such high infrastructure costs, and which seeks to keep ticket prices fair so the 300,000 or so people who go don't get gouged. The Festival has never been designed to make a massive profit. That isn't in the best interests of the hospitality businesses involved or the punters.

Our CEO Natalie O'Brien did a brilliant job arguing that the Festival brought tens of millions of dollars into the hospitality economy in Victoria. She had research to prove it too, as she was far more professional than me. When the Festival was declared one of the best tourism destination events across the globe by heavy-weight papers in the US and Canada, our case was made for us. The only other event in the Southern Hemisphere listed was Mardi Gras in Rio!

The media loved all the top chef stuff, but for us as organisers it was as much about driving people to eat and drink in the regions and shining a spotlight on the deliciousness Victoria has to offer all through the year. Hundreds of different hospitality businesses shaped the Festival with their own events. They sat proudly within the program alongside our huge logistical nightmares, like Australia's largest cellar door, with dozens of wineries showing their finest along the banks of the Yarra, and the World's Longest Lunch, which saw 1500 people sitting down together at one very long table at a different location each year.

For the latter event, we closed part of St Kilda Road outside the Arts Centre and the National Gallery of Victoria with a meal which took inspiration from Giovanni Battista Tiepolo's *The Banquet of Cleopatra* that hung inside the gallery. We also wound a table around the perimeter of Marvel Stadium in Melbourne's Docklands. In true footy style we even had a streaker and tried to get a hot air balloon shaped like a Sherrin football to float over the open-roofed stadium.

After these successes I was convinced that we should next take the World's Longest Lunch to the Yarra River. Our event gurus Ann and Ute tracked down forty-eight flat-topped barges lined with astroturf and I insisted that another newbie contact the Navy to see if they'd lend us divers to deliver food to the barges. Strangely, the two things that actually stymied this idea were the costs of insurance (undoubtedly people were going to fall into the Yarra – by accident or on purpose), and the sensible objections of some of the pleasure craft operators.

We also staged a new event over three nights we called 'Spice Bazaar'. This was at a time when an ugly anti-Arab undercurrent was prevalent, so we drew together Melbourne's Middle Eastern, North African and Spanish restaurants for a celebration of food from the Muslim Mediterranean in a massive shed under the Bolte Bridge. Turkish grandmothers sat cross-legged on the floor hand-rolling gozleme and the food was truly delicious.

Some 2500 people attended the event each night. We sold out the wine allocation on the first night. Our event manager Ann Houlihan and I both had nightmares before it started. I dreamt the beer was never delivered, she dreamt someone fell off the quay into the Yarra. This rather shows that the right woman was in charge!

39

I can remember exactly where she was standing when I first met her. The amethyst of her eyes. And the second time I saw her. And the dinner she cooked us. This would be three years before we finally got together.

A few months after the dust of my crumbled relationship with Ginger had blown off my shoes, I started to play tennis with the amethyst eyes.

It was pretty clear pretty quickly that I knew, or at least I think I knew, eventually, and after some thought, that I wanted to spend the rest of my life with her. With the greatest respect to all those who I'd dated, and even some-times loved . . . this was the first time I felt this so clearly. So confidently.

Emma was and is unlike any other woman I'd been with. I realised this the first time I came home very late and very drunk. I was already feeling guilty that I hadn't phoned to let her know that I was kicking on after work, but when my return was greeted by, 'Oh, good, you're home and safe. I was worried,' and not by recrimination and anger, my guilt climbed to the level of mortification.

Next time I made sure to phone.

Emma was an old school friend of Ginger. We started playing tennis together, just as friends, after the break-up with Ginger. I had no ulterior motive. After a game, Emma and I would go and sit at the big, shared table in the back room of Pellegrini's in Bourke Street – a venerable and very cheap Italian spot that was home to one of the city's first espresso machines. Think Bar Italia if you are a Londoner or Swati Snacks if you are from Mumbai. We'd order bowls of minestrone and slices of bread and marge. I remember being astonished that a woman this interesting, this funny, this beautiful, could be single.

It was a little uncomfortable at first given she and Ginger were friends, but it seemed that it was her and Ginger's friends who were more concerned about this than her or Ginger, who had already moved on by this point. One Sunday, three of Emma's friends took me out for yum cha and ruthlessly grilled me to determine if I was on the level. I must have passed. Two of them are still among my favourite people.

It wasn't all smooth sailing. Emma dumped me a few months in because she was convinced I was going to go back to London. I was stung but respected her decision.

Of course, I *did* make a trip to London and when I returned to Melbourne, I started hanging out with another woman, but I think both of us knew it was never going to last. I went to the footy to watch North Melbourne play one Friday night with Emma and some random French bloke who was trailing round after her. That sharpened my understanding that she was someone that my life would be incomplete without. I kissed her at Silver's discotheque after midnight and we've been together ever since – almost thirty years later.

If you are from Australia's AFL-playing south, you'll appreciate that discovering Emma's parents were Collingwood supporters was a huge bonus. Equally important was the fact that she was from Victoria's North East, as I had a mild obsession with Ned Kelly. To her credit she accompanied me when we tried to find the culvert through which the outlaws snuck unnoticed into Aaron Sherritt's mum's hut even though it was under heavy police surveillance from the hill above. She was there when we stood in the dock at the courts in Beechworth and Benalla where Ned had been charged, and when we trekked out past Greta searching for the unmarked location of the Kelly bark hut where he was accused of shooting Constable Fitzpatrick. 'Going above and beyond' I hear you nod and say.

There were two other factors (that contrary to popular family opinion do not include her mother Jude's ethereal quince jelly) that were like signs from above. Firstly, Emma made gnocchi lighter than any other human I have ever met. And secondly, while watching the highlights of a Chelsea game, I wondered aloud why our centre-back Michael Duberry wasn't playing. 'Out. Three weeks. Calf strain,' was Emma's response.

Damn, as if I couldn't be any more smitten.

*

Others also saw how special Emma was. Both my maternal grandfather Larry and his sister Anne independently took me to one side when we visited London for Christmas and explained in no uncertain terms why I'd be a fool a) not to marry her, and b) if I lost her. These two seldom agreed on anything. There were icicles dangling from the eaves in Hell that Christmas.

I proposed to Emma on the fairway of the fifth hole at Benalla's golf course, going down on one knee in the golf cart. Rather than this putting her off and giving me a chance against her, she played blissful, impeccable golf for the next four holes and then we went to tell her folks.

Her dad already knew. I'd done the old-fashioned thing but he hadn't made it easy, taking me round the back of the shed where he was band-sawing timber in the most ominous manner. I took this as a message, even if he wasn't that sort of bloke. His response of 'Are you fair dinkum?' was *Dad and Dave* perfect.

Emma's mother's response was a little less traditional, 'Ooh, we were convinced you were going to run off with a young blonde.'

Replying 'Oh, I didn't know that was an option' earnt, and deserved, a punch on the arm.

In 1999 we married in a paddock down by the Broken River in northern Victoria. A whole mob of my friends came over from London, and as I'd been a best man four times, I felt it was only fair to ask my four mates to reciprocate. The speeches went on for days. But Emma stole the show with her speech built around a quote from *Dirty Dancing*.

A year later we had our first son Jonathan and bought a rundown old house for a song in Malvern, one of Melbourne's leafier eastern suburbs. We only went to see it because Emma's boss had been raised there. He told us the old 1970s wallpaper was still intact. The place was pretty close to derelict and smelt so terrible that prospective buyers were walking round with their jumpers pulled up over their noses. The wallpaper was, however, extraordinary. We even kept the red and lilac paisley up in one room. It's where you'll stay if you come to visit one day.

A team of builders from Benalla, run by a bear of a man called Ross, who is about the most capable man I know, had the job of transforming the house from bombsite to family home. He and his team would drive down on Monday, live on site for the week, and return to the country each Friday after lunch. They finished the job in twelve weeks, including putting a new bedroom and two bathrooms in the attic and knocking over and replacing the back of the house. It was an astonishing feat. Baby Jonathan became adept at sleeping through the sound of nail guns. He can still sleep anywhere.

Jonathan was followed by William and then Sadie, leaving Emma with three under five. Why I say only 'Emma' will become evident very soon.

'Nothing prepares you for having kids' is such a banal cliché, but when you strap that first little bundle in the car seat for the journey home from the hospital and you're trying to remember which way is up, nothing truly can prepare you for the terror. Suddenly you are carrying something more precious than anything you've ever had before. And when you wave off your partner with your newborn for the first drive up to the grandparents', nothing can prepare you for the dread and fear you feel at being apart from them. I'd never had anything I was so afraid of losing. It took years to shake that fear.

Having kids is the best thing that has ever happened to me. Oh, there's another cliché almost as banal as the last. This isn't just because they have grown into fine upstanding characters who understand how to have a good time and have a high level of emotional intelligence, but because they made *me* grow up. Finally.

Selfishly, it took time for me to grasp the momentousness of the change after Jonathan arrived. Gentlemen or non-birth mothers, may I share some advice. If you are going out for work or play while your partner is alone with a small baby (and the dreadful sense that their life may now very much be over), don't, please, slam the door on your way out. In fact, maybe stop playing tennis and postpone going to the gym for the first few months as an act of solidarity. And then suggest your partner go and enjoy all of that before you do. I didn't do this and it was wrong.

Happily, though, with Emma working in a big job at an ad agency and me working from home, I was there for all of Jonathan's key moments – first step, first word – as well as sitting and writing at my computer with him gurgling in the bassinet beside me. Contentment had a new name.

*

If meeting the love of my life weren't reward enough for moving to the other side of the world, having three kids whom I adore but who aren't afraid to tease me when I'm being pompous or say 'bloody good' too much, who beat me at golf or cards, or who brutally take down some dish I'm developing with unerring truth, makes life pretty perfect too.

I could, however, have done without both the boys growing so much taller than me, and with my daughter developing the persuasive abilities of the best defence lawyer money can buy. Of course, you can have a kitten.

40

With three young kids and happily settled in Malvern, the next phase of my life was all about *MasterChef Australia*. I've already described in the Prologue that fateful trip to Paris when Emma and I received the news I'd been selected as one of the three judges.

We arrived at Perth's Exhibition Centre for the contestant auditions to find that Napoleon's army had rolled into town. It certainly wasn't glamorous. The make-up and wardrobe area ran along one side of the canteen, where the hundred or so crew would have breakfast each day. It's a TV truism that 'the talent' on a show are often seen as an unfortunate necessity. I'd learnt this back when I was writing for screen industry trade mag *Encore*. Us journos never ever talked to the onscreen 'warm props', 'meat puppets' or 'flesh scenery'. Only the crew mattered.

We spent the first few months of 2009 travelling round the country auditioning aspiring cooks who turned up with eskies full of ingredients and hearts full of dreams. Some just wanted to be on telly but had no idea what they could offer that was unique. Others had talent but crumbled with nerves. And a few simply blew us away.

At the Sydney audition, there was a mum from up Gosford way who looked a wee bit frazzled but cooked lamb like she was some sort of sheep savant. I gave her a hug and told her that she'd made a beautiful meal. Gary and George came down and joined me. We had discussed earlier how we all wanted to be Marcia Hines or Randy Jackson from *American Idol* – the nice and supportive judge who said things like 'you go, girl'. The woman who'd made that wonderful lamb dish, Julie Goodwin, received the first apron when we went to air. Thankfully, the producers realised that while our positive, warm attitude flew in the face of TV convention, it could make all the difference.

I know that I'm supposed to talk about how *MasterChef* became a hit because of the incredible team who made it in the studio and in the editing suites; the great publicists and the promo people who worked tirelessly each and every series; and our excellent lead-in on Network Ten, but that wouldn't be entirely true. Three very special blokes deserve the credit for the success. If you know TV, you'll know who they are . . . And no, it's not Gary, George or me!

The first was David Mott, the hitmaker at Network Ten who had commissioned *Australian Idol* and *Big Brother*. His push for *MasterChef* to replace *Big Brother* was vital, but scheduling us across the week like *Home and Away* or *Neighbours* was genius.

Then, none of it would have happened without the dogged determination of Mark Fennessy and his brother Carl at FremantleMedia Australia, who kept pitching *MasterChef* to

Mott until he finally said yes. Mark told me he'd been knocked back three or four times previously by Mott – and by the other networks as well.

And finally there was Paul Franklin, another hitmaker who led a great team including Jono Summerhayes. They reshaped the pedestrian UK version of the show and supersized it. What we saw when the show was broadcast was contestants living together in a house like *Big Brother* and team challenges like in Donald Trump's *The Apprentice*. Eliminations were either be at the hands of the judges in a pressure test or, *Survivor*-like, the contestants on the losing team would vote out the weakest link in a sort of kitchen tribal council. This was later changed, though, and I was happy about that as I didn't feel it fitted the supportive and collegiate nature of the show we were making. Like a shiny-headed shaman, Paul would prowl the floor after each of the auditions exhorting us, 'How will the audience fall in love with the contestants if you don't?'

For all the money that was being invested in *MasterChef*, or *MasterChef Australia*, as it is called in the rest of the world, by the time the twenty contestants were announced, the reaction to the show was as lukewarm as school milk left on a sunny step . . . For example, 'Nineteen of those contestants would never get cast on any other reality TV show – where are the ex-beauty queens and ripped tradies from Newcastle and the Gold Coast?'

Or, 'Who'll watch a show about cooking five nights a week?'

Or, 'On *Idol* you can hear the singing, on *So You Think You Can Dance* you can appreciate the rhythm, but you can't smell or taste on the telly.'

And my favourite, 'Why choose such fat ugly judges?'

A media-buying mate told me no one he knew was putting it on their schedules. Quite simply, it was dead in the water.

I suppose they had a point. We'd chosen contestants primarily based on their cooking ability. This meant we had the sort of diverse cast that reflected the Australia we lived in rather than that Stepford world loved by some other reality shows. We had mums and students; a pro golfer looking for a change of career; an ex-Navy petty officer who wanted to move from working on a sub to owning a pub; and a true gentleman who was a lawyer and dated a gallery curator and thus totally and thankfully confounded the TV stereotypes of Indigenous people. There was a chap who cooked in a pork pie hat and I think had finger-boned a quail for his audition dish, cooking it with flavours that roared. There was a girl next door who loved all things French and seemed to be able to wring 20 per cent more flavour out of the same ingredients than anyone else.

And then there was Poh Ling Yeow, a South Australian cook of Malaysian Chinese heritage who only scraped through after we gave her a second chance. Although quixotic and prone to failure, at her best Poh could win. As the voiceover for the show said: 'Australia's first *MasterChef* has to have that kind of genius that sometimes fails but sometimes succeeds extraordinarily.'

Less lucky was Kate Reid, a Formula 1 race car engineer who didn't get an apron for the Top 20. I took her to one side and told her how I reckoned she had the chops to make it in hospitality if she could put this setback behind her. And oh boy, didn't she just. Kate went on to invent the cruffin and launch the global success that is Lune Croissanterie, showing that she didn't need *MasterChef* to become a culinary star. She's the most successful *MasterChef* contestant that never was. Poh, Julie, Justine and so many others didn't do too badly either. In fact, a host of *MasterChef* contestants would go on to make their way very successfully into the food world, such as Hayden Quinn and Adam Liaw as TV presenters; Kylie Miller and Matt Sinclair as chefs; Andy Allen as both; or by creating a successful line of products, such as Diana Chan and Marion Gadsby.

It's another truism that when filming reality TV, the 'talent' makes paint for the editors to paint with. The editors made a warm show, but Gary, George and I also had no intention of giving them any knives to throw. We wanted to see the contestants succeed; we wanted any criticism to be constructive and of the food not of the person; and we wanted to make something that was ultimately uplifting. Even if Gordon Ramsay had recently had the number one show on TV for three nights of the week with his brand of culinary crucifixions, we wanted to represent a paradigm shift in how reality TV treated people. As executive producer Margie Bashfield would remark on news.com.au in 2015, 'I've been in TV nearly thirty years. I'd never walked into a show where the judges were calling the shots.' While I think this is overly generous as the producers and crew still drove the success of the show, we just wanted to persuade Australia to grate their own parmesan and stop using that dreadful pre-ground stuff that smells like vomit!

*

'Nice TV' wasn't enough, however, and the first time I realised that *MasterChef* might be more than that was in the second pressure test. Michelle Darlington, Sam Ciaravolo and Kate Rodrigues had to recreate a stuffed squid dish. Watching at home you could see both Kate's and Sam's dishes looked good and it was pretty clear that Michelle was going home . . . or was it?

I'd found an olive pit in my squid . . . a tooth-shattering, night-ending, $10,000-of-dental-work olive pit. I hid it under my hand as I interrogated Sam about how he'd gone. We asked him how bad it would be if someone hadn't carefully checked their olives. I think I even asked Gary how much the damages claim against a restaurateur could be for this kind of mistake. As the point of this overly egged line of questioning slowly dawned on Sam, we revealed . . . drum roll please, or at least perhaps the telltale *MasterChef* 'eve of disaster', sharpening-knives SFX . . . ''Twas the pit from *your* olive, Sam!'

Watching it was so compelling, so dramatic. That was when we knew we had something special on our hands. Who knew you could wring so much drama from one little olive pit?

In true reality TV style, I argued that Sam should be sent home for his misdemeanour. Gary and George, on the other hand, argued that Sam's squid was far tastier and as they didn't find a pit in their dishes, Michelle was the one who should go. And so she was wished well and waved goodbye. Majority always ruled.

There were so many other things that the producers got right that first series. Employing pastry chef Adriano Zumbo from Sydney's coolest pastry shop to make a croquembouche was one of the smartest. This turned into TV gold as Poh and

Julie excelled in a pressure test with Chris Badenoch and Tom Mosby. There was the drama of lifting the metal cone and the pain of the sugar burns up all the contestants' arms. Zumbo, who's a lovely bloke, oozed malevolence every time he walked through those doors after that, throwing future contestants into an instant funk. The episode also created a national demand for profiterole towers that made struggling pastry chefs a lot of money.

These pressure tests were high drama and very tense, and a month or so in, we had drunk enough Kool-Aid that we realised we truly cared about our motley crew of contestants. We saw the crushing of young cooks' dreams when we sent them home as a serious business.

Initially our ratings numbers were soft but there was one moment when I can remember it all started changing. I'd gone to watch my eldest son at an athletics carnival and when I arrived, around 180 kids from all over the track raced over and started to sing Katy Perry's hit 'Hot n Cold'. 'Jono's dad' was on the telly and they were watching. Across the country, kids were suddenly 'plating up' in the playground with sticks and stones, and scoring their parents' dishes at dinner. It was the kids who dragged in the rest of the family to watch *MasterChef*. And the fact that we refused to dumb down how we talked about food drew viewers not just from the other commercial channels but also from the ABC, in large numbers.

The other group of early adopters were Qantas air crew and it was lovely that a couple of them went on to become contestants. We were finally convinced this was becoming something far bigger than we expected when I was sitting quietly in a pub as a group of roadworkers in day-glo by the bar discussed the relative merits of different stuffed squids with the sort of passion usually reserved for a debate over which Rabbitohs forward had laid the heaviest tackle.

By July 2009, as the first series was nearing its end, the *Australian* newspaper reported that 79 per cent of metropolitan viewers had seen the show. Media buyers were praising it as 'that most desirable and valuable of content offerings: a high-quality entertainment franchise, delivering big ratings for an entire week, generating real viewer excitement and word of mouth, and multiple opportunities for advertiser involvement'.

And things were about to get even headier.

41

For our overseas trip in series 1, we took the show to Hong Kong.

I'd already spent a week there doing a story on the best places – both cheap and exxy – to eat, so we had a head start when it came to our R n R. And this was to be the model for all future overseas trips, at least for the three of us boys – to wring the most out of the experience and get our feet as far under the table at each location as we could.

One lunchtime we snuck off set to a tiny steam-filled room with tightly packed tables stacked high with towers of bamboo steamers. Back then, this dumpling house, Tim Ho Wan in Mong Kok, had just earnt a coveted Michelin star. You put your names down and waited outside until called. Two seats came up and Gary wasn't quick enough, undoubtedly chatting to someone else in the queue. Gary loves a chat. George and I were in, and Gaz was left out.

It then started raining. Not a light drizzle but a proper Hong Kong downpour, and all we could see as we got stuck into their famous fluffy bao with a crispy pork fat and sugar-glaze crust was Gary's sad, sodden face pressed up against the glass.

Don't worry, he eventually got in and we had a vicarious reprise as he went through the same blissful moments George and I had just experienced. When we left Hong Kong, we joked that if we walked through an X-ray machine all they'd see inside us were dumplings.

The pinnacle challenge of that week in Hong Kong involved sending contestants around the city to search for ingredients. We started them off on the spectacular Victoria Peak with the city and the harbour laid out far beneath us . . .

But the weather that day was bad and getting worse. The wind picked up to hurricane levels as we were about to send the contestants on their way. Our local fixer told me the history of this place, The Peak, and how local legend says we were standing on the head of a great dragon whose body curled back into the heart of China. From this vantage point, the old pirate kings who ruled the area would spot prey on the waters below to plunder. When we hit our marks the wind was blowing really ferociously, so much so it was hard to stand stationary. This inspired a sort of madness in me. I unleashed an unhinged, off-the-cuff monologue inspired by this 'dragon's breath' roaring around us. About how the three of us were like pirate kings sending the contestants out to 'plunder' the deliciousness of the city below and how that fierce wind was really dragon's breath. You can still find the rant on YouTube. It's one of my favourite moments on that first series – not least because you can see the contestants embracing the humour and madness of this moment.

The weather broke as night fell, and I'll never forget the sight of Julie Goodwin, curly hair drenched from the rain, as she laboured down a Wan Chai alley with the neon bouncing off the rain-rivered tarmac under her feet and a pig carcass over her shoulder.

Later we secretly made pirate eye patches for everyone on the crew in the tasting room to slip on before we recorded the intro to the tasting, as I'd likened us three judges to those ancient pirate kings, sending the contestants off to plunder the food and ideas of the city in the storm. 'Are we ready to film? We arrrrrrrrh!' Okay, we did take them off to film the tasting, out of respect.

Things were a little frosty with Gary during that first series. I suspect it was just that usual mongoose–cobra relationship between critic and chef. He didn't see why I should ever be in the kitchen. If that were the case, I didn't see why he should ever be in the dining room. Things weren't helped by the publicity that I was getting. I mean, here was a chef with decades of experience and yet people seemed more interested in some over-stuffed, rambling peacock. I should say at this point that over the years we grew very close. Today I regard him as the best and most trusted of friends. Gary is a top bloke and loyal to a fault.

Due to our filming schedules, host Sarah Wilson and I were largely apart during production. I was only there for the pressure tests, celeb chef cook-offs, mystery boxes and invention tests. But we still became friends – still are – even though we are very different in our approach to life. If I had an angel on one shoulder whispering in my ear what the right thing to do is, it would be Sarah. The imp on the other shoulder? That would just be a mini version of me, egging myself on to chase pleasure and short-term satisfaction!

Sarah and I shared the same tiny shipping container dressing room and became close enough that I even went shopping for bedlinen with her. I'm not sure she realised what a big thing this was for me, because linen shopping is even less fun than choosing gravel . . . stone by stone.

Sarah would end up leaving *MasterChef* after that first season. I couldn't be happier for the great success of her new career, writing *New York Times* bestsellers (including the mega-selling *I Quit Sugar*, the proceeds of which she donated to charity) and building a global health brand. Like I said, she's the perfect angel on my shoulder.

Now back to Poh Ling Yeow. She was eliminated for incorrectly identifying barley in a minestrone soup taste challenge, but someone had the bright idea of bringing her back for a second chance alongside Justine Schofield and Tom Mosby. Julie was happy but Chris Badenoch was miffed as he rightly suggested that those still there had earnt that spot.

Chris was in danger of turning into the villain in the pork pie hat with his combination of talent and confidence. On TV this can come across as arrogance. I thought it funny when he'd put up great dishes using one less ingredient from the pantry than everyone else. He did this so he could also grab a beer to drink when he finished before everyone else. And in fact over the years viewers have seen limits on pantry picks being phased out as we realised the key to the show was giving the contestants every chance to put up great food in the face of great pressure.

*

The idea of making these amateurs take on a top chef as a reward for the best invention test dish was a doozy, but initially the reward when they beat the chef was a double-edged sword. Sure, it meant they were fast-tracked to the finals, but only when we got to finals time did we realise that they'd suffered from not being fully part of the preceding weeks. They hadn't had a chance to develop like the other amateurs. In later series, an immunity pin was a far fairer and more valuable prize. Still, it was great TV when Julia Jenkins beat Pete Evans and Lucas Parsons beat Ben O'Donoghue.

After sixty-five episodes we reached the finals weeks. All contestants crashed and burned embarrassingly in a pie challenge, with Julie only saved by her savoury pie and the fact that her sweet 'puddle pie' tasted good even if it looked like someone had thrown it at the wall. Lucas was sent home. The next day went Julia.

After cooking a series of impressive dishes like a pig's head, Chris was sent home for undercooked beef cheeks. Justine Schofield had fallen apart the previous episode. That elimination literally made the front-page news. As judges, we were shocked too. Chris and Justine were regarded as the best cooks but as so many other excellent cooks would do in coming years, they wobbled on the brink of greatness. Still, it hasn't stopped Justine becoming an Australian culinary icon.

The finalists were Poh, who was on a roll since coming back into the competition, and Julie, perpetually harried but with a steel-spined resolve. Here you can cue any number of my thirty or so Poh puns that TV columnist Marieke Hardy called 'increasingly unhinged'. She was the 'Poh-llercoaster' for her up-and-down cooks; a disastrous dish from her was an 'A-Poh-calypse' for which we deserved an 'A-Poh-logy'. Or my favourite 'Oh no, oh Poh'. The days were long with not a lot really happening. We were bored. I was trying to keep our spirits up. Sometimes we'd sway around the room growling like those disturbed polar bears you see in zoos that are bored to distraction. TV can be like that . . . hours upon hours of waiting and then intense moments of high performance in a tightly constrained window. When a whinging celeb tells you how hard it is to make TV, however, take this with a pinch of salt. As I'd remind the boys, based on my previous experience, 'It's not digging ditches!' This became a motto of sorts over the years . . . every time one of us felt frustrated.

Poh lost the finale because her chocolate lacked the snap of proper tempering. I remember nudging guest judge Matt Moran's knee under the table as my spoon shattered Julie's version of the chocolate tube from Matt's curated finale dish. Julie won but they both came out winners. You know that already.

The great thing about *MasterChef* was that you didn't need to win to win. In *Idol* the runner-up often did better than the winner, but it ran deeper than that with *MasterChef*. Chris Badenoch went on to open restaurants with Julia Jenkins. Lucas Parsons' cafe thrived. Andre Ursini, who had been the most vocal about wanting to run a true Italian place in Adelaide, opened a couple of big successes over the years and delivered on his promise through hard work and dedication. And Justine

Schofield became one of TV's most prolific, best-loved cooks and longest-serving stars.

But it was ex-Navy petty officer Trevor Forster who launched the first restaurant – a 54-seater on Rockingham's beachfront in Western Australia. On that first series, he was perhaps best known for being at the centre of 'bait-gate', after he chose to use bait as an ingredient in one of his team's dishes, which made the food 'taste like the bottom of a boat'. It was the first of many '-gates' that would 'plague' the show in coming series.

As we sat, sipping cheap wine out of plastic cups after the finale wrapped, we were blissfully unaware about what was about to happen.

It was going to be big. Bigger than anyone could have imagined.

42

The finale of the first series broke all records. Its ratings were only eclipsed by the 2005 men's tennis Australian Open final and the 2003 Rugby World Cup final (and, since, by the Matildas' World Cup semifinal). It's still the second biggest non-sports broadcast ever.

The finale of the second series a year later would go one better and take out second place overall at that time, just a measly quarter of a percentage point behind the tennis.

That's the last thing I'll say about ratings for a while as it's hard to write this without sounding boasty, even though I'm sure everyone who worked on those first two series – the forty-four contestants, the two hundred or so crew and editors, all the big bosses, plus the host and three judges – feel the same way.

While the producers were the brains behind the show, I have always maintained that the contestants are the true stars. They deserve the plaudits. They are the ones you tune in to watch as they embark upon their culinary adventures. Gary, George and I were just the rails on which that journey ran for some eleven years and fifteen series.

And yes, occasionally too, we were also the bumps in the road.

About five years before *MasterChef*, in 2004, I'd been cast as the 'mystery critic' in the first series of *My Restaurant Rules* (not to be confused with the much later *My Kitchen Rules*) on the Seven Network. With my usual lack of judgement, I'd thought that as *My Restaurant Rules* wasn't doing so well in the ratings, no one would see me crash and burn if my appearances went badly. Needless to say, as soon as the elimination rounds started, the ratings jumped massively, my arrival a 'lucky' coincidence.

It seemed weird that, back then, none of the teams on the show ever worked out the mystery critic was me. I put it down to my *Seinfeld* disguise of 'jeans and white sneakers'. Even though I was anonymous, there was still a certain amount of pressure from the crew filming each restaurant because if that restaurant was eliminated then that crew no longer had jobs and got sent home. The chef in the Western Australian restaurant, which was the worst in my opinion, threatened onscreen to chase me down the street with a ladle. I think I can remember him saying he wanted to stab me through the heart with it but I might be wrong. In the end, the New South Wales restaurant run by a proto-hipster brother and sister who weren't battlers were sent home. Ah, different times!

The other key thing I learnt from my time on *My Restaurant Rules* was that being on a hit show makes you very visible. I discovered this while walking through Melbourne Airport one day. People pointed, people walked around me staring like I was a museum exhibit, and both the security scanning team *and* passport control guys said hello. Of course, this immediately went to my head and I acted like a dill for a month or so, which I suppose was another lesson learnt. If people thought I acted like a diva on *MasterChef*, they obviously hadn't met me after my short stint on *My Restaurant Rules*.

There was one other lesson from that early show. Under no circumstances should you allow yourself to be filmed sitting in the back of a taxi. It is never flattering!

With *MasterChef*'s growing status, the inevitable jibes began. The comedian and radio host Dave Hughes got stuck in about my 'greasy hair', while Kyle Sandilands called me a 'walrus in a neckerchief'. Dave came round when I was on air with him and pointed out that he'd forgotten we'd spent a long lunch together once when I interviewed him for *delicious*. 'Not so good at noticing the little people then, Dave?' was my riposte. I can't remember what happened with Kyle, but a year or so later they paid me to be an occasional correspondent on his and Jackie O's show, so things must have become more cordial. For all that might be said about Kyle, he is a very savvy (radio) operator.

For a brief moment, if you believe the media, I was 'dangerously close to becoming a fetish' (Miranda Devine), 'a breath of shiitake consommé–infused fresh air', and even, God forbid, 'an unlikely sex symbol'. I received marriage proposals from both men and women but Emma batted all this away like a pro when she told Wendy Squires at the *Australian Women's Weekly* that people would quickly stop feeling that way 'if they saw him in his underwear'. God, I love that woman. Okay, that's enough of that because it sounds boastful too and you're not here to read any more self-aggrandisement . . . Give us more dirt, give us pain.

When the second series rolled around, the jibes went up a notch. What seemed quaint and charmingly theatrical was suddenly lampooned as pompous and overblown. Someone was sawing at the stalk of this tall poppy. TV writer Holly Byrnes, whom I had always rather liked, referred to me as the 'prat in the cravat'. I was named second in a worst dressed list by some shoddy lads' mag (bested only by Tracy Grimshaw) and I even picked up a number of 'colourful' awards. I'm still waiting for the promised gold-plated tissue box that came with winning Wanker of the Year in another lads' mag. Those people, often complaining about how overexposed I was, were doing so in print and on radio and thus adding to the problem. Oh, the irony!

Not all awards were bad. At the 2010 Logies I was nominated for two gongs and the show for one. We were filming series 2 in London and I had to fly back through clouds of volcanic ash alone to attend the ceremony. The boys stayed to film the MasterClass and a challenge with Heston Blumenthal. Luckily, this meant I could take Emma with me on one of their tickets, and both Poh and Julie were there with us to hold my hand.

It was lovely sharing the night with these impressive women, but I was most excited that I could tick off another of the three dreams I'd mentioned to our publicists when I started on *MasterChef*. They were:

1. Go to the Logies
2. Appear on *Rove Live* (and not make a dick of myself), and, hardest of all
3. Get a guest role on *Neighbours* to impress my mum.

I'd already appeared on *Rove* the week before the finale. The 500,000 leap in audience to a record 1.6 million for that episode of *Rove* was not down to me but to the fact that PM Kevin Rudd was also on the show, as well as Sasha Baron Cohen (as Bruno) and Rove, both dressed in knitted woollen body suits complete with little knitted woollen penises. I basically was just the free air-freshener given out with a new Range Rover.

Backstage at *Rove*, I'd never seen more security, minders, fluffers, puffers and media liaisons. Their combined entourages were exactly a hundred times larger than mine. I know, I counted.

I watched that interview again recently and saw that I just about managed to avoid making a dick of myself. Adelaide's *Sunday Mail* said I held my own but the only quote I was actually proud of has been cut from the highlights reel, 'Some people say cravats are pretentious. To them I say, "Au contraire!"' Thank you, Monty Python.

But back to the Crown Palladium Ballroom and the Logies ceremony . . . and your host Shaun Micallef.

MasterChef won the Logie for Most Popular Reality Program, and after my mother's vote had tipped *Home and Away*'s Luke Mitchell over the line for Most Popular New Talent (male) rather than me, I was stunned to pick up the Graham Kennedy

Award for Most Outstanding New Talent. This was voted for by the industry and so my mother had no influence, which perhaps explains why I won. My speech seemed short enough to stop people yawning and I rather liked the idea of someone so old winning an award for a 'newcomer'. Shaun Micallef was suitably arch about that, complaining how that in doing so I had trampled on the hopes and dreams of the other, far younger nominees.

MasterChef went on to win the Reality Program Logie again the following year – and collecting it on stage with Gary and George made it all the more special. And then in 2019, we won for our tenth, and penultimate, series. We were proud that we'd helped bring the show back from the edge of extinction with a reaffirmation of good cooks and better cooking. The producers and crew also won the Best Reality TV AACTA in 2013, 2014, 2015, 2016, 2017, 2020, 2021 and 2022. This is an extraordinary record and confirmation that the *MasterChef* team was and is still the best in Australia. I don't want to seem churlish, so let me say for the record, I also had a smile when *MasterChef* took out the Most Popular Reality Logie in 2022 and 2023 with the three new judges at the helm.

The Logies and AACTAs weren't the only plaudits. There were more. I was shortlisted as a *GQ* Man of Style and picked up a *GQ* Man of the Year award the next year in the Critic of the Year category. It was jolly nice of them to create (what I think is) a one-off category just for me.

I also picked up a Nickelodeon orange blimp for winning their trophy for Awesome Oldie. This might be a way of saying thank you for the previous year where they had dressed me as Cupid complete with huge white wings and swung me from the highest rafters of the Sydney Entertainment Centre. I was under the impression that I would be a metre or so off the ground, but as I climbed flight after flight of stairs in my feather wings and hidden harness it slowly dawned on me that this might be a wee bit more terrifying.

Walking out onto the very narrow gantry high up in the roof was bad enough but, cable attached, swinging my legs over the handrail to step into the void some 35 metres above the stage was an act of faith. I'm not a fan of heights and uncurling my white knuckles from the rail took all my powers of concentration. I felt sick each time. Still do, thinking about it. This wasn't the sort of swinging from the rafters I was a fan of . . . After a couple of practice runs, they hung me up there for ten minutes as the show unfolded beneath me. Eventually, I was allowed to slowly descend from the gods to present Liam Hemsworth and Miley Cyrus with the award for Best Kiss of the Year.

Over the years I've become a fan of taking opportunities that scare you, or that seem well outside your comfort zone, and this is where that philosophy started to take shape. I had been genuinely terrified but the adrenaline rush afterwards was intense. And my oldest son, who was in the audience, not yet a teenager, thought it was funny, although I think he was more impressed that I'd met Sam and Freddie from *iCarly*, and that I got to slime people at the end of the show.

In fairness to the critics, I had been everywhere during 2009. So much so that I used to joke that even a narcissist like me was bored of seeing myself. There was more than a grain of truth to this, but the sun was shining and I was making just a little bit of hay.

I published a collection of my previous writing with Penguin Random House under the shameless title of *Cravat-A-Licious*. It was sold as a collection of my 'least worst' work. I signed up to do an ad for Handee paper towels, which helped take the brand from second place to number one. Then the nice people at Sony let me release a double CD of songs 'to cook and eat to' that initially sold like hotcakes . . . until Susan Boyle's LP hit the stores and blitzed us. I also found myself on a lot of magazine covers. There was a *MasterChef* magazine on the cards, too.

News Corp and Fairfax began bidding for my services. I went to News Corp because all those years ago Neale Whitaker had put me on the books and made me a staff member, while after ten years writing and winning awards for Fairfax, they still hadn't even given me so much as a contract for my column. 'Go with the company that has looked after you better' was Steve Vizard's advice. I've never looked back and am still happily ensconced there.

Later in 2009, we shot a celebrity version of *MasterChef* with a cast that included among others a state premier, a top AFL player, a test cricketer, that nice Kirk Pengilly from INXS, Josh Thomas, Indira Naidoo and Michelle Bridges. Gary clashed with Peter FitzSimons, which was like watching a pair of old silverbacks sizing each other up.

I was disappointed by George Negus's signature risotto of which he'd spoken so proudly. Before the show began airing,

I was talking about risotto being the 'death dish' in interviews. In George, it claimed another victim.

In the finale, swimmer Eamon Sullivan won in a huge turnaround, beating Kirk and model Rachael Finch. I'm not sure if we teased Eamon about going one better than his Olympic swim in Beijing the previous year, where he 'only' won two silvers (and a bronze). But we probably did. He's the sort of straight-up, knock-about bloke who'd take that and bat it back with a little extra curry.

En route we nearly broke the charming singer Alex Lloyd, and Swans premiership player Ryan O'Keefe likened the intensity of a cook in the *MasterChef* kitchen to that of a grand final. Queensland premier Anna Bligh was a delight – she was so happy cooking, perhaps because there were no advisors to hassle her and no phone calls to take during the challenges.

After wrapping series 1 and doing the celebrity version of *MasterChef*, we were already staring down the prospect of shooting series 2. The treadmill was starting to turn, but I was happy to be on it . . . in part because my lawyer David Vodicka's wise prediction that I'd have bargaining power for future series if the first show was a success had come to pass.

43

So much is written by the print media about the meticulous and Machiavellian planning of a reality TV series, but in my experience it's far more often seat-of-the-pants stuff. There's actually very little set in stone at the start. The idea that there might be some deep conspiracy afoot to preordain a winner is frankly unbelievable. Still, over the years, there were plenty of journalists and other keyboard warriors on Twitter who would declare that they knew the fix was in, and who was going to win. As we'd already shot so much of the show by the time it went to air, we'd know how wrong they were.

For a while I kept all their details on file so I could tweet them back after the broadcast of their 'definite' winner leaving in a black Hyundai had aired. I wanted to remind them how wrong they'd been and could we have an apology now, please? I soon realised that this was just a mark of how invested everyone had become. We *wanted* people to talk, to debate, and to cook . . . to help the show exist in people's lives for the hours when it wasn't onscreen.

*

If there was pressure making series 2, it was alleviated by how well Australia had reacted to series 1. That was a huge relief after all the early disbelief that anyone would tune in at all. I'm not sure about Gary and George, but I felt like a premiership player at the end of their career when they finally lift the trophy. If it all fell in a heap now, we could still walk away happy, knowing that we'd done our bit to promote the joy of sharing a meal, and we'd respected those who had cooked it. And, of course, sales of Microplane graters and wedges of real parmesan were up. Australia had sold out of ling, and of pasta machines. Friends were carping that they now had to make more of an effort in the kitchen. Talking about good food was no longer daggy and this all made us very happy.

Of course, we couldn't stop our new cooks seeing contestants from series 1 go on to achieve their food dreams. This made the newbies want it all the more. Gary, George and I encouraged this by getting them to buy into the process, to make them feel they were part of something big.

The freewheeling nature of series 1 gave way to an earnestness and a sense, both on the set and in the edit, that this stuff *mattered*. It was important. There was a concomitant danger that it could come across as pompous and any grandiloquence as self-obsession. I'm sure around this time I started using highfalutin words like 'concomitant' rather than just saying 'associated'.

The result was more tears from the contestants. And more stories about dead grandmas.

Donna Hay joined as a judge for the chef cook-offs. She received a brutal ride from some of the Twitterati, which seemed unfair given that she's a dead set legend. The media were full of stories about side projects or network moves I might, or might not, have in the pipeline. I did shoot a pilot with Anita Jacoby for Andrew Denton that I really liked. I was also apparently approached to join US *MasterChef* as a judge via Paul Franklin . . . He would later joke about sneakily not passing on my number so he could keep me on the Australian franchise.

There was no shortage of big moments in series 2 but none more shocking than the elimination of Marion Grasby. Even more shocking was the fact that she was eliminated on a satay sauce challenge against Twitter-dubbed 'beanie douche' Aaron Harvie, and she was half Thai. Besides being a great cook and one of the nicest people you could hope to meet, Marion was also the runaway favourite. There was a gag – probably in Ben Pobjie's very sharp and funny daily recap – that when Marion cooked, singing bluebirds flew round her shoulders like she was some Disney hero.

I wasn't there that day, and while I was sad she'd been elimi-nated, I was glad that the boys had stuck to their guns, as they would again in series 3, when the TV ratings–gold contestant Hayden Quinn was sent home earlier than hoped for, thanks to an over-seasoned dish. These 'shock' eliminations proved that the show stuck by the promise that what would eliminate you was cooking the worst dish. This was hardly ever something that Gary, George and I disagreed on.

I'm sure you've watched other reality TV shows and wondered how some contestants survive so long. You probably thought they had some kind of a guardian angel looking out for them . . . which in a way I suppose they did. Maybe their deal stipulates that they couldn't be eliminated for several weeks, or sometimes even that they could never lose a challenge! Maybe the producers are keeping them around for drama or for a belief that they'll bring ratings. Thankfully that never happened, to my knowledge, on *MasterChef*.

Eliminations such as Marion's and Hayden's were like the culinary equivalent of *Game of Thrones'* Red Wedding or Ned Stark's demise – the jolt that makes you re-engage with a favourite show, or perhaps howl at the screen.

In eleven series of *MasterChef*, we were never told who to save or who to lose. I respected our producers greatly for that. There might be, very occasionally, some out-loud musings about how good, for example, a young winner would be 'for the brand', but our record shows that if the dish wasn't there, then neither was the contestant. If the food gods wished it, so it would happen.

This concept of the 'food gods' was a brilliant construct of ours to reassure the producers. And strangely, it really seemed to play out. When we respected the food gods, respected the process, we were invariably rewarded with good, sometimes surprising, TV moments. Or with ratings that did exactly the opposite of the disaster predicted.

In coming series, TV gurus would predict that one contestant was TV gold and the other too boring. Guess which one became the crowd favourite – the 'boring' one! When Hayden Quinn left, some critics predicted a ratings catastrophe, but the numbers kept rising.

Every time we did the 'right thing' and respected the integrity of the process, we were rewarded by better numbers. There was a debate in the series 10 finale in 2018 that if Sashi Cheliah took an unassailable lead too early, viewers would switch off. Each of us still scored his starter of sambal prawns a perfect 10/10, and he ended up with an unassailable 16-point lead going into the final round. It was what the food gods would have wanted.

Instead of viewers switching off because the result was pretty much a forgone conclusion, the numbers actually grew. People *wanted* to see the much-loved Sashi declared the winner. They wanted to see his triumphant lap of honour with the last dish of the finale – and they wanted to see the contestant he had beaten in earlier rounds, Ben Borsht, redeem himself. Ben did a great job and Sashi walked out with the highest ever finale score: 93/100. It was a vindication of the essence of *MasterChef Australia*. Celebrate the wins, celebrate redemption, trust in the food gods and they will deliver.

Series 2 also saw the controversial decision to move a federal election debate because it clashed with the finale. Gary, George and I had a rare argument over whether Alvin Quah – one of that year's other best contestants – should be sent home over a pressure test centring around Adriano Zumbo's intricate, multi-level vanilla V8 cake. No one nailed it but, of the two worst contenders, I liked Alvin's version best. It was messy but it tasted more like the maestro's. Adriano wavered but sided with me. We argued for a couple of hours after the tasting, but in the end the boys got their way and the creator of one of the tastiest dishes in *MasterChef* history ('Alvin's Drunken

Chicken') went home. Still, what's the rule? It's only about the dish you've cooked on the day.

An ugly trope of reality cooking shows is when an angry judge throws a plate against a wall or in the bin. It's a deeply insulting thing to do and I cannot condone that sort of behaviour. But on Sunday 30 May 2010, I did it.

Aaron Harvie, the bloke who always wore a beanie, put up a dish of rare beauty and next-level tastiness in a pasta challenge. My oh my, his silky fennel and prawn tortellini with a chipotle oil was sublime. Gary and George tasted the dish and then I did. I then picked up the plate, held it out and dropped it, declaring, 'That dish was *disgusting* . . .' I let the moment hang for a beat and then flowed into saying, '. . . disgustingly *good*!' Cue cheers all round and a review full of praise for Aaron's pasta from me. The remains were all over the floor. Our DoP, Paul Mossy Moss, caught the whole thing.

The editors loved it, but the problems began when the promos started running. For a solid week all you saw was me smashing the plate, saying 'that's disgusting', and Aaron's crest-fallen face. That plate fell for seven long days until the final softening payoff was delivered on Sunday night. It just looked mean without the payoff – and rather than subverting the trope it ended up reinforcing it. Neither was my intention, but unintended consequences are what they are.

In retrospect it was still great TV, ratings jumped by almost 200,000 viewers for that episode, and it's the moment that a whole heap of kids who were pre-teens back then remember as 'iconic'. Now in their twenties, it's part of the reason why cut-outs of me, with that plate held out in the air, regularly pop up on doof sticks at music festivals around the country. Much to the consternation of my kids, who definitely don't want the image of their dad impinging on their downtime at 3 am at Beyond the Valley or Awakenings.

The plate moment was all part of our subconscious desire to play with, and subvert, the form. We sought to find other ways to say things in a different way if phrases risked becoming clichés. We tried to recap in a couple of ways so that the tedious repeat footage before and after each ad break might feel fresher to the audience, who would quickly tire of lazy repetition. Old-school reality TV always demanded an outcome, but now if two contestants both did really great jobs in an elimination cook-off, we would save them both. It caused a few planning issues but it felt more authentic for this very rare occurrence. That's when it worked. When you knew at home that this was the right thing to do.

Of course, we didn't always succeed even if our hearts were in the right place. Like when in *Junior MasterChef*, George and I scored at dish 11 out of 10 because Jack's choux buns were actually better than the ones made by Zumbo for the kids to recreate. What's better than 10? Well, 11 obviously. We'll come back to the stupidity (or brilliance) of this logic in a couple of chapters, so hold your anger or admiration until then!

We also tried to stop George saying 'yummy' all the time. Nigella Lawson outlawed 'delicious' as being an empty word, like 'nice', that conveyed no sense of why a dish was delicious. We might have ignored that too.

For me, delicious is such an evocative word. Everyone knows what it means. It's a very personal sense of perfection. It's the crunch of that perfectly seasoned golden crackle with that jellied rendered fat, soft on its underside. It's fish that flakes apart at the gentlest nudge of a knife. It's perfect salty caramel poured over tart roast apple with some crème fraîche ice cream to bring soft, cold creaminess against the riot of sour and sweet.

Other ways where we were more successful in playing with the reality TV rules were on those challenges when we were looking for multiple winners. We wouldn't always wait for the traditional reveal at the end of the show. We might announce a safe or winning contestant in the middle of a tasting if the dish was of such stellar quality that it was unlikely to be topped. Mix things up. Keep it interesting. Keep you on your toes!

In the final edit it was a great way of surprising an audience who often felt they knew what was coming next. The producers played the same game, introducing new challenges, constantly trying to improve the format, and bringing on increasingly bigger guests. The *Survivor*-style voting went, and new rounds were introduced so you now needed to cook badly twice in a row in order to be sent home.

We also insisted on celebrating the successes and mini-mising the pain of disasters. It was part and parcel of being supportive. I worked hard with the producers. We moved away from the traditional negative language of eliminations. I'm not sure anyone else ever noticed, but it all helped to push this idea of Gary, George and me being mentors as well as judges, people who genuinely cared about our contestants. It reso-nated because it was authentic. This was particularly true when we reached the top ten, but even in the earlier rounds it was important to allow people to leave with dignity.

On the way to the finale in series 2, we lost Jimmy Seervai (the first of many contestants to favour Indian techniques and flavours) in a cookbook challenge with Maggie Beer, and our final three contestants cooked dinner at Government House for then Governor-General Quentin Bryce and her guests (Claire Winton Burn went home).

Adam Liaw defeated Callum Hanh in the finale, after which we had a particularly wild wrap party at Luke Nguyen's Red Lantern in Surry Hills. I can't remember who we had to pour into a taxi to get them home. Or I can but I'm not saying. Buy me a beer next time we are out and I'll tell you. And no, it wasn't me.

The finale for series 2 peaked at 5.2 million viewers, and with an average of over 4 million, it became the second biggest Australian TV event since ratings began, and the biggest non-sports moment, with the previous finale in second place. *The Block*, *Australian Idol*, *The Voice* and *MKR* fill out the rest of the Australia's Top Five Shows Ever.

Media commentators estimated that *MasterChef* that year generated some $100 million in Australia alone, and sales of Peter Gilmore's snow egg – the finale dish that Adam excelled at, getting 9/10 all round – boomed at his Sydney restaurant, Quay.

With that sort of success, no wonder the copycat brands started coming.

44

The success of series 2 meant increased scrutiny – and more 'scandals'. The public had its eye on us, and every aspiring sleuth in the Twittersphere or the tabloids was watching to see if they could spot any cracks. I'm not going to discuss the contestant scandals – those are their stories to tell in their own books – but in terms of the production of the show, we always tried to be as transparent as possible about what we did and how we did it. We also tried to change our process whenever a 'glitch' occurred.

We ran an 'open set' so journalists could come and see that a one-hour challenge did in fact last for one hour, and that there wasn't a battalion of home economists off-camera helping the contestants with their dishes. Seriously, I've heard of this happening on some disreputable cooking-competition shows but far be it for me to name names. That's their deception and they have to live with it. They should have picked better cooks in the first place.

*

'Plate-gate' was probably the first glitch, when we allowed Callum Hann to put fresh ice cream on his dish because the stuff he'd had there at the end of the cook would have melted into a mess in the fridge otherwise (and we couldn't store his whole dessert in the freezer for obvious reasons). This became the norm in the future for all desserts.

Similarly, we had to find a way to deal with the issues of keeping tastings – especially large tastings – fair. If we started tasting immediately at the end of the cook, the first five dishes would be warm but the rest increasingly cool. That prejudiced those whose dishes were tasted at the end.

One solution was to taste all the dishes cold. This would allow the post-cook mayhem of the kitchen to be cleaned down before the judging started but was far from ideal when it came to assessing dishes whose textures might change. The best solution we came up with was to get each cook to plate up a second rough version of their dish to be tasted warm and fresh immediately after time was called. This could be a mad rush, but it was incredibly useful. Especially as we also constantly tasted and assessed elements of each dish as we did our bench visits during the cook, and tasted it again in the formal tasting. This improved things dramatically.

George and I had a lot in common. We both loved football. Him: Carlton, Man United and Melbourne Victory. Me: Collingwood, Chelsea and Melbourne Victory. And while Gary was the traditionalist, George and I were both a little bit dazzled by the new culinary wonderland. Gary was a classicist and a master of technique. George was the creative one.

Looking back, I'm surprised the producers didn't seek to try to divide us. The longer we worked together and the more experiences we shared (whether these were marvellous contestant dishes or just from being three blokes set adrift from our families in Sydney), the tighter our bond became. I think it was indie English rock band Alt-J that once said the triangle was the strongest of all shapes. Gary, George and I became that triangle.

Being a trio also meant that there were always two others to pull the one playing up back into line. When Gary complained about having to take a taxi to the airport in Adelaide, we called him 'limo boy' for a week. When I was getting too wanky about a dish, Gary would just ask me whether I'd order it again in a restaurant. Usually I wouldn't; the cleverness of the concept had blinded me to the blandness of the flavour. George would try to keep Gary away from the cheese board set up for crew snacks in the afternoon and he'd try to stop me ordering the whole menu when we lunched together. He'd usually weaken, however, when we reached dessert. And they both teased me about ordering weird amphora-aged wines made by Josko Gravner in Friuli in Italy when Gary never wanted to spend more than $100 – and 'Could we have a nice oaky chardonnay instead, please?' Well, I did have to admit it tasted much nicer . . .

In series 2, the judges started to physically fall apart. Gary did his hand in a mountain bike accident filming for his other TV show *Boys Weekend* and then ripped a quadricep muscle clean from the bone when a new but unmarked step was installed at the door of our new, less leaky green room. His scream was piercing as he went over and the muscle rolled up to the top of his thigh like a spring-loaded blind. George meanwhile was suffering from a pinched nerve and a dodgy disc in his back. I developed sciatica.

Yes, I can see that tiny violin you are playing there, but the days *were* bloody long and I had a destructive habit of standing with my left hip cocked. Gee it could ache! This meant that during a cook you might spot me on the camera side of the *MasterChef* kitchen flat on my back stretching out my hip flexors and lower back like some big old Galapagos turtle flipped over in distress.

Trying to fix the problem, I visited Sydney's best acupuncturist, as well as a leading NRL sports masseuse. He was a short walk from the *MasterChef* kitchen so I could pop round and he'd free me up for a while. Ironically, it was a tiny, gentle physio magician near my home in Melbourne who finally gave me some permanent relief.

More seriously, I developed a mystery affliction, something between vertigo, spatial displacement and agoraphobia. It came on towards the end of series 2 and would reach a peak during *Junior MasterChef*. At some points it made it almost unbearable to be on set without some sense of an anchor point.

It started when I had a weird turn one day and had to be taken away in an ambulance. In emergency they suspected a stroke, sent me off for an MRI and took a sky-high blood pressure reading. Nothing untoward was found and my blood pressure dropped back to normal within twenty-four hours.

I began training with a wonderful fitness and nutrition expert, Amelia, losing 18 kilos, thinking this might help, but still the wobbles persisted. I ran on treadmills to check my heart function with a top cardiologist. Nothing wrong there. I wore a bulky heart and blood pressure monitor on set to check for either hypertension (too high) or hypotension (too low) – there was a theory that blood was pooling in my legs from standing around for so long, which might lead to the latter. Again, all good.

As it didn't happen when we were filming outside or on location, I even researched the effects of 50 Hz and 100 Hz light flicker from the various studio lights.

In the end, after all the specialists, and all the specialists discussing my case with other specialist friends in different fields, we never found out what caused it. And just when I felt it was becoming so unpleasant that I really didn't want to ever go back into the *MasterChef* kitchen, it stopped. The relief was palpable.

It did return a few years ago during a period of high stress. This, combined with the fact that it didn't happen when I was doing other shows, made me think that even though I never felt under pressure while filming *MasterChef* (and I didn't notice the way people stared at me when I was out in public anymore, either), perhaps my mind was feeling otherwise. Especially as the wobbles would return at times when I felt exposed, overly visible or vulnerable. Anxiety can cause all the symptoms I had – agoraphobia, dizziness and light-headedness – and I now realise that even when you don't actually consciously feel stressed, anxiety can still be weighing you down.

45

When you find yourself in the peculiar situation of being on a hit TV show, the media develops an appetite for reporting anything about you – good, bad or totally speculative. The journos whose work I respect the most are those who actually get hold of a real story. Sure, that's often inconvenient but I respect it.

Most of the time, the fear of litigation and Australians' natural discretion and a desire 'not to dob' keeps the stuff celebs really want to hide out of the media. That's one of the reasons I'm in a couple of dining clubs with other journos, so we can gossip about what's *actually* going on. Good evening, Road Trip Club members, and thanks for coming.

The other challenge is the paparazzi. I actually don't mind getting snapped at the airport after a thirty-two-hour flight (unless I have my kids in tow). What I don't like is when, after posing for that blurry-eyed snap, the pap sneaks behind some foliage to try to make it look like they ambushed you.

The worst of these was a guy who parked outside my house every Saturday morning and then followed my daughter and me around trying to get an embarrassing 'gotcha moment' as I drove her to netball . . . you know, a '*MasterChef* judge feeds child junk food' sort of thing. Still, when a mate told me a photo like that was worth between $10,000 and $40,000 I could see why the pap was there. This all stopped after he ran a couple of red lights following me one day and I reported him to the police. Yes, of course I'd slowed right down turning left at the lights so I went through at the very last glow of green, but he still followed.

George moved out of his lovely flat in Sydney's Bondi Beach because there was always a pap outside his door. When his bags were packed, he found out that the pap was actually staking out Lara Bingle's apartment down the road. I don't think the bloke even knew who George Calombaris was.

A cardinal rule (that we came up with) was to be careful of any photographers bearing props. For what seems like a good idea at the time ends up with you looking like a dill on page 5. We developed a 'code red' phrase for such asks: 'Think this might be an ice cream moment, lads.' We'd turn it down. Just like we'd never sit on a couch for a photo shoot (it's too much like the back seat of a taxi and unflattering for the larger-figured).

The ice cream lesson came after we shot for a magazine cover where they gave George an ice cream to hold. When the image came out in the magazine of him licking it, his ribald mates artfully turned it into a phallus. Oh, how they laughed.

On a more uplifting note, most of the fans who watched *MasterChef*, whether they were in Australia, the Netherlands or Portugal, treated us like a neighbour you've bumped into on holiday. This was great. They would say hi as they walked past you in the street in Adelaide, Amsterdam or Lisbon, or just smile and wave. They wanted to tell you where to go to eat. Or show you photos of something they were proud to have cooked. These interactions were easy and friendly most of the time.

Kids who wanted a chat or a photo were invariably polite and respectful and a credit to whoever brought them up. They'd also often ask the most insightful questions. There is something joyous about meeting people – especially young people – who share a love of food. This is perhaps one of the greatest gifts that my time on *MasterChef* gave me. Not just all these conversations but all those that are yet to come.

In fact, the only unwelcome interactions are when some guy in a suit is close-talking to you at a million miles an hour, wanting to tell you what you could be doing better, late on a Friday night. So convinced of his own opinions. So uninterested in discourse or discussion. It's the same depressing behaviour that you see in political extremists. Why don't they all listen a bit more, and channel some of their energy into trying to understand the other side?

Whenever I'd see them approach – those close-talking suits – I'd try to quietly slip away. With this in mind, I am eternally grateful for a bit of advice Ian 'Dicko' Dickson gave me before starting *MasterChef*: always leave the pub or club before 10.30 pm because *nothing* good will happen after that. I abided by that most of the time. And when I didn't, the bad that happened was still pretty good.

The other bit of advice about fame came from the late, great Tony Bourdain. He wisely suggested never signing a fan's body part or allowing people to sit on your knee for a photo. He told a story about an early book signing, probably for *Kitchen Confidential*, when a lovely, slightly frail grandmother asked for a photo. When Tony said yes she asked if she could perch on his lap for the shot. He was very tall and she was bird-like tiny. But he agreed. As the shutter clicked she grabbed his face and give him a big sloppy, snaking tongue'n'all kiss on the mouth. Beware!

For the first four seasons, *MasterChef* was shot in Sydney. This was a huge sacrifice – most of all for our families. It had been core to me taking the gig that Emma was happy and willing for me to be absent four days a week, seven or so months a year.

We'd all get back to Melbourne as often as we could during series 3 – Gary and George also had restaurants to run and services to lead – and occasionally our families would come to visit. We laughed at the irony when Gary's wife Mandy insisted on leaving pictures of herself and their daughter all over his Coogee apartment. For Gary is someone about whom there are absolutely no rumours of womanising.

Mandy and George's partner, Nat, would eventually relocate to Sydney. I preferred heading back to Melbourne every weekend and keeping the kids' routine as normal as possible. They were in primary school and playing a lot of sport. Sadie played basketball for a while, but then thankfully moved to AFL Goal Kick after one basketball game when I turned up hungover. The sound of two dozen pairs of runners squeaking on glossed wooden floors and the endless booming, bounce, bounce, bouncing was too painful to ever risk again.

There was also more support for Emma in Melbourne. We'd made a pact early on that I wouldn't do any gigs or corporate events on the weekends. Those two days were to be kept sacrosanct for family. Thank heavens, for this became my happy place and my respite. Whether it was just dagging about in the back garden playing games, walking the dog with Sadie, seeing Jono's under-9s team – the mighty Gladiators – beat Fitzroy, or seeing William score a hat-trick playing futsal. Needless to say, by the age of ten my kids had eclipsed my modest sporting achievements.

There is also power in turning down a Saturday night gig, even though I would have earnt in one night what a few years earlier I'd earnt in a month. I now preferred to spend the weekends with my family. It's a luxury I have always appreciated. And a choice I've never regretted making.

In 2010, we shot the first series of *Junior MasterChef*. The infectiously effervescent Anna Gare joined the team, which I think stopped the producers from worrying that I would scare the children. Little did they know that most kids saw me as a cartoon character – somewhere between Shrek, Humphrey B. Bear and Barney the Dinosaur.

My fashion choices were certainly a joy to some of them. I introduced a 'cheflings' choice', where they could suggest which of my vast array of stupidly bright coloured pants I should wear the next day . . . hot pink, eye-searing lemon yellow, strawberry, silver-and-peach snakeskin.

Having kids under twelve cooking meant the days were shorter, we had to take regular breaks and every bench had safety officers on hand to ensure no teeny digits were lopped off by accident. Our critiques of their dishes were softer but still honest, and those kids whose time was up left with, I pray, dignity and a little hope, along with the sadness.

The problem with *Junior MasterChef* was that there just wasn't the same 'jeopardy'. There was no dream future at stake. And the kids were generally more sensible than the adults. They had their ratios and techniques firmly lodged in their brains and when they were given a recipe to follow they did just that . . . follow it. Part of the fun of giving adults a recipe is that they usually second-guess it, or go and check the freezer to see if the ice cream has set every thirty seconds, letting in warmth each time they open the door so instead it sets more slowly. Kids just take it out after the allotted time specified in the recipe and, guess what, the ice cream is perfect.

In the series finale, our junior cooks had to replicate a streusel-topped choux bun from Adriano Zumbo known as Pear Perfection. Isabella Bliss did it perfectly. It tasted just like Adriano's. She had to get a 10/10.

Trouble is when we tasted young Jack Lark's version it was noticeably better than Isabella's. Better even than the archetype from the Dark Prince of Pastry himself. Zumbo even agreed it was. This is one of only two occasions I can remember this happening.

So, if something is better than perfect, better even than the version baked by the creator himself – something he himself admitted on camera – then surely Jack deserved 11/10. Three people – Adriano, George and me – gave him this score. Oh, the controversy! For those of you who want to vent at our flawed logic, I should point out that, ultimately, the very talented Isabella pipped Jack at the post by three points anyway. A deserved winner.

46

In series 3 of *MasterChef*, Caroline Spencer stepped up to join Margie Bashfield as executive producer and the changes they brought about were immediate. You knew this series was going to be special when the auditions for the top twenty-four were held in an old industrial complex on Cockatoo Island in the middle of Sydney Harbour. Instead of placing the first mystery box on each contestant's bench, one monster box was helicoptered in. This required not one but two helicopters: one to haul the huge *MasterChef* logo'd wooden crate and the other to film it with the Bridge, Opera House and vast expanse of blue-green water glistening behind it. It felt like the show had reached heights that no other food show in the world had ever reached before – either in terms of drama or gloss on the screen. This feeling was confirmed by the fact that for the first time I could remember, the dynamic Caroline Spencer had the show and its challenges mapped out before the cameras even started rolling, which appealed to my nerdy, pre-planning magazine-making brain. It was also perhaps why there were more jaw-dropping moments in this season than any other.

Chef Matt Moran joined the team as an extra judge. He immediately started in with pot shots at the new Seven Network show *My Kitchen Rules*, describing it as a 'poorer version' of *MasterChef*. Gary called it 'chewing gum for the eyes'. Certainly the initial ratings of a show that I felt was part *Come Dine With Me*, part *MasterChef* rather than just a cheap knockoff were weak.

This would change once *My Kitchen Rules*' producers realised that there was gold in having bitchy drama at the dining table. They would eventually overtake our numbers. We'd mutter that this was because they were on a far bigger network with far higher base numbers anyway. Manu Feildel and Pete Evans would snipe back at us that the big difference was that *My Kitchen Rules* had good-looking judges while *MasterChef*'s were fat and ugly!

The truth was, Manu was a close friend of Gary, and I'd known Pete since his days running a cafe in the Melbourne beachside suburb of Brighton. Both had appeared on the first series of *MasterChef* so they were part of the family. Having two food shows elevating Australian food culture and topping the ratings was great, and we were glad that a couple of mates were part of it. Yes, there may have been a few ructions when they started to wear the same Arthur Galan evening wear as George and fire off similar glitter cannons in their finale, but the fact was, *My Kitchen Rules* was another Australian TV success story being watched around the world. At least until *Married at First Sight* took the bitchiness of the dining table to whole new heights – or should that be depths – and the differences between Pete's personal views and those of the show reached such a point that he, ahem, moved on . . .

*

With series 3 of *MasterChef*, the boys and I were delighted when we found out that the contentious returning of eliminated contestants was axed, and that elimination after a team challenge was now going to be decided by a cooking challenge. We'd long felt that it should take two bad cooks in a row for a contestant to be eliminated. And that this would help the more consistent and better cooks to go further than the less skilled.

The guests were *great* too, with homegrown talent like Maggie Beer, Colin Fassnidge and Neil Perry joined by a cavalcade of international superstars including Nigella Lawson, Rick Stein, The French Laundry's Thomas Keller, Andoni Aduriz from Mugaritz outside San Sebastián (the then third best restaurant in the world), Heston Blumenthal (then fifth best and previously number one), David Chang, Anthony Bourdain, Shane Osborn and the world's best chef at the time, René Redzepi from Noma in Copenhagen.

Andoni Aduriz was the quiet poet of modern Spanish food. I'd first met him at Spain's big culinary conference, Madrid Fusion, and warmed to him immediately. He told me through his Scottish interpreter that his innovative introduction of tweezers to the kitchen was not for fine and fiddly work but actually to slow down his chefs so they would plate more mindfully. So many others would follow his lead but never fully understand the reasoning. I'd then invited him to the Melbourne Food and Wine Festival, and even though he was a culinary giant running one of the best kitchens in the world, he took the time to debrief Festival organiser Ute Biefang and me on his experiences and share his thoughts on how we could make the Festival better. His insights showed this wasn't something off the cuff but carefully thought out.

The first time I met Heston Blumenthal was also at a food conference but this time it was in Milan. I'd eaten at his restaurant The Fat Duck on my first trip back to the UK and loved his humour and his iconoclastic approach to the kitchen. Here was a man who thought about food in ways others hadn't. He wanted to work out how to make dinner taste better as much through understanding neuroscience and flavour chemistry as cooking. We spent most of that first time together discussing his dream of making an ice cream that would catch fire but not melt. The next time I was back at the restaurant, a surprise addition to the menu had appeared. Lo and behold if the ice cream didn't flicker with flame but still stay cold and unmelted when you ate it. Kitchen alchemy at its finest.

I'd later play straight man for Heston's live shows in Australia. It was a role I also enjoyed performing for stage shows with El Bulli's Ferran Adrià, Jamie Oliver and Nigella Lawson. I find spending time with intense creative minds truly liberating, but then the likes of Heston, Andoni, Ferran and René are very rare and very special. Truly unique culinary thinkers. Too many who are heralded as such are just mere copycats.

René Redzepi's way of thinking may not have delivered dishes that pop, fizz and burst into flames with dusts and foams, but his passion for championing the food of where you are has probably had a longer influence on how we eat here in Australia than any of the others. René also always manages to confront and to force diners to interrogate what they will or won't eat in intelligent ways.

When he first came to Australia he was astonished at how few Indigenous ingredients he saw on menus. It was as though we were a culinary colony of France, Italy or South-East Asia. When he returned with his whole restaurant for a residency in Sydney, he aggressively targeted an intensely local menu that championed ingredients familiar to First Nations people. I was a wee bit ashamed that it took someone from Copenhagen to do this. Yes, there had been champions of local foodstuffs before, such as Red Ochre Grill's Andrew Fielke and Mark Olive on SBS and the ABC, but in a throwback to the bad old days of culinary cringe it took a foreigner to spark a new wave of appreciation of Indigenous ingredients.

René was also a lot of fun to hang out with. During the Melbourne Food and Wine Festival he asked me to introduce him to the Victorian Minister for Tourism so he could tell him how valuable the Festival was internationally. On another trip here we spent a morning urban foraging as he looked to create a truly Australian dish using local fish and bitter leaves foraged from parks, rough patches and verges around the Sydney fish market. Don't try this at home, kids, unless you know what you are doing.

Also don't try to do what René did back in Copenhagen . . . starting the city's own culinary convivium in a circus tent on a docklands wasteland. It's way too much work! MAD was an incredible culinary wonderland of new food ideas. It was here that Alex Atala shocked the world by suggesting we should eat more insects and I had the pleasure of lunching with Dan Barber from Blue Hill in New York's Greenwich Village and listening to his ideas on food sustainability and what would become some of the premise of *The Third Plate*. I also met a slightly crazy but amusing Scot by the name of Roddy Sloan who dived for sea urchins in the icy waters near Tromsø in Norway.

Tony Bourdain was almost as much fun to hang out with as Roddy, whether he was telling you the best place to hide a body on the New Jersey turnpike or how to win a game of Melbourne's most obscure sport, Trugo. I was a little snaky that I didn't get to film with Tony in series 3 of *MasterChef* – I think Matt Moran nabbed that honour – but I'd already shot an episode of *No Reservations* with him in Melbourne so felt as though I'd had my fair share. Tony was a chef who loved chefs, but almost as fascinating as talking about food was talking to him about the process of making TV in a fresher, more authentic and faster way. He liked to involve the editor of each show in the actual shot as an extra/third camera person. This meant they already knew the story they were going to cut when they flew back to the US at the end of the trip. Brilliant.

But enough with the superstar chefs . . . we also welcomed to the *MasterChef* kitchen George's mum and, thanks to Kylie Kwong's support, our contestants got to cook for none other than His Holiness the Dalai Lama! This was a very special and slightly surreal appearance which some contestants found overwhelming. Sensing their tension, His Holiness grasped their hands to calm them down. I was tasked with greeting him and taking the blessing when he arrived. While having the Dalai Lama on the show was a huge coup, he didn't feel comfortable comparing or judging the food, which presented us with a slight challenge. When the cameras stopped rolling we did, however, get to talk about his childhood and the food he fondly remembered his mother cooking for him.

For some, this was the episode that 'jumped the shark', proof that in spite of our success, we'd disappeared completely up our own fundaments. Those critics were wrong. It had actually happened earlier in the series, back on Cockatoo Island. In a *Gilligan's Island*-style themed challenge, the producers had set us up with sand, a beached rowing boat and palms. Gary was wearing a captain's hat like the Skipper's and George was sporting a bucket hat like Gilligan's. Neither was particularly overjoyed by this. As I always got about looking like Thurston Howell III, I didn't need to dress up at all.

Anyway, the art department had decorated the set with buckets and spades, large plastic crabs and, behind a palm tree, a large inflatable shark. It was too good an opportunity to miss and Caroline Spencer and I took photos of us leaping over it. Shark jumped!

All this alone would have made series 3 not just the biggest food competition show in Australia but also the world, but then we went to New York. And what a trip it was.

Our contestants got to cook soul food at the famous Harlem restaurant Sylvia's, and meet matriarch Sylvia Woods and the rest of her family. Like Sugar Plum Fairy in Lou Reed's 'Walk on the Wild Side' (who was also looking for soul food and a place to eat), I hit the streets to make a pilgrimage round the corner to the famous Apollo Theatre. Next door I bought a couple of magnificent suits worthy of Huggy Bear at his most flamboyant. Emma would later burst into tears when

I unpacked them, crying at their gaudy polyester shine and at their cheapness (which – wrongly it seems – I saw as a plus). She knew then she was destined to spend her life with a man who buys (and dresses in) embarrassing rubbish.

Restaurateur and TV celebrity Lidia Bastianich joined us to judge an immunity challenge at an open-air kitchen in Central Park. French chef and restaurateur Daniel Boulud stopped by for a MasterClass, and Éric Ripert of Le Bernardin helped judge a New York boroughs food challenge. This contest was most notable for Dani Venn's whoopie-pie (bad), Michael Weldon's taco (good), and for the way Éric Ripert ate off his knife during the tasting. George quietly leant over to me and said, 'You see, all the top chefs do it.' I knew we'd now never get him to change this habit of his – even when later Nigella, shocked and appalled, ticked him off onscreen.

Our New York week had opened with the Statue of Liberty towering above us, and the Manhattan skyline under black glowering storm clouds as our backdrop. We'd set up well before the opening hours of Liberty Island and having such a world-famous icon to ourselves was magical.

Later in the week our contestants were invited to cook for a reception at the United Nations. If this wasn't special enough, the production team had somehow secured *MasterChef Australia* permission to film inside the General Assembly. We were the first TV show ever to do this. Under that huge domed ceiling, and in front of that giant gilt seal, Gary, George and I stood on the podium where so many history-making speeches had been made. I still get chills thinking about it . . . and can remember the intense desire not to screw up what I had to say in such historic surroundings.

*

Before we left NYC, George and I went with director Michael
Venables to eat hot dogs and watch French striker Thierry
Henry play for the New York Red Bulls. We also lunched at
Le Bernardin (enjoying one of the most Swiss-watch-perfect
meals I have ever experienced), and with Gary by our side chased
down burgers and 'concretes' (thick shakes) at the original Shake
Shack in Central Park in the shadow of the Flatiron Building,
and ate pork buns at David Chang's Ssäm Bar.

Our biggest night, though, was at a burlesque club known
as The Box. Stringy, our wardrobe queen at the time, knew the
MC and organised a couple of booths for us and the crew. It
was bottle service at the tables, much was ordered, we danced,
and we cheered when Gary was dragged onstage by some
burlesque performers with a large can of shaving cream and
malicious intent on their minds. Gary was mortified – fearing
the salacious headlines back home – which made it even
funnier. As the crew left as the night wore on, some chucked
in $50 towards the bill. Around 5.30 am we decided to call it
a night. I had about $1200 cash in my pocket from the whip-
round. Trouble was, the bill was over $3000. Ouch! But then
the manager pointed out that she needed to add 10 per cent
sales tax plus 20 per cent mandatory service charge. The total
bill came to more than $4200.

In the grand scheme of things it was a small price to pay for
one of the great nights of my life. And there's no doubt that's
not even a tenth of what I owed our extraordinary crew for the
show's success.

*

Perhaps the most bizarre thing about the third series was the finale between Michael Weldon and eventual winner Kate Bracks. Not because the contestants were forced to make a very twee snowman rather than one of René Redzepi's other, more iconic, desserts, but because of how the episode aired.

Network Ten had invested heavily in another show modelled on *MasterChef* and made by the same production company but with home renovators rather than cooks as the focus. It was called *The Renovators*. This show might not have had an actual challenge where you watched paint dry, but sometimes it felt like that.

It just wasn't resonating with audiences, so someone came up with the bright idea of splitting the *MasterChef* finale in half and putting an episode of *The Renovators* in the middle! Our finale was already long and waiting that extra hour to see the winner announced was going to put it way past many of our youngest viewers' bedtimes. We weren't happy.

It was said that some 1.6 million people turned over or off when *The Renovators* aired in the middle of our finale. Not all of them returned for the winner's announcement and our numbers were dramatically down on the previous series' finale. It was enough to allow both the finales of *The Block* and *Australia's Got Talent* that year to outrate us. The vultures in the media started to circle.

Yet another TV truism is that hit shows have a ratings life that looks a bit like an upside down hockey stick. The second series goes up, the third plateaus or drops slightly, and then the numbers steadily fall away.

This was where it now seemed *MasterChef* was heading. The media landscape was very different in 2011 from when we'd launched in 2009. Where once we were the only prime-time commercial show crazy enough to be all about food, everyone was now crowbarring cooking challenges or food segments into their shows to capitalise on Australia's latest obsession. We also had a serious rival in *My Kitchen Rules*, and there was a concern that eighty-five episodes of *MasterChef* and spin-off formats like *Celebrity* or *Junior* was just too much of a good thing.

I'm not sure if this is the reason why the second series of *Junior MasterChef* did so badly later in 2011. The show launched with less than half the numbers of the first series, barely tipping a million viewers. Some episodes dipped below 700,000, a figure that had never previously been contemplated.

As I wasn't asked to be one of the hosts, I can't say it upset me all that much. Apparently people had been told that I wanted to concentrate on my work as a critic, which is interesting as I'd ceased doing that back in 2010 when I was no longer based full-time in Melbourne. Now I was just a food writer and recipe developer.

As I stewed about being overlooked, I told myself that my absence must have been why over a million viewers didn't tune in this time. If I were a Bond villain, I'd have been in my volcano lair plotting revenge.

47

There is no doubt in my mind that we got it right with the contestants in series 4. Finally, our 'no dickhead' policy seemed to be paying off. There were knockabout lads such as electrician Andy Allen and teacher Ben Milbourne; roller derby queen Tregan Borg; Amina Elshafei, one of the nicest women ever to walk into the kitchen; Wade Drummond with the impressive eyebrows, who set up a successful Western Australian crumpet business; finalist Audra Morrice, who called herself 'spider monkey' and went on to present *MasterChef Asia* and *MasterChef Singapore*; and Mindy Woods, who was arguably the best cook of the lot but fell just short of the finale, joining a long list of similarly talented types who we judges had picked as favourites but who stumbled before the final hurdle.

Then there was a woman in glasses who claimed to be into paleo way before Pete Evans and who now works alongside me at the ABC. Alice Zaslavsky might not have made the finals but she is one of our most successful contestants. She now fronts a food segment on ABC *News Breakfast*, hosts *Saturday Breakfast* on ABC Melbourne, has presented multiple series of her own kids cooking quiz show, and has written a bestselling, award-winning cookbook.

Perhaps the biggest culinary success of all, however, was a one-time swimmer and physio student, Kylie Millar. Acclaimed British pastry chef Darren Purchese took Kylie under his wing after she left the show. Always first in and last out, Kylie's insatiable thirst for knowledge and experience was ignited by her time on *MasterChef*. She is also who I'll credit with popularising the salty caramel trend and moving it on from an esoteric Thomas Keller dessert to something much more everyday. She went on to work with some of the great chefs of the world – Andoni Aduriz at Mugaritz and then Dan Barber at Blue Hill.

The winner of series 4, Andy Allen, has gone from strength to strength too and is now one of the current judges of *MasterChef*. But Kylie (who left in sixth place) and Alice (who left in seventh place) proved the point that you didn't need to win the show to come out a winner.

The final round of auditions took place in Melbourne. Life was so much better when I was sleeping in my own bed and going home each day to kiss the kids goodnight. It was all well and good, me constantly twisting my wedding rings when I was filming on the set of MasterChef in Sydney to let the woman I love know I was thinking of her back in Melbourne, but being there was so much better.

This was something I appreciated even more after having had those extra months off with not having to shoot the second series of *Junior MasterChef*. That time made me realise how much I'd missed being home.

Auditions can be dull for the audience as they've no vested interest in any of the cooks yet, so we were always looking for authentic ways to challenge the expected; make the hum a little less drum. In among the usual cooks followed by tastings, we sent a group of aspirants down the Mornington Peninsula to find great produce and then return to cook it in the grand surrounds of Melbourne's Royal Exhibition Building. The contestants who already had their name on a white apron and who were through to the final twenty-four watched on from one of the balconies. After tasting Audra Morrice's spectacular chocolate tart topped with local raspberries, I carried a couple of slices up to the balcony. Gary and George took turns at fighting over the remains.

This dark moody tart was really rather special; all bitter, satin-smooth ganache and the sweet–sour bite of the rasp-berries. Up in the balcony, with the other already-selected contestants' faces smeared with their guilty tasting, we started the chant, 'Apron, apron, apron.' Mob rule. The boys caught on and soon Audra was through and up on the balcony with the rest of us, resplendent in her crisp new apron. The produc-ers had the good grace to accept us going rogue like that. That's not common in TV world.

The handing over of the apron had become as much a vote of confidence in a cook's ability as a ticket to the *MasterChef* kitchen in Sydney. Some contestants would try again and again to get in. We loved that someone would listen to our advice and then come back a year later a more formidable cook.

The challenge was that at the audition stage there were always far more talented women cooks than men. I suspect this was partly because they'd been cooking family dinners for years, or grew up with the baking gene, or they were the offspring of a generation of parents who persisted in thinking that their female children should be in the kitchen and the males should be on the cricket pitch or footy field.

This was about to change as those kids who'd grown up watching those early days of Julie and Poh, Alvin and Adam started to apply. They were fierce with YouTube knowledge and as skilled with the sous vide machine and the crémeaux as the previous generation were with old-school bush cookery and pikelets and cupcakes.

This female–male talent bias was tricky, but by series 4 we had accepted it. Fourteen of the twenty-four contestants were women. That was not a cause for concern, although having five of the final six contestants as women did have the bigwigs a little nervous. We reminded them to have faith in the food gods . . .

I had also begun to notice how fast the good male cooks could develop. When he started out in series 2, Adam Liaw talked a great game but was pretty mediocre on the tools at first. So much so that he began referring to himself as the 'unfavoured Asian', given how much tastier we found Alvin Quah's cooking. The thing is, Adam managed to stick around long enough to become good. Really good. That was the joy of shooting each series over many months. With nothing else to do in the contestants' house other than cook and talk about food, and then practise and share what they were learning, contestants who were willing to put in the hard yards could improve dramatically during the run of the series. It was something that you just didn't see on our rivals' shows.

Adam's culinary awakening was heralded by a spectacular prawn scotch egg with a coconut chilli sambal, and a series of skewers at an invention test challenge judged by the late, great Margaret Fulton. After that, we forgave him for his 'three-course pizza' (meaning three courses on one base), which Gary saw as an affront to everything he thought holy, and which I thought funny but just not tasty.

In series 4, Andy Allen was the same. He just squeaked through a few eliminations but then in the finale wowed us with a seafood platter. Then the momentum was all his.

And, of course, there was plenty of good food in series 4: Audra's delicious pork belly braised in Chinese black vinegar with hand-pulled noodles; Mindy Woods' crispy-skinned duck with red curry and lychees; Emma O'Shaughnessy's five-spice flourless chocolate cake; and pretty much all of Julia Taylor's desserts are just some that stand out. The nosh was good, people cared and the collegiate nature between the contestants was unlike any other show.

Andy Allen and Ben Milbourne's was a bromance that captured the hearts of the nation. Some contestants allegedly made booze in the air conditioning vents and some once even volunteered to go into an elimination cook instead of Emma one day because they felt she wanted to stay the most. Quite extraordinary. I think Ben Milbourne led that revolution. In the end it was a step too far for the showrunners, but I loved to see this.

*

While the stellar quality of series 3's international guest chefs would have been impossible to match, in series 4 we did have Jamie Oliver spend time in the *MasterChef* kitchen, taking on (and beating) three contestants – Tregan Borg, Alice Zaslavsky and Jules Pike – *at the same time*! I don't think I've seen anyone as happy and terrified as Tregan when she heard who she'd be cooking against. She actually dropped to her knees in shock. This was a much better reaction than those early days when I'd introduce a little-heralded local chef and all the contestants would just go, 'Huh? Who?'

George was equally excited at having American cake boss Buddy Valastro in. He spent the weeks before and after bellowing one of Buddy's catch phrases at the top of his voice whenever Buddy's name was mentioned: 'You got to bake the cake!'

I'm indebted to Buddy for some advice he gave me when we were both on the bill at a big food festival in South Africa: 'No one is here to see you cook, they want to hear your stories, they want to be entertained by you.' Wise words indeed . . .

Series 4 set out to be 'back to basics' with a tone that was a little less Churchillian and a little more hokey and home-style. While initially George and Gary had wanted to find a winner who'd end up a chef and go on to run their own restaurant, we'd seen that this was unrealistic for a number of reasons:

1. Six months in the *MasterChef* kitchen was no alternative to an apprenticeship and three years working in a successful restaurant.

2. Cooking in a restaurant requires a very different skill set, and is more about timing, logistics and accurate repetition service after service, week after week, than freestyling a couple of plates every couple of days.

3. Most restaurant food is a lot more populist and a lot less 'brave', or fun to cook, than what our best contestants were putting up.

4. Few young *MasterChef* cooks wanted to head back to the bottom rung of a professional kitchen and peel peas all day – while occasionally getting shouted at – after six months of being a reality TV star. And yes, I do mean 'peel' peas. That's precisely what I once watched thirty stagiaires do in the Noma prep kitchen. I guess that's the sort of skin-free detail you expect in the world's best restaurants.

5. And lastly, most of the chefs I knew were desperate to get *out* of the kitchen and on to TV, or sign a cookbook deal, or do ads for a cheap parmesan that they'd never use in a million years. It hardly inspired a sense that being a chef was a cool or worthwhile profession . . . being a successful *MasterChef* contestant was far cooler.

In the first ten series, more than twenty *MasterChef* contestants went on to have their own TV show. This told us that after their time with us, they might have become far better cooks, but what the show really excelled at was training them for careers in front of the camera rather than behind the stove.

Naturally, there were some exceptions. Andre Ursini from series 1 and Philip Vakos from series 2 became restaurateurs rather than chefs. For them, it made more financial sense to employ a professional than do it yourself. Andy Allen, Sashi Cheliah, Mindy Woods, Laura Sharrad and Matt Sinclair all went on to helm their own successful kitchens – and I am sure there have been more. Pip Sumbak, for example, still cooks professionally (but in a looser way, with her catering business Pip's Plate), as does Ava Stangherlin, and of course Kylie Millar has a CV most Aussie chefs would lust after. The majority of contestants, however, went on to do catering or pop-ups, a bit of TV, or run cooking schools. Some went on to develop recipes and dishes for magazines or corporate food businesses. Others became influencers, or bloggers, or brand ambassadors as they turned a dollar doing what they loved. I really enjoyed seeing all this blossoming – I loved that so many of these young, and occasionally not so young, kids ended up doing something they were passionate about after their time with us. It's these guys who are the legacy of which I'm most proud . . .

Sure, it was great helping change the food culture of Australia (something that the media laid at our door), although I'd argue that we were standing on the shoulders of giants who were already shifting it in this direction . . . Here I am thinking of Jamie (whose TV show on Network Ten had championed a more relaxed Italian style of cooking and saw many more boys become interested in cooking). And of the great magazine gurus who also deserve to be known by their first names alone: Valli (Little) and Jill (Dupleix), Michelle (Southan) and Donna (Hay). It was as if they had been pounding at the door of the kitchen to create a truly relaxed Australian cuisine with a sunny sense of place. *MasterChef* just turned the key, opened the door and beckoned far more of Australia to enter.

With this belief in a more food-focused future rather than a restaurant kitchen future for our contestants, we had argued that we wanted the next series to be more about the contestants' adventures in culinary failure and success rather than grandiose and unobtainable fine dining flights of fancy.

We'd started with a trip to Tasmania, where I'd finally discovered the value of a close professional relationship with the story team (particularly Plum Stubbings and Carly Schmidt) as they spent so much more time with the contestants and were loaded with valuable insights that made me better at my job of drawing truth and dreams out of the contestants to help mentor them. The production team, however, took things up a notch with our series 4 overseas trip. We headed to Italy. Our contestants got to cook for two of my favourite people, the late Antonio Carluccio and the genius Massimo Bottura, who was on the verge of becoming the world's number one chef. With Antonio we ate our way across Florence, this great bear of a man dropping ribald jokes and displaying a true trencherman's love of food. To watch him order dinner at the famous Buca Lapi, conducting the waiters like a maestro, was a privilege . . . 'Some pappardelle? Perhaps with wild boar? Yes! The bistecca alla fiorentina? Well, obviously!'

I'd been lucky enough to spend a bit of time with Antonio over the years. During an interview for an article I wrote about him, he sat whittling a walking stick in the vineyard at de Bortoli in the Yarra Valley; during another, he and the great Michel Roux traded barbs over lunch about whether Italian or French food was the greatest. Roux, always the gentleman;

Carluccio, ever the rogue with a twinkle in his eye, making the most inflammatory statements possible; Roux getting increasingly frustrated when many of his undeniably true contentions were mischievously ignored.

Whether at food festivals or just hanging out, Antonio was always generous but also happy to stand his ground if he felt he wasn't being treated fairly. Not only did he teach me how to cook pasta (huge pot, water as salty as the sea) and a spectacular wild mushroom risotto, he also taught me the responsibility that came with being a much-loved public figure. You owed your fans. At a huge Melbourne Food and Wine Festival dinner in among the cornucopia of stalls at the Prahran Market, I watched as he walked round every single table dispensing bonhomie. I seem to remember he was a little lame at the time and puffing from the cigarettes he loved to smoke. The effort required didn't faze him. He seemed to really derive joy from these interactions. And, gee, he gave so much joy in doing it!

For our challenge with him in Italy, we sat down to taste in the grand ballroom of a Renaissance summer villa that apparently had once been owned by a Borgia. Antonio owned the space like the Pontiff of Porcini that he was. All that was missing were the scarlet robes and ermine.

Massimo Bottura is an altogether different character but a similar impishness was evident the first time I met him. He talked about how, to be creative, a chef must 'plant his feet in the furrows but keep his head in the clouds'. It's a beautiful line that neatly encapsulates his twin passions: an uncompromising dedication to procuring the very best produce of his area of Italy (balsamic, prosciutto, parmesan and so forth), and a lyrical and artful way of putting food on the plate.

Massimo invited us to eat a sensational pasta carbonara and an amatriciana in a deli near Rome's Campo de' Fiori. The dishes began with the freshest mozzarella that had only been milk a couple of hours before. He talked incessantly and with an infectious enthusiasm, as he did when he was trying the contestants' dishes. Massimo is that rare thing: a chef whose enthusiasm is as contagious as it is authentic.

He also showed us how to make the perfect cacio e pepe pasta but swore us to secrecy. Which is a pity, because I would have loved to have shared that with you here . . . gee, it is just so clever. He had already shown me the perfect rolling technique for tossing pasta in the pan with both sauce and a little cooking water to perfectly emulsify the dish. Both tricks I'm happy to share if you bump into me out and about!

None of these off-the-clock moments, however, could match Heinz Beck's three-Michelin-star restaurant for pomp and ceremony. On a sweltering summer's night, the ancient majesty of Rome in the shimmering twilight haze laid out beneath us, we marvelled at the vast range of champagnes on the restaurant's champagne chariot, at all the fresh herbs that would be snipped with gold scissors at your table for a tisane made using an accurately but different prescribed temperature for each herb, and at the kitchen's enormous bank of extraction fans. Or, at least, Gary did. 'It's a chef thing. You wouldn't understand,' Gary said, beaming. Heinz was equally as excited by Gary and their shared appreciation of a million dollars' worth of ventilation.

'Gary, Gary, Gary,' Heinz would chorus. We might have teased Gaz about that later . . .

The trip had started especially well, as we had flown to Italy via London so I could take George on a double-decker bus with a bunch of mates to Wembley to see Chelsea win the FA Cup. I'm not sure George understood why a couple of lads jumped off the bus in Harlesden High Street to buy a box of celery, but rest assured, it's a Chelsea thing. Chelsea is the only football club in the world to have a top-level chant about the aphrodisiacal properties of a loaf of celery.

The following day we flew to Milan, where George reciprocated the favour by organising tickets for us and our series producer Tim Toni to the famous Derby della Madonnina. We stood awestruck in the San Siro Stadium as Inter took on AC Milan, surrounded by the Nerazzurri fans of the Curva Nord waving huge flags, lighting flares and constantly singing, singing, singing. It was like a scene from a medieval battle and almost as chaotic.

Once past the police cordon, the young Milanese kids were going through the turnstiles two at a time and the Inter part of the ground ended up being about 40 per cent over capacity. The stand's upper levels – made of solid concrete – bowed and bounced as the crowd jumped as one. In the stairwells of the stadium's signature towers, in between piles of burning rubbish, little piss waterfalls ran down the steps from the multitude who couldn't be bothered to queue for the urinals. It was rough. It was passionate. Inter won 4:2. Ibrahimovic scored twice but Milito got a hat-trick.

There was one sour note to the game. Those pissy steps weren't nearly as distasteful as the racist chants Milan's Kevin-Prince Boateng was subjected to, chants that had mostly been driven out of the English and Australian game.

Italy was also when the production was shut down due to sickness. Roughly two minutes after I'd received a call from executive producer Margie telling me that she was locking down the show and would I like to stay in my room in the hotel, please, Gary rang. 'Right,' he said, 'where are we having lunch?' Close call.

Filming was delayed a few days but there aren't many better places to be than Rome in early summer. We were happy, we were healthy and gee we had an appetite. We lunched well and dined better. We'd take picnics up to the Palatine Hill where the noise of the traffic honking round the Circus Maximus was just a distant cicada-like buzz. A rug, the best cured meats, a hunk of taleggio cheese so ripe its sides were collapsing, and fat slices of the ruddiest tomatoes picked for the intensity of their fragrance were loaded onto roughly torn bread. We drank chilled Tuscan Frescobaldi among the long grasses and wild poppies. It would have been quite romantic if I hadn't been with Gary and George.

We went to see Inter play Lazio in a far calmer atmosphere at Rome's Stadio Olimpico. A day earlier we had wandered over there in the midday heat to sit among the fascist/homoerotic sculpture of Mussolini's Foro Italico to watch some clay court tennis at the Rome Open. Aussie Commonwealth Games gold medallist Anastasia Rodionova was playing and we wanted to show our support. I'd met her and her talented doubles-playing sister Arina years before and had traded tennis lessons for cooking lessons. She laughed out loud when she saw me serve for the first time. In fact, they both laughed, and when we ended up in the players' dining room with them at Wimbledon a year later, they called over other tennis pros just to tell them how embarrassing my serve was . . . Not just any pros either, but the likes of Angelique Kerber and Martina Hingis. We had got in on 'family' passes as their nearest and dearest. My wife Emma remarked that they treated me with the same brutality as my own sisters, so 'family' was about right.

We sat with Arina in the bleachers at the Rome Open in our usual *MasterChef* order: Gary, then George, then me. The way we always lined up on set for *MasterChef* would become the way we'd sit on flights or in some dark, packed theatre waiting to be told about the award we hadn't won. Bizarre.

About halfway through her service game, Anastasia looked up to see us sitting there like birds on a wire. She did a visible double take, shook her head and tried to refocus. Arina smelt trouble. If this put her sister off her game . . . Anastasia is pretty scary when mad. Word is, even Tennis Australia were frightened of her.

Thankfully she won, but I still got sliced in two with a look after cheering too loudly at one point. She made me carry all her tennis bags as punishment afterwards . . . it was hot and she had a *lot* of racquets.

We did film some television too eventually. I, however, had to return from Italy early as I had a commitment at the Noosa

Food and Wine Festival. I have never been more tempted to do the wrong thing than diverting to Munich on the way home. Why? It was the Champions League Final. Chelsea had made it and were up against Bayern Munich and I'd been offered a ticket by one of the blokes on the FA Cup bus ride. But I did the right thing and consoled myself with lunch alone at Massimo Bottura's magnificent Osteria Francescana in Modena on the way to the airport. Chelsea won in a dramatic penalty shoot-out, by the way. But I wasn't complaining.

The rest of the series went pretty much as planned, bar a minor hiccough or two. UK *MasterChef* host and Melbourne-born chef John Torode was our guest judge in the second elimination in finals week, and someone had the fine idea of putting me and a 550-kilogram steer in the pantry as a 'surprise' for him. Now, as you might imagine our steer was not happy being enclosed in a windowless pantry with a complete stranger. I was holding him by a halter but as soon as the door slid shut, he started to dip his head and twist into me with his horns. I've seen enough horrific images of matadors with severed femoral arteries to know what could come next – it's as if the bull instinctively knows where to gore for maximum impact. But then if you were a bull who has to line up against a whole team of blokes with swords, lances and one in a very annoying cape, you'd pass the word around your bovine brothers about where the enemy was softest.

Thankfully I got out with my femoral artery intact.

We enjoyed hanging out with John Torode and hearing how the UK version of *MasterChef* was made. For starters, it was a much leaner production with fewer cameras and a smaller crew. They also used far fewer words in their commentary on dishes. John's 'sweet lamb, irony spinach and popping peas. I like the dish but I don't love it' became our benchmark comment from then on. Gary, George and I were only that concise on fourteen occasions over the almost 400 episodes we ended up shooting. One of those was when we were presented with a lamb dish . . . with peas and spinach. It was just too good an opportunity to pass up. We had to do it and each repeated John's signature line, one after the other. Well, at least we found it funny.

'Popping peas' became a shorthand reminder for us to try not to ramble. It largely failed. Gary was famous for the lengthy but unofficial and unsanctioned MasterClasses that he'd conduct at the tasting table even though no one else was listening. I became notorious for 'going for a canter', where I'd unleash university-thesis-length discourses about the almond growers of Willunga, or some such historical irrelevance, that had even less chance of making the cut than George's snoozing – something that happened quite a lot during the long days of filming.

George has the uncanny ability to sleep anywhere, and immediately. As do I. I am sure Gary could develop the same skill if he wasn't always talking to random strangers about anything from local geological formations to the comparative performance of Royal Enfield engines. Gaz doesn't just love a chat, he lives for one.

As I mentioned earlier, Andy Allen won series 4. Shortly after the finale, I started to wonder whether this should be my last series of *MasterChef*. I'd done four, plus an *All Star*, a *Celebrity* and the first of the *Junior* spin-offs, and I was starting to feel as though I needed to get back to my family. Back to Melbourne. On a trip home one weekend near the end of filming the series, I'd caught my then six-year-old daughter Sadie playing a wish-fulfilment game of 'Daddy's going to take you to the zoo tomorrow, but probably won't'. Ouch. The poignancy of getting on a plane back to Sydney that night was not lost on me. And there really aren't any more depressing flights than the last one out of Melbourne on a Sunday full of sad-eyed road warriors gearing up for another week away in an alien city.

Hearing Sadie play that game had been a hammer blow to the solar plexus driven with a power that an absentee parent feels double. But the final straw was catching myself calling Sydney 'home'. Home should be where your family is. Sydney was no longer an alien city to me. It was a place seemingly free from responsibilities. A holiday. A treat. And if you start thinking like that, and that home is where your family *isn't*, then you're in trouble.

That old warning friends had made four years ago about how moving interstate to make TV can destroy a relationship was ringing loudly in my ears. It felt as if it was getting a whole lot closer. So far, I'd avoided the lure of young blondes with bags of white powder on the pool deck of the Ivy, but there were traps and pitfalls everywhere you looked.

It was clear as daylight. I needed to go home. My *real* home. I needed to move back to my family, back to Melbourne, even if it meant quitting *MasterChef*.

48

If I was going to walk away from *MasterChef*, then my decision to hang on to my day job as a food writer now seemed eminently sensible. Food TV is what I had found myself doing but food writing is what I do. It's how I'd defined myself, and still do twenty-five years on. I'd grown to really appreciate the purity of getting the message from writer to reader without having it go through all the hands that are necessarily involved in making TV. This directness is now also part of what I love about doing live radio.

I also realised that with food writing you can put most of yourself on the page while TV can only ever show a small part of who you really are. Live radio was the perfect foil for this problem. It was a better way of showing people the 'true' you. Of course, it's important to acknowledge (and own) that the onscreen you is still you. TV can only show what you have willingly given – us 'flesh props' are seldom victims of editing in that sense. So yes, that's you on the screen, but it is just not *all* of you.

While doing a chat on a sports radio station one day, I could see all the texts coming in as I was introduced and began to speak. It was the usual deluge from down-to-earth blokes who seldom watched *MasterChef* . . . the words 'pompous' and 'wanker' were in high rotation with reference to me, if I remember correctly. But once we started talking about me growing up watching Chelsea FC from the Shed End, and my abiding love for Vic Park and the 'black and white army', the tone changed markedly. When I mentioned former AFL player Rene Kink, the text line nearly melted down. I'd gone from 'pompous wanker' to 'not a bad bloke really' in the space of seven minutes. Lesson learnt. Letting them shoot you down for who you are is far less painful than getting shot down for who you are not. That said, there's probably 20 per cent of who you are that is *always* best left hidden from public view. Of course this book breaks that rule, but what is a memoir if it doesn't show at least a few weaknesses and flaws? Thankfully the lawyers have ensured that at least the worst 13 per cent have been left hidden!

As I say, I'd always written about food and said as much when some ageing boomer radio presenter asked me why I was writing a cookbook when I wasn't a chef. The naivety of this question was as breathtaking as diving into a frozen Alpine lake. I pointed out that if you wanted to know what to cook at home then a home cook was who to go to, rather than a chef, and that if you wanted a book to read, maybe using a writer wasn't a bad idea either. Fortunately, when you look at cookbook sales you'll see that it's mostly cooks rather than chefs who dominate the charts.

*

I spoke with a few book publishers but ended up going with publisher Mary Small at Pan Macmillan for that first cookbook. *Matt Preston's 100 Best Recipes* was released in time for Christmas 2012 and was full of my most-cooked and beloved home recipes. There were old family favourites including my mother's trusty bolognaise, new recipes and recipes collated from friends. It had a distinctly homey, almost 'bush' feel about it.

As with any cookbook, it took an entire village to produce: mums from the local primary school helped test and develop recipes – the talented Marnie Rowe and cake whisperer Kate Quincerot the stars; there were stylists, a photographer (Mark Roper, with whom I'd travelled extensively with shooting stories of *Vogue Entertaining + Travel*, and *delicious.*), lots of editors. A cast of thousands. And all utterly brilliant at what they do. I'd learnt from having written weekly columns for the *Taste* food section in News Corp's metro mastheads that you needed to be 'expansive' in your method when you were writing recipes. When you were cooking a dish, it had to feel as though I was talking directly to you, a voice on your shoulder, calmly advising you want to do and what to look for. Wise advice indeed from editor Jana Frawley.

Marnie Rowe was one of those amazing school mums. A prodigious cook with an approach to bold flavours spookily similar to my own, but who possesses a masterful way with plating (unlike me!). She would become a regular partner in crime both on those early cookbooks and on our trips cooking overseas. I think our first trip to India nearly broke her, but the young lads in the kitchen who worked with us were both inspired and besotted by her skills. I knew how they felt. Marnie had worked with one of my favourite chefs, Karen Martini, and was a huge part of the success of my cookbooks. Some of the best recipes, like Marnie's Thighs, were hers. Kate Quincerot, whose son played in the same footy team as Marnie's son and mine, helped massively with the baking and French ideas in those books. Kate is a perfectionist who earnt the title 'cake whisperer' for her skill, and for making every sweet taste better.

Another revelation from the process of creating the book was that I had to learn to stop being a 'foodie wanker'. Here, Jana Frawley was also a great help. In my early days writing food columns syndicated in the *Herald Sun*, *Daily Telegraph*, *Courier Mail*, *Advertiser* and *Mercury*, I'd tried to impress people with my 'clever' ideas. When I published an article which included a fail-safe recipe for poached eggs that avoided the unwelcome tang of vinegar, the volume of positive feedback made it crystal clear that what people really wanted was crafty insider tips central to simply cooking better. So from then on I tracked down loads of 'hack' dishes and nifty shortcuts. An instant three-ingredient ice cream. An instant mayo I customised in all manner of flavours. A two-ingredient ice cream bread, two-ingredient flatbread and three-ingredient fresh baked loaf first created in Brooklyn that would end up everywhere a few years later.

All eight of my cookbooks went on to sell well, both in Australia and abroad. There were several European editions and respectable sales in the UK, South Africa and New Zealand. At one point Dutch sales made up a quarter of the global numbers. Indeed, *Yummy, Easy, Quick* was a top five bestseller in the Netherlands. On a trip to promote the Portuguese edition of one of the books, more than two thousand people turned up for a signing. It went on for more than four hours and broke some sort of a record, apparently. That was also something of a headfuck. Its success was due to the smart insights of my new publisher at Pan Macmillan, Ingrid Ohlsson, and to working with Michelle Southan – the food director of taste.com.au and my long-term recipe collaborator in that magazine. Michelle is an encyclopedia of recipe wisdom, and she took on the role of my food muse across this and subsequent cookbooks as a side project.

Incidentally, the title *Yummy, Easy, Quick* was coined by my daughter, Sadie, when I was struggling for inspiration . . . 'That's your food, Dad – it's yummy, it's easy and it's quick.' With clarity like that, she's got a future in publishing!

49

Now, before we get on to the problem child that was series 5, my mother always said that rather than talking about things you *don't* like, it was far better to talk about something you *do* like . . . like cake!

Personally, I am a Victoria sponge sort of a guy, which probably says something Jungian about me (I'm a traditionalist), but I also don't mind a kirsch-soaked and plump cherry-laden Black Forest cake, so maybe I'm a traditionalist who likes a little decadence too. Sounds about right. In fact, if you'll allow me this short digression, I'd like to bring in cake-baking guru Natalie Paull from Beatrix Bakes to work out what *your* favourite cake says about you . . .

What your choice of cake says about you

Victoria sponge

I say: You are a traditionalist who appreciates elegance and good manners. You might be my posh Grandmother Vivienne . . . or me.

Nat says: Sponges are fluffy and ethereal, so sponge lovers are multi-dimensional beings with both a serious and a sweet side. They might be dreamers too.

Fruit cake

I say: The cake for tweed wearers and those who like to go for long winter walks with their dogs – probably Labradors – on windswept beaches. You might take a hipflask with you.

Nat says: Fruit cake lovers are traditional. They are likely to be older or to have an old person living inside their soul.

Chocolate cake

I say: This cake tells me you are the dependable type who likes their luxury to be within strict bounds. You're a rule follower too.

Nat says: Very straight and narrow. There is only one cake for them. If it's a simple chocolate cake then it's probably for a tracksuit wearer on the couch watching Netflix, or if it is multi-layered and with lots of frou-frou on top it's appealing to those cakers who love to partaaaay.

Chocolate mud cake

I say: You are decadent, greedy and will bend the rules to get your way. Most likely you'll cheat on your taxes too . . . Sorry, what I meant to say is, you'll have a 'tax minimisation plan in place'.

Nat says: Mud cake lovers tend to be secretive about their love for them, often because they think they are a bit common and daggy. Like the mud cake they crave, they are not as exciting as they pretend to be . . . They like hugs and doing their taxes on time. They like spreadsheets.

[In the interests of transparency, Nat loves mud. Her go-to is a caramel mud cake.]

Red velvet

I say: You are wacky on the surface, but at your heart you are really the sort of dependable soul who likes their luxury contained within strict parameters. Most likely you'll dye your hair pink once you reach the age of forty.

Nat says: Those who love red velvet love pineapple on their pizza and Adam Sandler movies. They can never tell you what they love about it but they are resolute nevertheless.

Carrot cake

I say: You are earthy and generous. You probably like to wear hessian or linen. You might also favour tribal prints of some form. You secretly hope that carrot cake is healthy when we all know it is not – even if it is made with vegetables. So you are probably prone to denial as well. In your youth you used henna on your hair, and possibly played guitar. I like you very much!

Nat says: Carrot cake lovers are living a small lie . . . they are really only there for the cream cheese frosting. They also need to be reminded that it is *not* a serve of veg.

Lumberjack

I say: You love getting out in the bush. You possibly fell trees for a living. You're more likely to be a prepper and male but otherwise similar to the carrot cake lover as you both love life and want it to be generous.

Nat says: They love taking a walk on the wild side and while I hate the idea that cakes might appeal to one sex more than another, you can usually spot who's going to head for the Lumberjack cake and they are more likely to be male.

Tea cake

I say: You are serious, functional, good at replacing washers in taps and a person of habit. The presence of sparse simple icing does nothing to hide your utilitarianism. You also like a nice cup of tea or an instant coffee.

Nat says: Why bother with tea cake? It doesn't appeal to me but I see tea cake lovers as being a little prim. The sort of folk who make their bed every morning, are into meal prep and pay their taxes on time.

Lemon drizzle cake

I say: You have a wicked mischievous side and love to have a good laugh. You are living your best life in spite of everything. You might not have much money but you know how to get the most out of very little. You're also likely to be more fun than the tea cake lover at a party . . .

Nat says: Lovers of the lemon drizzle are explorers. They are adventurous. They like the sweet familiarity of a tea cake but it is only palatable when it comes with something exciting like that intense tangy kick of lemon. There is something of the 'pioneer woman' about them.

Cheesecake

I say: Liar . . . you know that's not really a cake.

Nat says: They might be living a lie thinking cheesecake is a cake but I see cheesecake lovers as a cross between Uma Thurman and Joan Chen. They know how to wear bright red lipstick.

Okay, enough with the cake. Back to *MasterChef*!

Towards the end of 2012, we received some news that, on face value, was very welcome. For series 5, we would be relocating to our home town of Melbourne! I don't know what dark deals had been done to secure the move, but we were told we'd be making the show in the old chook shed at the Showgrounds out by Flemington Racecourse.

With a new CEO, James Warburton, at the helm at Network Ten, I'd signed a contract to co-host the series along with a spin-off they'd call *MasterChef Australia: The Professionals*. James had been the sales gun at rival Seven Network. Now that he was at Ten, I felt valued and appreciated. Naturally, I shelved any plans to leave.

I co-hosted *Professionals* alongside Marco Pierre White, but the best thing about *MasterChef* moving to Victoria was the fabulous new Melbourne crew. My wardrobe also lifted to new 'heights'. Most everything I got to wear was bespoke, apart from a selection of diamond-patterned golf pants for $90 that I found online (and which helped reduce the average cost).

In the off season, wardrobe queen Charmaine De Pasquale and I would send each other snaps of looks we liked that we'd seen on the street when travelling, or on TV in shows like *Deadwood* or *Downton Abbey*, or in movies like *Night of the Hunted* or *Goodfellas*. Nothing was off limits in that planning phase, although a lot of the more outlandish and expensive stuff was ultimately nixed.

Some bizarre choices did make it through, though, like the procession of dusty pastel-pink suits, and a number of striking tartans and checks, including a double-breasted suit with gold buttons in a garish red royal Stewart tartan. The cloths available for tailoring when I'd started on the show had basically been blue, black or charcoal. Over time they became dramatically more exciting as we continued to push the boundaries. I like vainly to think of us as early fashion influencers. A version of the pink suit that we commissioned ended up on the Gucci runway a few years later, and those frock coats I got about in wound up on Harry Styles in a One Direction video. I particularly loved the online commentary about my dress sense – good or bad, it was always funny, whether I was being likened to a Colombian drug cartel boss or Barney the Dinosaur.

One of my best finds was a range of broad, candy-striped curtain material in IKEA at a measly $10 a metre. We made a suit of bold pants in stripes of white and red, or black, or pink, or grey, or blue, or yellow. My cravats were also cheap, occasionally material from vintage fabric suppliers but more often than not random lengths picked up from high-street fabric stores' bargain bins. We always favoured using local Aussie businesses wherever possible. Hence a lot of my suits were made by Pino Prinzi in Carlton (now in Brunswick), and the shirts were made by Ganton, one of the last shirt makers in Australia. The Aussie theme continued with the boots and belts I wore, which came from R. M. Williams, while the workwear, colourful shirts and jeans came from Pilbara.

There was really only one rule when it came to my onscreen fashion: dress for the occasion. If Nigella Lawson was in doing a custard challenge, then my wide-striped, yellow-and-white pants made from that IKEA curtain material were okay, but on the day of an elimination I'd wear something more muted, sombre and respectful.

Once we'd ordered and chosen the wardrobe, I'd leave it up to Charmaine to pick the day's outfit. Very occasionally we'd bicker over cravats that looked like a 'disco bin liner' or 'old ladies' La Perla underwear', or change a white shirt for a fuchsia shirt, and even more rarely I'd trash the whole look because I didn't feel right in it. That might have caused some friction but the thing to remember about TV is that no matter how long we'd prevaricate doing make-up or choosing what to wear (or not wear), we'd still be waiting a while before filming started. If you want to see a selection of these outfits, do check out @masterdressed on Insta!

When it came to call times, Gary was always early. He lived around the corner from me and so the journey to our new home out by the racecourse was the same, but he usually had a call time after mine. Most days I'd pass him crossing the Bolte Bridge. I'd phone him and tell him to stop for a coffee in a vain effort to train him to be more like me. Fashionably late – as I like to call it. Some might have used a different F word. Especially when I produced a log on *The Professionals* of how almost every time I was early we finished late and when I was late we far more often than not wrapped early.

I took the attitude that as long as you don't keep the crew waiting on set, that's okay. That was probably as irritating as in the early series when we used to chant 'That's a wrap!' the minute we'd finished filming a challenge denouement. Needless to say, there would always be hours and hours' more work for departments like art. They were understandably peeved because we were basically boasting that the day was done and we were going home (or to the pub). After being quietly taken aside by a friend on the crew and told the lie of the land, we never uttered that particular chant again.

50

Despite our happiness at being back in Melbourne, series 5 of *MasterChef* was a mess.

With no on-screen auditions, as previously, we were presented with a pre-picked cast. We did manage to do a few 'surprise' turn-ups at homes to at least see potential contestants in their own kitchens. On one such trip, we found ourselves in remote Port Hedland in Western Australia, where we'd planned to visit stay-at-home mum Liliana Battle. Unfortunately, the trip was notable for rather different reasons. When we checked in at the motel and asked about the lovely stretch of beach out front, the bloke behind the counter gave us a funny look. He then advised against going anywhere near the beach for several, rather alarming, reasons:

1. There were deadly blue-ring octopuses.
2. There were deadly cone shells.
3. There were huge bull sharks.
4. There were monstrous saltwater crocodiles.

5. There were evil box jellyfish that could melt your face off, and, most terrifyingly of all . . .
6. Local miners might not take kindly to pale, soft-handed TV types prancing along their precious patch of sand. The wall behind the bar in the local pub was plastered with photos of who had been banned as a suitable reminder of this.

That night, George wedged an easily splintered, cheap wooden chair against the door handle in his room just to be on the safe side. You can never be too careful: those blue-ring octopuses are clever critters.

We did also check out eventual winner Emma Dean's house in the inner northern Melbourne suburb of Northcote and had some very nice 'millionaire's shortbread' after a short spell filming in her impressive vegie garden. Little did we know this was probably the best thing we'd eat all series.

I suppose the writing was on the wall from the very first cook. The series was built around each week having a theme. This wasn't a terrible idea in and of itself, but the dated 1950s sitcom idea for week 1 – 'boys versus girls' – was the first misstep. Where we'd once promised to sow unity and a sense of collegiate harmony, here we were presaging discord and drama in the series promos. As you'd expect, there were unhappy mutterings from the press and on social media.

This was, however, like the beating of butterfly wings compared to what went down when the first episode eventually aired. Having all the contestants crowd around a 'boy' and a 'girl' both whipping egg whites in the middle of the MCG looked impressive but it was pointless – there was no team relay challenge, no drama, no sense of who these new contestants truly were.

Even worse, it soon became clear that some on the boys' team weren't great cooks. The giveaway was when they couldn't make a simple pumpkin soup (cook pumpkin in stock and blend would be the easiest way) or meringues (whip egg whites with sugar and then bake at a low heat). At one point, Gary leant over to me and said, 'I think we might be in trouble here.' Facebook was far blunter. There were more than a thousand comments on our Facebook page. I read them all. The response was unequivocal: well over 90 per cent of our viewers weren't going to watch the second episode because, and I paraphrase here, 'These muppets can't cook.'

The premiere launched at 1.1 million viewers. That was bad. The following night fewer than 740,000 tuned in. That was worse and as Gary had pointed out, we really were in trouble. The food was average and the audience reaction in some quarters was downright ugly. The producers were convinced that a daggy dad from Sydney was going to be the hapless hero of the show, but unfortunately Daniel Kelty was subject to some ugliness from the public, on the street and online. He wasn't the first to experience this sort of thing; I think Joanne Zalm in series 2 also had that unpleasant honour. It's weird how invested – in a bad way – some fans can get.

There were good cooks like Pip Sumbak, Emma Dean, Rishi Desai and Lucy Wallrock, and the audience ultimately warmed to their down-to-earth, girl/boy-next-door demeanours. But they couldn't save us. The show limped on with some bad food and worse ratings. A particular low point was in the Barossa Valley where we judged a mess of a lamb stir-fry dish that included almost every ingredient in the pantry in a sort of confused grey sludge. It was the worst thing I tasted on the show. It was even worse than Andre Ursini's strawberry risotto in series 1 that I archly suggested I only swallowed 'because I liked him'.

The situation deteriorated even further when we went to Dubai in week 11. Gary got sick eating two-day-old hummus and George passed out from heatstroke on the famous helipad at the Burj Al Arab hotel some 200 metres above sea level. (It was so hot even my shins started sweating. And my lovely aquamarine suit looked as if it had been tie-dyed.) Gary and I caught his slumped body under the armpits before he hit the deck and dragged him off towards some shade. We had to wrap him in cold damp towels and bombard him with fluids to revive him.

On the upside, I did get a very nice photo of me in a soft mint pastel suit in the middle of the desert with a peregrine falcon on one fist and a camel held by the reins in the other! The purpling light as dusk descended was divine. George was a little scared of the camel so I led it round after him. That was funny. Also funny was the fact that the teams had to cook camel meat. Well, that wasn't funny, that was culturally appropriate given we had Emirati guests. What was funny was that the camel shoulder was stamped 'product of Australia'.

The show averaged about 570,000 viewers. A disaster. And none of us had enjoyed making it. It wasn't the *MasterChef* we had signed up for. When we got home, Gary, George and I had a summit meeting at Pizza Espresso in Carlton and seriously debated walking away. We decided to give it one more year. If series 6 was as bad as series 5, we'd leave – or maybe the network would just quietly put the whole sorry mess out of its misery.

While series 5 of *MasterChef* was a bit of a nightmare, there were some contestants I really liked. I'm still in contact with Pip, Emma, Lynton Tapp and Dan Churchill (who has done very well for himself in the US after almost beating Heston Blumenthal in a cook-off). And, after a long absence, finalist Samira El Khafir joined me on the radio recently and was terrific. We share a love of shoes and of the Collingwood Football Club as well as eating well.

I was also given a regular slot in the MasterClass, which was shot at the end of each week in front of a live audience. I loved doing my simple, tasty versions of the sort of food everyone wanted to eat. It was also nice being able to show people that I could actually cook, and I was delighted when the download figures revealed that seven out of the top ten recipes of the series were mine. I know it sounds impressive but I was just playing the numbers. Working for *taste* and *delicious.*, I knew what recipes people were looking for at different times of the year. It's winter? Let's do pumpkin soup. It's always easier to get someone to buy something they are already looking for.

Oh, and in case you were wondering, the ice cream I made with Heston Blumenthal using Passiona and dry ice wasn't one of those seven MasterClass dishes, but gee it was fun playing in the kitchen with a bona fide culinary pioneer.

51

The dismal performance of series 5 spelt inevitable changes for the next series, but these were mostly changes for the better. Preliminary audition rounds meant Gary, George and I could try and 'tilt' the aprons towards the better cooks; the presence of the five previous *MasterChef* winners in an early round reminded people of the food-focused legacy of the show; the wonderful Kylie Kwong joined as a mentor and occasional judge; and the immunity pin challenge was now a two-round process with three contestants competing for the right to cook off against a top chef. That all made for a far more compelling show in my opinion. But before we got underway, I headed off on the publicity trail to do the mea culpa for the previous series. As we'd been universally unhappy with how it had turned out, this had some authenticity.

Series 6 launched with 874,000 viewers but by the end of that first week we had over 1 million watching in the five major cities. We were back, baby! I loved the fact that in spite of the 'problem child' that was series 5, the *MasterChef* audience still had a real ownership over the show. They had spanked us when we strayed from the tried-and-true format, but now that we were back on the straight and narrow they returned in droves.

As well as being a generally lovely bunch of humans, the series 6 contestants really delivered in the kitchen. Kira Westwick was a gun, Emelia Jackson was wonderful with pastry, and Sarah Todd cooked a Scotch quail's egg that made us sit up and take notice. It is to their credit, and their hard work, that Laura Cassai, Kira, Emelia, Sarah (who would return as the series 14 runner-up in 2022), Sean Baxter, Emily Loo, Tracy Collins, Colin Sheppard and Byron Finnerty (who, like Colin, was one of the nicest blokes you could hope to meet) all went on to forge solid careers in food, whether talking nutrition and health, writing recipes or perhaps setting up their own places.

Heston Blumenthal returned and spent a whole week with us. He was at the peak of his powers at the time and had a profound effect on conceptual dishes like bobcat-operator Brent Owens's very tasty chocolate mud dessert which hid all manner of delicious surprises.

Less welcome was the arrival of the 'power apron' concept, which gave the winner extra advantages in subsequent challenges. And again we were faced with the uncomfortable elimination of a contestant who had to cook using an ingredient she couldn't taste – on this occasion, Deepali Behar in a beef challenge. Amina Elshafei had the same problem back in series 4 if we had a pork challenge. Religious restrictions were one thing, but medical conditions such as contestants who were coeliacs or had an ethical position like not eating animal protein meant that keeping the competition fair became increasingly difficult.

There were also some nice new challenge concepts in series 6, like one of my all-time favourites, the time auction. Here contestants bid for ingredients paying in minutes taken off their cook time. Perhaps the best part of the challenge was that I got to bang a gavel and wear my most outlandish, 1960s second-hand car-dealer check suit.

Then there was the snapper challenge, where the contestants had to be judicious about how they butchered their one allocated fish. It had to last over three rounds and three dishes if their first two dishes weren't successful in saving them. It was a great concept for an elimination, or so we thought until inflight manager Nicole Cleave decided to roll the dice and do the *whole* fish in her first dish. If it worked she'd be safe, but if she wasn't in the top five that first round she'd have nothing left to cook with in the subsequent rounds. This would mean instant elimination.

Suddenly those three rounds, which were supposed to stretch over an hour or more, looked like turning into one single round. The producers became anxious. We were sent out to try to persuade Nicole not to do it given the risk. Nope, she was convinced she wanted to put all her eggs – or should I say fish – in the one basket. By this stage, the producers had begun to panic. What if Nicole's fish dish bombed? How would they fill the show without letting everyone know that she was going home? This would become pretty clear around the halfway mark when the first-round cook was still onscreen and we'd have no time to fit in any more rounds!

I can't remember if there was any pressure to wave Nicole's dish through for the good of the show – which suggests to me that there wasn't. This would have solved the problem, but in the end once again our 'trust the food gods' philosophy prevailed. And the ratings didn't suffer when Nicole's oil-seared fish didn't match the dishes from Tash Shan, Emily Loo, Laura Cassai, Rachael Ciesiolka and Amy Shields and she was immediately sent home. Rather than being a disaster, the entire episode became just another piece of *MasterChef*'s unique reality TV history. Another truly 'real' moment.

During every series, one ingredient or aspect of the show always seemed to trend. In the early years it was all about your nonna's tortellini (even if your nonna was actually from Cork or Krakow), an impressive croquembouche or, always an interest of mine when it came to food, the heritage of our cooks. This became increasingly important as we tried to mentor our contestants into developing their own unique food voice.

Sometimes this was a function of strategy. For example, everyone started doing pasta, especially filled pastas, when they realised it was an easy dish to make in a mystery box challenge where you had an under-bench pantry full of supplementary staples like flour, eggs and milk or cream. That's also why, as the show evolved over the years, you'd see so many ice creams, parfaits and cakes.

But sometimes an idea just seemed to capture the imagination of the nation. For example, the year 2010 was all about pastry wizard Adriano Zumbo's marvellous macarons; 2011 saw Kylie Millar turn salty caramel into an Australia-wide obsession; while 2012 highlighted smoky chipotle chilli – that's 'chi-pot-lay', not 'chip-ottle' as Gary and I used to say – as well as the sweet and salty pleasure of 'dude food'.

Just like in series 4, the theme for series 6 was 'back to basics' (in spite of Heston being there), and we saw quick pickling and smoking come to the fore. For dessert, we had loads of white chocolate, pannacottas and berries – especially blackberries and strawberries. These were used in both sweet and savoury dishes, with blackberry popping up rather deliciously with beetroot and ash-coated goat's cheese, as well as in game dishes.

The pannacotta was one of those pantry-staple-friendly ideas, as was using milk to make everything from buttermilk and whey sauces to butter and cheese. The pannacotta trend would get so big that viewers (and us judges) started to get a bit jack of it. It was like when we moved into the era of the parfait or ice cream – even if the ice cream was as good as that which series 9 contestant Ben Ungermann made.

With our charges sharing techniques and discussing flavour pairings in the *MasterChef* house, it's not surprising that these trends would continue throughout the other series. We moved on to savoury ice creams and herbs in desserts, which became easier and more common once Gary or George began saying 'the garden is in play'. That garden plot through the double doors at the end of the *MasterChef* kitchen could be relied on for anything from edible flowers and obscure herbs to even eggplants or chillies. The 'garden' era would be properly ushered in with a challenge with Maggie Beer in series 7. That's also the season where Reynold Poernomo made crémeaux happen. In series 8, Korean flavours, soy and miso caramels and smoking dairy were all the rage, with kimchi and more pickling along for the ride.

We saw similar trends in the types of equipment being used. During the early series pasta machines kept selling out as they were getting so much exposure on the show, but then as the food became more aspirational it was all smoking guns and sous vide machines. More recently, it's seemed that you can't grill anything unless you have a charcoal-fuelled Japanese hibachi on your bench.

Going into the final rounds of series 6, we were left with Brent Owens, Laura Cassai and Emelia Jackson, who was the short-priced favourite to win. Laura put up a couple of ripping dishes, peaking with her 'chestnut forest' dessert, which took her through to the finale. Gary noted she'd cleverly worked out the way to our hearts by adding sweet and sour (or agrodolce) elements to her savoury dishes. Over the years Gary, George and I had started to exhibit weaknesses for certain foods. Good pork crackling, onion rings, a great gravy, agrodolce onions or pickles, or a well-made classical sauce would all make us smile and leave us with a warm feeling that would be reflected in our comments. Smart contestants like Laura had decoded this and in coming series we'd be more wary of such obvious bribes!

In the semi-final, a restaurant challenge, Laura's first dish of quail with a chestnut cream was tremendous. Emelia's first dish was even better – glazed beef cheeks with a Jerusalem arti-choke puree and a little citrus zest to alleviate the richness. We'd expected a good savoury dish from Brent and he delivered with pork, golden crackling (the classic judge bribe) and a vinegar gel. Surely dessert-guru Emelia would have him covered in the dessert stakes. Trouble was, Brent put up a cracking sweet dish based around apple, pistachio and fennel with a sour cream ice cream and an apple cloud. To use the old *MasterChef* cliché, it was 'restaurant quality', and not from one of those dour communist restaurants you might find in 1970s Omsk or Novosibirsk. It was modern, fancy and excitingly tasty.

Surprisingly, Emelia's whipped chocolate ganache crumb and fig leaf custard was underwhelming due to her mandarin curd failing. Adding cream helped but it also deadened the floral citrus note and sourness the dish needed. When we sent her home after that semi-final we were all in tears. As had happened before, and would happen again, the favourite had faltered. She would, however, get her moment in the sun, winning series 12 in 2020 and writing a very fine cake cookbook a couple of years later.

Brent won the finale. Laura went on to start up a couple of very fine restaurants in Adelaide (Nido pasta bar and Fugazzi), so no harm done there.

Series 6 was the season in which I started putting up even more hacks in my MasterClass segments, like the three-ingredient peanut cookies, a two-ingredient Nutella cake and an instant ice cream made in a blender with nothing more than frozen fruit and egg whites (or aquafaba) and a little sugar as required.

This was also the series when I debuted the cheat's flatbread made with yoghurt, self-raising flour and an instant mayonnaise that the winner of the 2009 series of UK *MasterChef*, Mat Follas, had shared with me after he watched me demo the cheat's quick bread the year before. These two recipes would become regular fixtures for contestants in coming series.

52

TV shows bouncing back from a long and slow decline are rare but not unheard of. In the US, *American Idol* achieved it once when they changed judges, as did *MasterChef Australia* in 2020 with the 'All Stars/Back to Win' season that aired in the middle of the COVID-19 madness. Maybe its success was down to the new judges there too?

Anyway, at the end of series 6, it seemed *MasterChef* was back. Our finale ratings were up over 50 per cent on the previous year's disastrous results. It was as though we'd somehow recalibrated the show and reclaimed the glory days of series 1. *MasterChef* was being re-embraced, and in series 7 we ended up with 2.2 million (metro) people watching the announcement of Billie McKay's win. It became the biggest non-sports show of the year again. Even sweeter was beating the self-proclaimed 'better-looking' judges on *My Kitchen Rules*, especially as we did so by the barest of margins. Not that I'm one to boast, but we also beat that other TV powerhouse *The Block*. I should note, by way of disclosure, that is the fifth time the word 'boast' has featured in this book so far, which is quite a lot for someone who isn't inclined to boast.

There is no doubt in my mind that cutting the various spin-off series helped reduce audience fatigue. And the strategy of getting 'back to basics' again made series 6 and 7 more relatable – even if we did still have Heston Blumenthal's high-end wackiness as part of the mix. We said goodbye to Kylie Kwong and welcomed Shannon Bennett on board as a mentor for the immunity challenges. With the likes of Heston, Shannon and Darren Purchese coming back as regulars, the show started to feel like a real family affair.

There's a lot of tosh talked in the media about how this or that production is 'like a family'. What they don't say is that it can be like the most dysfunctional family imaginable, where the hosts are at each other's throats and bullying is rife. In all the years I filmed with *MasterChef* in Melbourne, I never felt that. I remember one of our talented camera team saying the atmosphere we had on set was pretty unique. He felt it was anchored by the shared challenges and the pleasures of the annual overseas trip.

Naturally, there were some contestant scandals in series 7. One of our top twenty-four was shown the door after the producers discovered he'd cooked professionally, if only for a short time, but more than the allowable six weeks. Jessie Spiby replaced him and not only made the top seven but went on to set up the rather wonderful cafe My Grandma Ben in Adelaide, a city that has always been really supportive of its *MasterChef* alums.

However, this scandal paled in comparison to John Carasig's decision to rewrite his team's dish in a relay challenge in week 3.

Choosing to ignore all advice – and all that was laid out on the bench in front of him – John proceeded to make a white chocolate velouté . . . when the dish his teammates Jarrod Trigg and Fiona Grindlay had started was . . . mussels!

It was the sort of marvellous madness that quickly became a cult moment in popular culture, captured in memes and in hashtags. For one wild minute, it had Australia screaming at their screens in frustration and rage. The entire team found themselves at risk of elimination in spite of Georgia Barnes's valiant effort pulling together pan-fried prawns with a scallop ceviche in the few minutes she had. John's white chocolate velouté stayed on the pot on the stove for the tasting. Some 1,127,000 people watched the mayhem unfold.

Georgia went on to make the finale. She cooked great, achievable stuff like her delicious and quick Monte Carlos and her lemon and thyme ice cream sandwiches. Both dishes still make my mouth water when I think of them.

Trouble was, she ran into the cooking machine that is Billie McKay.

Mild mannered and charming, Billie's cooking had become quite extraordinary over the course of the series. Her dessert that riffed on cornflakes, lemon verbena mousse and saffron was one of my favourites. And this was in a year when Reynold Poernomo put up some truly top-end, restaurant-quality sweet dishes such as his combo passionfruit mousse and sphere with coconut that married cold and hot elements brilliantly (and scored him the perfect 30/30 against one of Australia's best pastry chefs), or any number of desserts where he championed crémeaux, making it one of the words of the series, along with 'sphere'.

Series 7 made it abundantly clear that Gary, George and I were but simple souls who were happiest when the contestants were talented and the food was good . . . And there was a *lot* of good food, as well as contestants with great flair and great knowledge who could have easily won in previous series. Ava Stangherlin was brilliant, as was Anna Webster, even if they never quite found their true groove on the show. Anna's now a good friend and I am sure she wouldn't mind me saying that. Both she and Ava went on to carve out solid foodie careers.

We were also happiest when surrounded by our inspiring guest chefs: personal favourites like Rick Stein and Massimo Bottura, and Nottingham's Sat Bains, with whom George became great mates.

Overall it was a very good year. The show was flying. Our director was on fire with his creative time calls that ranged from the most ridiculous puns to the sharpest insights. Our big boss in Sydney, Pete Newman, was happy too, even though his beloved Spurs were still rubbish. And the extracurricular activities were a hoot: George and I ended up at the Asian Cup Final in Sydney where Australia beat South Korea. I'd also love to say loads more positive things here about the EPs that had joined us – Marty Benson and David McDonald – because they really were brilliant TV minds and central to the renewed success of the show but to do so and provide on-set evidence of this would be contrary to the confidentiality clauses in my contract. Good people but also the best at TV. Sadly, you'll just have to take my word for it in the absence of proffering evidence!

*

With the problems of our first series shooting in Melbourne well behind us, we now found ourselves in the midst of perhaps our happiest time together. Gary, George and I had always felt like three lads from 'south of the border', musketeers cut adrift in the Emerald City, supporting each other as best we could. As we'd learnt way back at the start, a triangle was the strongest shape. Now we were really taking pleasure in each other's company, both on set and off. I think it was around this time that we started referring to ourselves as 'the chubby trio'.

It is hard to think of another finale where one contestant was ultimately so dominant. Sashi Cheliah winning series 10 is about the only other one who comes to mind. But watching Billie McKay's performance in the series 7 finale was something else. In the third round of the cook, Billie and Georgia faced off in a pressure test where they had to recreate a dessert from Heston's three-Michelin-star restaurant, The Fat Duck. They had five hours to complete this highly technical dish, yet Billie was utterly formidable.

Her performance was enough to wrestle the lead from Georgia and so impressed Heston that he offered her a job on the spot. This was in addition to the $250,000 prize money, a column in *delicious*.magazine and an Alfa Romeo Giulietta!

The next morning we all rejoiced. The ratings for series 7 were up, our contestants had produced some truly wonderful food, and Gary, George and I seemed to have found our sweet spot.

53

In 2016, almost 1.9 million people watched the series 8 finale. The numbers had been strong throughout, bubbling around the 1 million mark following our first episode in May when 1,012,000 tuned in across the five cities. *MasterChef* was the biggest show on Network Ten by some way and was ultimately only pipped by the grand finales of *My Kitchen Rules* and *The Block*.

Given that Ten had a lower base audience than the bigger Seven or Nine networks, this was a significant achievement. It meant that we could argue we were still dragging more eyeballs to our network than those other two shows . . . many of who were switching over from the ABC, a desirable and hard-to-reach demographic for advertisers.

Our series 8 winner, the New South Wales teacher Elena Duggan, was a very good cook with a heart of gold, but the runner-up Matt Sinclair was the true star of the show, not just for a succession of excellent dishes but also because he was a straight shooter who wore his heart on his sleeve and was willing to admit his vulnerability. His interviews about the challenges made for compelling viewing. It was as though he was the unofficial narrator of the show.

Matt broke a number of hearts in the control room when the two halves of Heston's 'Verjus in egg' that he was making in the grand finale pressure test very slowly fell apart. We'd not seen such a dramatic moment – when someone's dreams literally evaporated right in front of your eyes – since the finale of series 1 when Poh's chocolate half pipe hadn't shattered like Julie's beautifully tempered one.

While there is a sense that coming second on *MasterChef* tends to allow contestants to chase their dreams without the distractions associated with being the winner – and Matt was to go on to set up the very successful Sum Yung Guys restaurant in Sunshine Beach, just down the road from Noosa – these moments are also part of the lore that the best dishes always win. Elena did the best job on the day so she won.

This transparency and honesty was an essential part of the show's credibility. It also meant that often our internal predictions about who would win were frequently wide of the mark. It's hard to understand how the pressure increases once a contestant admits to themselves that they could, in fact, win. How they react to this pressure can be the difference between victory and defeat.

Our series 8 contestants were, by and large, a fun, funny and emotionally intelligent bunch. We had a brother and sister competing for the first time (Theresa Visintin and Jimmy

Wong) and an airline pilot, Brett Carter, who was a great chap.

The contestants also cooked some truly memorable food. To this day I can still taste Anastasia Zolotarev's tarragon prawns and fried fennel pesto; Trent Harvey's red wine sauce for steak made with a smoked butter and teamed with beetroots and crispy kale; Harry Foster's cobia with a Korean gochujang sauce; and Nidhi Mahajan's finger-licking cream pepper chicken with paratha. And how could I forget Elena Duggan's Spanish-inspired 'rice and pork'. It truly was one of the best things I'd ever eaten on *MasterChef* . . . there was pork floss and a pork caramel, and there was loads of sunny saffron in the rice that came with the Pedro Ximénez cooked pork. Yum!

Desserts were strong in 2016 too, whether it was Mimi Baines's chocolate aero mousse made during the challenge at Curtis Stone's restaurant Maude in Beverly Hills in California, or Elise Franciskovic's pretty fennel nougat parfait with apple jelly, or her quandong tart and mastic ice cream. Elise also managed to work crickets into a parfait, bringing together in a tasty culinary collision two of *MasterChef*'s big trends that season.

While Matt Sinclair's blackberry sorbet with tempered chocolate and port jelly was another winner, it was his savoury cooking that blew us away, whether that was a hot 'n' sour prawn head broth, or a crispy skin kingfish which he cooked in an immunity challenge (and that only lost because guest chef Victor Liong's roast crayfish was perfect).

As if heeding the message that you'd need to attain perfection to win, Matt Sinclair and Elena Duggan both put up sublime dishes when they met in the grand finale, making, respectively, a crispy skin barramundi with prawn and pancetta sauce and twice-cooked lamb and smoked vegetables.

Finally Nigella Lawson was persuaded to join us on the judging panel for a week. This was a coup. I'd worked with Nigella when she was out for the Melbourne Food and Wine Festival in 2011 and had seen first-hand how she connected with audiences in a way that seldom seems to happen with chefs. There was adulation. There were tears. There was a willingness to wait for hours just to have a moment with her.

I'd been a fan of Nigella forever, as much for the elegance and depth of her writing as the tastiness of her recipes. Working with her on *MasterChef* was a dream come true. And she did not disappoint. I loved how she came in and immediately banned us from saying 'delicious' when talking about a dish because it was lazy and not particularly evocative. She was also no shrinking violet when it came to prosecuting her case on the floor, or after tastings in what we called the 'deliberation room'. She renamed it the 'room of pointless meetings'. The name stuck.

Sure, we'd bicker about whether doughnuts or a pannacotta could be served for breakfast (as they were back then in Melbourne), and she was distinctly unimpressed by my love of white chocolate – but even less impressed by George's table manners. Overall, it felt as though we had another sister joining the family.

During the time she was with us, Matt Sinclair cooked her rather good koftas, we threw a village fete for over 1000 people at the Showgrounds, which the contestants catered, and the two of us dropped into the contestants' house together to get them to make us a midnight snack. Harry Foster's 'brookies' – a cross between a brownie and a cookie – won. It's weeks like this that make you realise that judging a cooking show isn't really a job, and more of a tasty privilege.

We also had Heston back for a week and he was a little more manic than usual. As we'd talk, ideas and insights would come tumbling forth in a seemingly ceaseless torrent. A few years later he'd be diagnosed with ADHD, but at this point, while that sort of energy was excellent and stimulating when having a chat over dinner, it's the enemy of TV, where the producers like to deal in concise sound bites.

For the first challenge in week 9, we found ourselves standing on the roof of a carpark in Melbourne's Docklands as night fell. Under the Milky Way, our cooks were about to set up the 'world's largest pop-up restaurant' in the pods of the Melbourne Star, a huge 120-metre-high observation wheel (a bit like the London Eye if you're from that part of the world). The theme of the challenge, set by Heston, was 'outer space'.

When asked what his inspiration was, he began talking rather eloquently about the stars above us, and how tens of thousands of years ago Australia's First Nations people would have sat beneath them to cook their dinner. It was poetic. It was evocative. And it went on far too long. I had absolutely no intention, however, of telling one of the greatest minds in food to stop yapping.

In the end, Theresa's 'black hole' dessert was voted the dish of the day.

*

In week 11, we took a trip to California. The production team put together two weeks of filming the length of the state with great aplomb. The contestants cooked in Dominique Crenn's restaurant Atelier Crenn in San Francisco, and at Curtis Stone's Maude. Away from the cameras, we cooked and ate an obscene amount of oysters together at Hog Island on Tomales Bay, throwing them on the grill after discovering that none of us was fast enough at shucking to match the pace of our appetites. We also ticked off a few more items on our bucket lists such as Alice Waters' Chez Panisse in Berkeley and eating original fish tacos in San Diego, after which I stunned George by showing him just how much Carhartt clothing one man can buy. I couldn't resist: it was so cheap there! I think the store location deep in San Diego suburbia as part of a huge warehouse of giant reels of fake lawn was also wigging him out.

We had a very big night in LA that ended with a mob of us back in George's room with a motley selection of crew and chefs and even Gary's *Boys Weekend* castmate Miguel Maestre, after we were chucked out of Soho House in West Hollywood in the less wee small hours. Wiser, I had avoided getting stuck with the bill there.

There was dancing and gin and mezcal. The night started with lunch, then a trip to see the LA Galaxy football team play and eat the shittiest runny cheese and jalapeno nachos on the terraces, followed by a street-truck blizzard of tacos al pastor in a part of town where we probably shouldn't have been. That night was the first time I saw the 'other' Gary. The Gary on fire and insisting everyone go for pancakes as soon as the sun was up . . . it was like our roles had reversed . . . usually it was him sneaking off to bed after a couple of beers, leaving George and me to kick on.

We really enjoyed filming again in LA with Curtis Stone. We all love Curtis . . . and, with his regular appearances on the show over the years thanks to his (and the show's) close relationship with the Coles supermarket chain, we felt very comfortable together.

Curtis suggested we take our lunch break off set and, strangely, we were allowed to wander off together without a minder from production. We ended up in the back room of a deli up the road from Maude that was once a secret haunt of the Hollywood top brass. With one of the owners, we ate well and drank better. We got back about thirty minutes *after* our call time. Usually there were always delays, especially on location shoots like this, but this time . . . there weren't. Apparently when no one knew where we were, and we were late, panic had started to set in.

It's a bad idea to lose any of your judges mid-episode, but it wouldn't be the last time. After a pizza night in Tokyo when filming there a couple of years later, George and a few of the contestants went AWOL. I was there then to witness the panic first-hand.

In June of 2016, after series 8 wrapped, Gary, George and I headed to Bengaluru with our teams to headline a new Indian food festival, World on a Plate. Our profile had been rising on the subcontinent over the previous five or six years, and as the Indian middle class had ballooned, so had the audience for our little show made in a shed on the outskirts of Melbourne. I'd been to Mumbai a few times and had noticed the deep connection Indian fans seemed to have to the positive nature and good food of *MasterChef*. The first time I was there, I was told it was one of the biggest English-language broadcasts in India, eclipsing even hit dramas of the time like *Desperate Housewives*. By our tenth series, Indian broadcasters were regularly citing audiences of 6 to 7 million an episode.

Travelling for food festivals, or doing cooking appearances to promote the cookbooks, you'd meet passionate *MasterChef* fans from every corner of the globe. When the show switched cable channels in the UK it started to boom there too. We heard from devotees in Ireland, and Pakistan, and Venezuela. *MasterChef* wasn't broadcast in the US, but still around 5 per cent of my social media followers were from there – they'd found it through other routes, and they were enthusiastic correspondents. One day while I was at an animal sanctuary in Sri Lanka washing an elephant, three huge Bulgarians came over to say hello. In fact, they just said one word, '*MasterChef*?', and smiled. Portugal is another of my favourite places to visit because of this connection. This is a true food lovers' country and they are a beautifully hospitable people. When I visited pre-COVID, there seemed to be an obsessive interest in the show, and far too much media coverage for my ugly mug to justify.

Gary and George had a similar experience in India when around 3000 people turned up for a signing. It was so overwhelming, they had to be snuck out of a side door when the crush became too much. The Bengaluru event enjoyed the same sort of madness. The crowds were overwhelming.

Actually, the entire trip was overwhelming. We would find that a simple night out dancing at a club seemed to have been sold on social media (without our knowledge) as a live appearance with a cover charge. People would thrust their three-month-old babies at me through closing lift doors to hold . . . 'He's your greatest fan!' Lady, he's three months old!

On an earlier visit to Mumbai, my cravat had trended on Twitter and I'd made the front page of the two major English-language papers. I'd walk into smart restaurants and people would freeze and stare, forks poised halfway to their mouths. It was like a scene out of some old cartoon.

Holidaying in Sri Lanka on one occasion with my family, we'd swung into our huge Colombo hotel and were greeted by a bank of paparazzi and seemingly every chef from the hotel's kitchens, and the neighbouring restaurants too. We faced a wall of about 300 chefs in crisp white jackets and tall white toques. It was more than humbling – I had a supreme and uncomfortable feeling of not being worthy. How could I live up to this . . . be big enough, loud enough, impressive enough to justify the show? I couldn't.

This feeling was heightened by the fact that I'd been up all night dealing with my sick daughter, who'd been volcanic at both ends. I looked dog-tired and was wearing Birks, a pair of loose, pink, drawstring pants and an old, crushed grey T-shirt. A million miles from my onscreen persona. I felt I'd let them down. I was embarrassed even . . . and all those eyes . . . Still I muscled through . . . smiled . . . took all the photos required, and there were many . . . and discussed their secrets for the perfect seeni sambol or miris malu, which was, I suppose, my purpose, my way of repaying their kindness.

Celebrity overseas is very different to being known where you live. In Australia, if people see me in the street they usually react like they've bumped into the bloke who runs the corner store, in a surprising place (that is, not the corner store). And I love that. The whole screaming and pushing and treating us like we matter feels slightly uncomfortable. Scream at Harry Styles, not this old bloke . . . and Harry's probably swagger-jacked my style better anyway.

Still, it's a weird thrill to be in places like Krakow, Lisbon or Naples and to be recognised in the street by people who love the show, who want a photo, who have the need to share the one place you *must* eat at while you are in their city. It's never a chore and always a privilege. I usually end up asking more questions of them than they have of me. Sometimes you can see their eyes glaze over and they try to sidle away. This wasn't the way they expected the encounter to go!

At its peak, *MasterChef* was so big that my sister could walk out of her hotel room in Delhi after the Commonwealth Games and leave Gary cooking rice pudding on her telly there, only to walk into her flat in London some sixteen hours later, turn on the telly and see Gary still cooking the same rice pudding!

The only real difference was how some countries made subtle tweaks to the show when they broadcast it in their region. In the Middle East any pork products mentioned – and we did love our crackling and bacon – were bleeped out like swear words, and when we were dubbed in Arabic I was given a very high-pitched voice. This has greatly amused friends travelling there over the years.

The show was also popular in Italy, where I've been confronted everywhere from the market in Rome to the back streets of Naples with the words, 'Giudice? [Judge?] *MasterChef*?' Heston Blumenthal tells a story of being in Milan and a fan approaching him to talk about his TV work. Rather than *In Search of Perfection* or *Fantastical Food*, they wanted to speak about his appearances on you know what.

I filmed a guest appearance on Dutch *MasterChef* once and Gary, George and I were in a brilliant but weird promo for *MasterChef*'s launch in Korea. I also flew to Milan and Krakow to film with the local versions of the show there too. This was like some bizarre acid trip where you step through the looking glass and everything is the same but different. The logo, the gantry, the benches, the language, the backdrop where you stand. All the same but all just a little bit skewed.

I saw this as a tremendous lark and loved every moment. There's something marvellous about appearing in a mock-up of the show you've worked on for eight years but in another language and with another set of judges. Interestingly, there was always an overly dressed, loud one like me . . . possibly wearing some sort of scarf or wacky bow-tie. In Poland she was a woman with huge back-combed blonde hair. And there was always a quirky little one who looked like a Mossad agent, and a bloke dressed like a bank manager who did the heavy lifting. Check out the photos of the judges in France or Malaysia and you'll see what I mean.

Before *MasterChef Australia* came along, the UK format of the show – which had been running since 1990 – had not been sold in any other territories. After the show's success in Australia it was recreated in more than sixty countries around the world. No surprise, then, that in 2017 it was named the most successful cookery television format of all time by the fine folk at Guinness World Records.

And the legacy continues. Over 500 series of *MasterChef* have now been made and in 2020 the Australian format was named the Most In-Demand Reality Series at the Global TV Demand Awards, with all twelve series streaming somewhere or other on the planet!

Smart of *Time* magazine then, way back in 2010, to name *MasterChef Australia* one of the top ten TV formats for the next ten years alongside the UK's *EastEnders*, Afghanistan's *Afghan Star*, and India's *Yeh Rishta Kya Kehlata Hai*.

The growth of cable, streaming and satellite TV was perfect for *MasterChef*'s huge number of episodes, multiple series and straightforward culinary competition format. Over the years those numbers continued to grow. It seems that everyone loves good food and the clean, fresh brand of top nosh and the great outdoors that Australia represents.

On our various trips overseas, we started to get a sense of how many people were watching. Either we were given ratings like the 2.5 million who watched in South Africa and the 1 million or so who watched in the Netherlands and Portugal, or we were told facts, such as when *MasterChef Australia* ran on the cable channel in Malaysia their viewing numbers doubled. In 2018, I started totting up the numbers for a bit of fun . . . With 6 to 7 million viewers in India and all those viewers in South Africa, Portugal, Italy, the UK, the Netherlands, Scandinavia, Canada, the Middle East and Ireland, and dozens of other countries each throwing in a few hundred thousand more, it looked like our biggest shows might have reached some 18 million viewers globally.

What quickly became clear was that Australia was not even close to being our biggest market. It was more like fourth or fifth. This huge global success was a great credit to everyone who has made the show what it is, from crew and editors, to contestants, network peeps and all the producers. I'll say it again, we were just the hood ornament, the Silver Lady on the bonnet of a TV Rolls-Royce.

The Indian food festival World on a Plate was punishing for a number of reasons, not least of which included having to dress up like a maharaja – very culturally insensitive, I felt, but our Indian hosts loved it – but also for the fact that Gary had to play peacemaker between George and me at the start of the trip, thanks to a flippant throwaway remark to which George took umbrage.

Later, while in India, I apologised for any lingering offence I might have caused and the air was cleared. Little did I know what was happening behind the scenes in George's life.

54

Series 9 started out fairly well with more viewers tuning in for the first episode than the year before. The trouble was that the finale crashed by over 30 per cent.

'Why?' was a point of much conjecture. How come the numbers started to drop, reaching new lows, through the show? This wasn't the new era of *MasterChef* we were used to.

Was it the guests? Well, sure, there was no Nigella and she was one of the few international guests who actually bumped audience ratings in a meaningful way . . . but Yotam Otto-lenghi was a delight to spend time with and had a big influence on how the contestants thought about food.

And of course Heston was back at his quirky best with a week of episodes shot across Victoria themed around the four elements. We did 'water' on the banks of the mighty Murray in Swan Hill (I remember Sam Goodwin doing a fine job there). We did 'air' on the salt flats outside Mildura and 'earth' by the painted silos of Brim in the Mallee, where a hot wind blew so hard elements were whipped off dishes and the sprinkling of herbs was an act of trigonometry that required you to be a fair way upwind from the plate so that they'd land where you wanted them. And 'fire' was done at the old gunpowder and explosives store at Jack's Magazine on the Maribyrnong River.

Was it the overseas trip? I thought going to Japan was a stroke of genius. We were there for cherry blossom season, and the memory of shooting with the iconic Mount Fuji in the background will live with me for a long time. Offscreen we ate too many katsu sandwiches, were introduced to some incredible sushi places, tried the infamous fugu pufferfish (but didn't tell the producers in case one of us died), ate grilled and lacquered eel in rustling brown paper bags and our bodyweight in ramen of all forms.

We also snuck off to Kyoto on the bullet train for a side trip full of calming temples, flaring grills and chilled beers. The only downside was that Gary and I had to share a bed as George refused to have anyone else in his room. The bed was big. We didn't cuddle.

We also took the contestants out for pizza – there are a couple of excellent hardcore Neapolitan-style pizza places in Tokyo – and ate at the Japanese offshoot of Sydney's Apollo, where George told everyone it was my birthday so I got a cake and the whole packed place sang to me. It wasn't my birthday, of course, but there was nothing else I could do but run with it.

The highlight of Kyoto was a young chef's tiny degustation restaurant where we were instructed before turning up not to be barbarians or do any of the following: 1) laugh loudly, 2) raise out voices above a whisper, 3) belch, and 3) wear aftershave. It was okay, we knew what we were about . . . earlier in the trip we had seen the look of horror on the faces of customers and staff alike when we rocked up to a tiny yakitori joint, unmarked and hidden in a basement around the corner from the touristy place where Uma Thurman dispatched the Crazy 88 gang in the Tarantino film *Kill Bill*.

Gary, George and I filled the doorway like a bad omen. There were some seats at the bar and they ushered us in as though they were welcoming yōkai who could not be ignored. By the end of the meal, and having ordered enough skewers of chicken bits both prosaic and exotic – chicken knee cartilage, anyone? – to reassemble a complete chicken jigsaw, we did get a nod, if not quite a smile, upon leaving.

Was it that Australia's collective heart broke when our eighteen-year-old contestant Callan Smith was sent home? It is true that the numbers were particularly soft after that elimination. And Callan was both so fresh-faced and so innocent we all felt his loss keenly. It was like the guilt after eating veal. It's lovely to see him, as charming and as solicitous as ever, ruling the floor at Neil Perry's Margaret in Sydney.

Was it the casting or the contestants? I found this hard to believe because I think we not only had several of the best contestants we'd seen from any of the series but we also saw some of the very best food. Oh my gosh the food.

Sarah Tiong's play on bak kut teh with tea-braised pork belly, vegetables and bean curd cooked in a tea plantation under the lee of Mount Fuji still brings tears to my eyes, as much for her evocative storytelling as for the brilliant way she referenced, but progressed, this legendary dish. Her pork 'steamboat' with mushrooms, taro and wombok was equally special.

Karlie Verkerk was also extremely talented, and her cooked oysters with oyster cream, cucumber granita, gin and fennel was like an elegant beachside holiday. It was perhaps ironic that her spicy XO pork belly with rice cakes was one of the dishes that saw Sarah sent home so close to the finale. Karlie spent a bit of time working with me after the show, writing recipes and helping out on shoots with myself or superstar offsider Warren Mendes before she headed off to *Gourmet Traveller*.

The rest weren't slouches either. Tamara Graffen's macaron parfait sandwiches with strawberries continued the parfait craze, while Eliza Wilson's 'peach ember' and Eloise Praino's rhubarb sorbet with smoked Italian meringue were memorable. Even Arum Nixon, who was often in the middle of the pack, impressed with a totally mad but unexpectedly delicious steak with liquorice gravy and a smoked swede puree.

So was it the finale? Was the pairing of the talented Diana Chan and Ben Ungermann, who had been lambasted on social media for making too many ice creams, just not appealing enough? Certainly, I was expecting either Karlie Verkerk or Sarah Tiong to make the finale as they were among the best cooks we'd ever had.

That said, the food Diana and Ben put up was good – Diana's green dish of abalone with a nasturtium leaf juice, crispy spatchcock skin, shiitake and bamboo shoots was perfect, her take on classic buttery oatmeal prawns utterly delicious and, in spite of cutting himself, Ben put up an interesting dish of a cardamom coffee ice cream with butternut squash three ways.

Was it viewer fatigue or *MasterChef* getting tired? Sure, nine series is a long time on the telly – especially for a show with so many episodes and spin-offs over the years.

Was it the judges? That is a distinct possibility!

Series 9's ratings weren't great but little did I know that a far more ominous storm was brewing – a veritable maelstrom from which one of our number would not so easily recover.

55

In early April 2017 the MAdE Establishment restaurant group – which owned Melbourne's Press Club among others, and of which George was the group's very public face even though he was only a minor shareholder and director – made a shock announcement. Due to 'historically poor processes', 162 employees had been underpaid $2.6 million.

I'm not going to dwell too much on this episode, as it's George's story to tell – I was just a bystander. If you are interested, the Fair Work Ombudsman's long and detailed report into their investigations is online and worth a read. But, to be clear, I feel that underpayment of staff is never acceptable. And doubly so in industries that employ vulnerable workers like new migrants and students. I applaud the work that Fair Work Australia has done over the years to get these workers paid what they are due. Paying any shortfalls is not heroic, it is the bare minimum. Correctly remunerating your staff is one of the fundamental duties of an employer.

*

There was no doubt George was under an enormous amount of pressure. But then, on 7 May, less than a month later, things got a whole lot worse.

At the end of the A-League grand final at Sydney's Moore Park – which incidentally Melbourne Victory lost to Sydney FC on penalties – George and the rest of us were walking through the crowd to get to the Victory rooms, when the Sydney FC fans started chanting insults at him.

I told him to ignore them . . . and he did. Melbourne Victory had played so well, we were so proud of them, and the atmosphere in the rooms afterwards was electric and emotional. I think I had tears in my eyes when I was talking to goalkeeper Lawrence Thomas and Victory director Mario Biasin. After a few minutes, chef Shannon Bennett and I wandered out after George. We stopped to congratulate Football Federation Australia CEO David Gallop on the game. George kept on walking.

Next thing I knew, he was involved in an altercation in the stands. George argued with one fan and shoved him in the chest. Of course, it was all caught on film. He then spoke with the police standing nearby, who up to that point hadn't seemed all that interested in what was going on. I walked over and could see straight away how upset George was. 'He called my mum a cunt! You can't call someone's mum a cunt!' he told me. We swiftly ushered him up an aisle and out of the ground.

George was immediately remorseful about what had happened. He's simply not that sort of guy. I'd known him for over a decade and had never seen him like that. We'd joke that he was the one more likely to hide behind Gary than step up to a threat. He was understandably worried about what the ramifications might be following the incident.

These days it seems that the size of a story is directly related to the amount of visual imagery available of the event, and as I mentioned, someone in the crowd had filmed the whole thing. It became a huge story. It didn't look good for George and got worse when it turned out that the fan who he'd shoved was a teenager – albeit a nineteen-year-old who was much bigger than him.

Again, I want to make it clear that I do not regard confrontation or violence ever as a valid way to resolve conflict, and I regret to this day that I didn't stick closer to George so I could have kept him away from those fans. That's what I'd done earlier walking through the crowds of chanting Sydney supporters. But dealing mentally with a mass chant is easier than with a single insult from a person you can see. This can cut harder as it's far more personal.

To their credit, Network Ten stood by George. He copped a $1000 fine and an assault conviction, which was quashed on appeal. According to Georgina Mitchell's report in the *Sydney Morning Herald* in early 2018, Judge Andrew Scotting overturned the decision, finding that George had been provoked and had a genuine belief that his mother had been seriously denigrated. The bigger cost, however, was the loss of reputation.

Thankfully the memory of that moment of madness at the A-League grand final would fade. The same could not be said for the underpayment scandal at MAdE Establishment.

56

In spite of the offscreen woes, reaching the tenth series of *MasterChef* seemed like an achievement. Well, I suppose it was; not only did we have celebrity chefs who refused to do other reality shows, or even other *MasterChef* franchises, willing to appear on our version, but we'd found ourselves filming – and eating in – some truly extraordinary places.

The show had nearly died but we had all together – producers, crew, post and contestants – resurrected it and there was a real pleasure in making it now. We were comfortable with the format, enjoyed watching the contestants develop and accomplish things they never thought they could, and the veracity of our onscreen relationships were supported by the relationships we had with past contestants offscreen. When I'd go to an event in Adelaide, for example, I'd be disappointed if I didn't catch up with Poh, Callum, Eloise, Laura, Jessie and the rest of the old crew.

Series 10 was really set apart by two very special guests (other than Nigella, of course, who returned for another week of keeping us on our toes). The first was Gordon Ramsay, who the team had been chasing for years. He finally agreed. I had a certain amount of trepidation having Gordon on because when we started *MasterChef* his onscreen approach had been part of the reason we went in the opposite direction. I was worried he'd start haranguing our contestants, putting a slice of white bread on either side of their head and calling them an idiot sandwich. The version of *MasterChef* that he made for Fox in the US was very much in that old style of reality TV competition with plates being thrown when you didn't like things rather than when you did.

What actually transpired was a pleasant surprise. Gordon was extremely engaged in the production, constantly asking questions about why we were doing things in a certain way, seeing what he could glean to improve his version of the show. He'd done his homework on Gary, George and me, which was the sort of professionalism you don't expect, and he even engaged in conversations that weren't just about him! He was sharp, he was quick, he was very funny. It was great seeing that side of him. He also knew his food and had a wonderful palate to match his broad-based knowledge. Again, this is not always the case with the professionals. Best of all, he treated our amateur cooks with humour rather than abuse. My fears had been unfounded.

The other highlight of series 10 was a trip to the Northern Territory where our contestants got to cook for (then) Prince Charles and 150 of his guests at a cocktail party for the Royal Flying Doctor Service in Darwin. This was an extraordinary coup pulled off by one of the great TV producers of our age, Mr Tim Toni. As if Nigella and Gordon weren't enough!

Camilla, the then Duchess of Cornwall, briefed Gary on the heir to the throne's likes and dislikes. She was the one who had persuaded Charles to take part as she was apparently a fan of the show. But they shouldn't have had much objection from his advisors on the Privy Council, as we'd heard rumours that some of them were also avid *MasterChef* watchers. Then there was one other link. Many of our crew had worked for Camilla's restaurant critic son, Tom Parker Bowles, when he was in Melbourne filming *Family Food Fight* for the Nine Network. I'd met him too and he was a lovely bloke.

King Charles has always had an interest in food and was an early proponent of organic and sustainable farming practices. He was also really curious about Indigenous ingredients and the food of our First Nations people. In the end, that formed the brief for the canapes our contestants cooked for him in the team challenge on a Darwin quayside.

It was perilously hot out in the kitchen marquees and the wind picked up as the weather looked to change. It added to the unreal atmosphere; a slightly unhinged tension clattering in the air. Knowing who was going to taste the food amped up the pressure on everyone, including the judges. As if meeting the prince wasn't stressful enough, our time with him was going to be strictly limited. We only had a few minutes to get some usable quotes when he joined us at the tasting table.

Oh, did I mention the guns? Knowing there was a highly trained and seriously armed protection squad poised behind a door next to where we were standing didn't help our nerves either. 'If that door over there opens just hit the deck immediately, then you should be all right' was the advice from one of the close protection officers. We prayed that there would be no reason for that door to open.

Watching the prince work the crowd as he wended his way towards us was a masterclass all of its own. Prince Charles had the knack of making people feel at ease, getting them laughing. The event had an incredibly diverse crowd but he seemed to have the right thing to say to each and every group. It was masterful and inclusive.

When he eventually reached Gary, George and me, we talked about the fizzy lemony pleasure of eating green ants and the other unique Indigenous ingredients that the teams had used. He seemed genuinely engaged and had a good sense of humour. Even though he'd been up since 5 am and had been to two other appointments that day hundreds of kilometres apart, he told his team that he wanted to stay on after his allotted time so he could meet the contestants who had cooked for his event. He was even happy to do photos with them. That was an extra yard none of us expected. We took pictures, he chatted, and it was sensational.

I have no memory of who won the challenge and why, but that didn't really seem to be the point . . . there could be no greater seal of approval for a TV show than to have had two characters as diverse as the Dalai Lama and the future king of England both agree to be on the show. The Prince of Wales' appearance seemed a fitting way to mark our tenth anniversary.

While in Darwin we ate some really delicious, sweet, sticky dried shredded squid at Little Miss Korea. If you ever get there, ask them if they have their ojingeochae bokkeum. Sorry, these things matter to me and surely a memoir should include that which dominates your memory of a time or a place – like that stunning dried squid.

We then drove south and filmed a challenge at Nitmiluk (Katherine Gorge). There was no better way to follow that royal episode than with something a little more down to earth and truly Australian like this. The only thing bigger than royalty is the majesty of the Australian landscape.

On the drive down we stopped at Mayse's Cafe in Pine Creek to sample their famous homemade sausage rolls with mango chutney, and had a couple of very, very cold ones at the open bar of the Pine Creek Hotel, where we all fell in love with the ingenuity of a local bloke who drove his ride-on mower to the pub. Apparently you can't lose your licence on a mower.

I should also note that we'd already had a very nice fish supper at Rachael Ciesiolka's fish shack, another example of an ex-*MasterChef* contestant – Rachael was in series 6 – who may not have won but who was now making their home town a tastier place to be.

At Nitmiluk, it was hot. My wardrobe queen Charmaine and I had one of our rare rows about whether or not it was suitable to wear my white Birkenstocks as the temperature was expected to exceed 40°C. But while filming the reveal at the end of the day, the gorge was suddenly flushed with the best evening light, soaking the rock faces in reds, and ambers, and purple. It was memorable. It was magical. It was majestic. And it was the perfect backdrop for white Birkenstocks!

We tasted dishes on a boat, trying not to think too much about the huge crocodile traps that lay along the waterways. This shoot was one of those examples of when the whole crew came together as one, in this case to muscle the giant jib and its camera off a boat and carry it up into the gorge to a suitable position where its long neck could sweep across the contestants as they awaited their fate. They were all there helping: the camera team, story team, producers, make-up, wardrobe, sound, lighting, art, runners. It was an epic feat. Recently when I was talking to a colleague from that time, they cited, unprompted, that moment in Nitmiluk as an example of the unique sense of family on the show.

I am ashamed to say that I couldn't help as I was wearing my white Birks and they weren't closed-toed. I was worried about stubbing a toe. Typical spoilt 'talent'!

Those highlights really gave series 10 a special air, as did having the nine previous winners on hand in the first episode to help mentor the aspiring contestants to win an apron – and a place in the competition. This was also a great way of seeing which of them might have the onscreen presence to become a more regular fixture on the show. We would go on to have Matt Sinclair, Poh Ling Yeow and Billie McKay mentoring in the immunity challenges in series 11 and that seemed to work well. I felt that when the day came for Gary, George and me to leave, a new judging panel solely made up of ex-contestants who had gone on to make careers in food would make for the perfect replacements. Who better to understand and care for the contestants than ex-contestants themselves?

The boys and I had discussed moving on a couple of times after that fateful meeting at the end of the doomed series 5. There was a general feeling between us that it should be one out, all out; that it would be weird continuing without the others. This also fitted with a growing sense of the three of us being a unit. A magical triangle where the strengths of the others covered the weaknesses of the one.

Series 10 started with auditions and a very special moment. I met an Italian great-grandmother, Nonna Celia, when she accompanied her daughter (and a grandmother in her own right), Nonna Gina. This tiny woman was greatly enamoured of my cravats and was a tougher judge of her daughter's cooking than we could ever be.

The second challenge of the series was a blind tasting of dishes to win an apron. Some fans had long been arguing for more blind tastings to stop any bias in the judging. These were often the same fans you'd see declaring on social media that the fix was in and that Eliza Wilson, or Sara Oteri, or Georgia Barnes were going to be crowned because the judges loved them. Yup, you'll notice that none of those names are engraved on the *MasterChef* trophy. We did, however, love the one-eyed passion of some viewers for their favourite contestants. It meant that they were connecting and feeling the same emotions when we had to send someone home – especially when we'd spent a couple of months with them and got to know and love them.

I don't mind a blind tasting, although it would have made it harder for us to mentor the contestants if we weren't allowed in the kitchen when they were cooking. If we'd seen what they were doing, and what ingredients they were using, it wouldn't have been a blind tasting.

*

Once again, our 'no dickheads' policy meant we'd ended up with a terrific bunch of contestants, but Sashi Cheliah was hard to beat. Before long he had won two immunity pins and was consistently putting up great dishes. Here was another stand-out performer like Marion Grasby in series 2, but we all knew how that could turn out.

Apart from Sashi, Hoda Kobeissi was a series 10 star, cooking some beautiful dishes, including a date and molasses ice cream cornet with pistachio halva, a hand-pulled cotton candy and a unique take on knafeh. I also enjoyed Sarah Clare's, Jenny Lam's and Samira Damirova's food sensibilities, one of the reasons why I still follow them on social media. Brendan Pang was a beautiful human; a social worker who cooked us one of the best dishes ever on the show with his poached lobster with carrot dressing and bonito bavarois. He made good dump-lings too, something that Perth now benefits from along with Jenny's excellent banh mi that she started selling from her cafe Bunn Mee in Leederville. She also has a Vietnamese tapas place next door called Phat Lon.

Khanh Ong would be one of our three finalists but he took a bit of time to get going, only really emerging from the pack after we spent a week cooking in Adelaide. He finally came good with a kangaroo dish he put up in a South Australian producer challenge.

In retrospect, the story arc of series 10 was the 'will he or won't he' of Sashi Cheliah, the cook with the thousand-watt smile, an endearing intensity when it came to food, and a surprising special forces and prison guard background.

As the show neared finals week, Ben Borsht emerged as Sashi's main competition. He cooked a beautiful piece of barramundi paired with an outstanding lemon beurre blanc at Nitmiluk National Park and this set him on a roll. As Ben grew stronger, Sashi started to wobble. His lamb curry with smoked cauliflower was eclipsed by Ben's seared coral trout with a ginger carrot puree and a parsley vinaigrette. And then, in a challenge at Icebergs Dining Room overlooking Bondi Beach, a lacklustre pasta dish almost sent Sashi packing. He just managed to hold out against young pastry whizz Jess Liemantara and Khanh to make it to the finale, where Ben stood waiting.

For all Ben's skill cooking fish, and with all his elegance at making simple classic sauces to go with them, the finale was a brutal affair. Sashi seemingly awoke from his culinary slumber and crushed it. He was dominant. The flavour of his sambal prawns with crispy prawn heads was perfect and his fish curry with cumin rice was only a tad shy of that. Damn they were both such good dishes! The sort of food that makes you forget there are half a dozen cameras and thirty-five people watching you obliviously crunch and slurp.

The pressure of the finale must have got to Ben as his avocado and crab dish was mushy and the coating on his deep-fried whiting a problem.

Going into the final round, Sashi had a virtually unassailable lead of sixteen points. That's a TV no-no anywhere else, but our audience was different. Even though they knew Sashi had won, they stuck around to see him lift the trophy and watch Ben redeem himself with an excellent rendition of Heston's complex nineteen-ingredient dessert in the final pressure test.

For once, the favourite had won, and Sashi had done so in style with the highest ever finale score of 93 out of 100.

57

Series 11 of *MasterChef* had all the classic elements that had made the show so beloved around the world. There were the mystery boxes and the invention tests that had always started off the week, and the immunity challenges against a top chef who was often (and surprisingly) floored, both by the difficulties of cooking in a strange kitchen and the restraints imposed on their access to ingredients. This was something the contestants quickly became used to.

And, of course, the pressure tests were back. When that cloche was lifted and you saw the look on the contestants' faces at what horrors awaited them, at home you were convinced it was seemingly impossible for an amateur to master such culinary complexity. Yet hours of painstaking testing back of house by our food team ensured the task was hard but could be achieved in the time allotted – just – but only if the contestants attempting it worked like stink. The planning of each challenge was crucial as the time allotted had to be just right. Too little and you ended up with the disappointment of unfinished dishes. Too much and there was no drama, no time pressure, and a lot of hanging out when everything was done waiting for the clock to run down.

Then there were our guest chefs, who once again helped ensure that even contestants who were eliminated early went home with stories of the time they cooked for Yotam, Heston or Nigella.

And of course there were the judges. Gary, George and I weren't just there to direct the traffic and look ravishing in the promos; we also needed to convey to you what the dishes tasted like and why they were good or bad. We had to keep you abreast of all the action in the cook and identify where to look among all those stovetops to find those one or two compelling stories. There was that fine line of the bench visit where your role as a judge and a mentor was to nudge but never tell; to enthuse, encourage and inspire but also to warn; to walk away hinting at the catastrophe that was about to unfold . . . just after this ad break. In the game, this is called 'setting jeopardy' and if you do it well when filming you are rewarded with the ultimate TV accolade . . . the moment of hanging tension that's broken only with a fireball and prompts to the ad break. 'Are you sure crème de menthe is the secret to a great soufflé, Gabrielle? Have you got time to finish *all* the elements?' The camera then cuts to Gabrielle looking really nervy. Fireball! Ad! You know the drill.

And finally, there was that one unwavering essential ingredient of any and every episode of *MasterChef Australia*: great contestants. Series 11 was a far more even affair when it came to culinary skills. Rather than a couple of front runners, or just one, this series saw many great dishes shared across many great contestants. One thing remained the same, however – the remarkable diversity of professions that were represented. This had been a feature of *MasterChef* since the beginning, but in 2019 our very diverse group included a gardener, a theatre manager, a travel agent, an IT manager, a criminal statistician, a barman, a student, a stay-at-home mum and a couple of pharmacists!

And what about the food? Well, office manager Dee Williams fed us a wonderful Sri Lankan crab curry while financial analyst Derek Lau made us excellent crunchy Korean chicken wings tossed in a sweet and spicy sauce. Then there were the turmeric garlic prawns cooked by homewares buyer Abbey Rose in the Noosa Surf Club challenge. Yum!

Other memorable contestants included Walleed Rasheed (the self-styled Prince of Baklava), Sandeep Pandit who had an angelic touch with spices, and Tim Bone who looked like Prince Harry, had one of the best smiles we've ever had on the show and was in love with toasties, which I felt was a noble culinary pursuit. There was also a formidable trio of cooks from South East Queensland who all made the top seven. Christina Laker impressed us with her Chinese-inspired duck broth and Nicole Scott with her baby beetroot dish, but Tessa Boersma's cheese and onion millefeuille topped the lot. She was a criminal statistician, and a worthy finalist against restaurant manager Larissa Takchi and barman Simon Toohey, who'd done a valiant job championing vegetables throughout his time on the show.

Larissa was the cook though with the momentum, having beaten top chef Adam D'Sylva in the last immunity challenge before finals week. After that, she made an exquisitely good dessert to take out the crown and the finale. Little did we know that her Szechuan pavlova with beetroot and blackberry was the last dish Gary, George and I would ever taste in the *MasterChef* kitchen. It was, in retrospect, the perfect way to finish our astonishing eleven-year feast. The best degustation ever!

58

Sadly, while Larissa Takchi was a deserved winner, her crowning would ultimately be overshadowed by what happened on the day the series 10 finale went to air. I always felt that was a little unfair. She deserved her moment in the sun. She was a most worthy winner. Let's take a moment to make up for that now . . .

Yay, Larissa!

Okay, now we've celebrated Larissa a little bit, back to the story. I was sitting in a car with a Ten publicist about to go on Mick Molloy and Jane Kennedy's radio show on Triple M to talk about that night's finale. The one that Larissa would win . . .

Yay, Larissa!

My phone beeped. I had been sent a screenshot of an Instagram post from Network Ten informing the world that the three judges of *MasterChef Australia* – Gary, George and I – would *not* be returning for the next series. I showed the publicist the screenshot. We agreed that doing the radio show probably wasn't a good idea. The publicist was more shocked than me, because I can't say that the news came as a great surprise. Disappointing, yes. A surprise, no.

The media would report that our contract negotiations had broken down. It all seemed reasonably straightforward – bar one complication. The week before the finale, MAdE Establishment announced they had back paid $7.8 million to their past and present staff. The reaction to this bombshell was brutal and instantaneous. Very quickly the narrative turned, not to the fact that MAdE had back paid all this money, but that there had been $7.8 million of underpayments in the first place. The social media hounds started baying for blood, and as the public face of MAdE George quickly became the poster boy for wage theft. There were calls for him to be sacked from *MasterChef*, and reports that some of his commercial partners severed their links.

Gary and I were onlookers through all this mayhem and anger, but when asked about it at the time while on ABC Radio I publicly made it clear again that I supported Fair Work's desire to ensure that all workers are paid what they are due.

I also said that rulings like this from Fair Work Australia were increasingly common and that such underpayments were almost becoming endemic. By the end of 2019, a long list of big names including Bunnings, Qantas, Woolworths, Rockpool Dining Group, Suncorp, University of Technology Sydney and Super Retail Group would all come to the attention of Fair Work Australia over underpayments ranging from a few thousand dollars to millions.

As for the breakdown in our contract negotiations, I don't want to waste too much space on a retread of the whole we said/they said territory as it's all available to read in the media archives, but basically, hand in hand with the news that Network Ten would be looking for new judges for *MasterChef,* Ten came out and publicly stated that George's current problems had *not* played a role in their decision to get rid of us. The *Australian*'s Nick Tabakoff had spoken with the network's CEO Paul Anderson and in the following day's paper wrote, 'Despite the Calombaris scandal, Ten's decision not to renew the trio's contracts is about money.' Our position was that we were happy with the money that Ten were offering, but couldn't reach agreement on the terms of the contract. The long and the short of this was that our time in the *MasterChef* kitchen was over.

I didn't feel any rancour over Ten's decision. It's just business. That's all. It was their call to make, and that's the nature of these negotiations. If a deal doesn't make sense to you, you don't need to sign it. And that cuts both ways.

I also don't think Ten really had a choice. While international numbers on the show were strong, the Australian ratings were dropping. The numbers for the finale I saw were down from 1.3 million in 2017 to 992,000. I think they did the right thing for them – and it worked out well. The new judges and the 'Back to Win' concept of much-loved former contestants returning made for perfect, warm, familiar COVID-lockdown viewing. *MasterChef* powered on. Rejuvenating.

When something like this happens in your life, the danger is that you let it consume you, but it was the undeniable truth that Gary, George and I had had an incredible time over a long period at Network Ten. I genuinely enjoyed working with the people there, loved some of them even. It's a good network, why would I have let the current woes get in the way of all those great memories? All those great times? And all the great things we achieved together?

Also, it has to be said, I had pushed hard on the contract because I was probably ready to go. Those eleven years had been magnificent. We had done so much and I still loved making the show, but I dreaded becoming jaded and growing to resent doing what was still, in my opinion, one of the best jobs in the world.

It had also been made clear to me that *MasterChef* was the only show in my future if I stayed. I had a yen to try other things before I drifted off into that oblivion where ageing TV talent goes to polish their Logies and gaze wistfully at photos of how good-looking they once were. Especially as I couldn't do either. I've only got one Logie and none of those photos.

My only regret was that I never got to say goodbye face to face to our wonderfully loyal and long-standing crew. They had been central to the success of the show over the years. Instead, I wrote them a farewell love letter in my column in *Stellar* magazine. You can read it on delicious.com.au if you can be bothered. They really were the best bunch of people.

One last thing before we move on. If I'm being totally honest, it did sting a bit when Ten announced that the next series of *MasterChef* would see a bevy of ex-contestants – our friends, our charges, our own *MasterChef* family – returning to compete. I would have loved for George, Gary and me to have been there for a reunion in the kitchen with so many of our old friends. But by then, of course, there were other fish in the sea to fry, steam or sashimi and serve with a little wasabi, soy sauce and pickled ginger.

59

You know that old cliché about how when one door closes, another opens? Well, that nice James Warburton from Ten had joined the Seven Network as CEO in August of 2019 and he kindly opened his front door. I think he was looking to make a statement as the new boss and, fortuitously for us, that statement included signing Gary and me for a cooking show. Not only that, we'd be working alongside Manu Feildel, star of *My Kitchen Rules* and the man who had come so close to taking George's role on *MasterChef* all those years earlier.

Sadly, George was still in a bind. James Warburton said 'never say never' but at that stage there was no place for our third musketeer. A major problem was that his Network Ten contract's 'hold back' clause forbade him from working for anyone else for several months after the agreement ran out. The clause reached deep into 2020 and so he couldn't join us anyway, as Seven wanted us to start work on the new project before the end of summer.

Gary, George and I spoke with an Indian production company about doing something over there as the *MasterChef* audience was still huge on the subcontinent, but in spite of some initial enthusiasm, nothing came of it. Then, while we were in Pretoria, South Africa, headlining a stadium food festival, we discussed splitting up 'the chubby trio', at least for the time being. Although George was upset that he wouldn't be coming with us to Seven, he gave us his blessing.

Of course, George had other issues to sort out before he'd be fully accepted again by the Australian viewing public and the media, but that is his story to tell. And when he does tell it, it will be quite a read.

Channel Seven had the Olympic broadcasting rights and James Warburton wanted to make a feelgood food show to run after the Games to capitalise on the eyeballs that would be turning Seven's way. And so *Plate of Origin* was born. It would be a knock-out competition where teams of two representing their chosen country competed to see 'whose cuisine ruled supreme'. It was to be about national pride and a celebration of the food of your heritage and, while some on the left carped about what they called 'primary school multiculturalism', I loved it, as back then it was rare to see so many people of Cameroonian, Vietnamese, Colombian, Indian or even Chinese or Vietnamese heritage on prime-time commercial TV – other than on *MasterChef*.

There were a few rather good cooks, such as Thanh Truong and Duncan Lu from Team Vietnam, Ash Vola from the Cameroonian team, the wise matriarchs who led the Lebanese and the Italian teams, and the Chinese team of Mandy Chai and Chrys Hong who blew us away from the very first cook. Dezi Madafferi and Penny Kerasiotis from Team Greece also shone and ultimately took out the title. They've both since gone on to be a force on social media.

I still keep in touch with or follow quite a few of the contestants. Thanh (as the Fruit Nerd) is a regular guest on my ABC Radio show and Ash has come in to talk about the Cameroonian food she serves at her Vola Foods pop-up in Melbourne. Tragically, the talented Chrys Hong died from cancer soon after *Plate of Origin* aired. She was only thirty. That just seemed so wrong. It still does.

The tone of *Plate of Origin* was warm and positive, though we did need some villains and the French team of Austine Dall and Leo Garnier fitted the bill. It was never nasty, just a bit of pantomime. We made one episode that was such a joyous affair that a long-term *My Kitchen Rules* producer marvelled at the power and pleasure of making such affirmative TV.

Manu was happy to be back in production after the network had canned *My Kitchen Rules* due to low ratings. He was a joy to work with – knowledgeable, funny and a true performer. I think he was also energised by the absence of any bitchiness. Gary and I teased him a bit, but that was only because 1) he was better looking, 2) he thought French food was the culinary pinnacle, and 3) as the long-running incumbent Seven talent there was a feeling that he was the star of the show.

When *Plate of Origin* went to air at the end of August, the reviews of the judges and our chemistry were great, but there was criticism of other parts of the show.

After a solid start (almost 700,000 viewers – consolidated), our ratings drifted to the levels that *My Kitchen Rules* had sunk to near its end. There was one big problem for *Plate of Origin* and that was totally out of our control. The cancellation of the summer Olympics due to the pandemic removed part of our raison d'être and nixed that perfect promotional platform which would have enabled us to reach a huge audience. There were other issues which to a lesser or greater extent affected the show as well.

Some felt *Plate of Origin* fell between two stools, being neither *My Kitchen Rules* nor *MasterChef*. We could debate that. It certainly didn't help that when the name of the show was announced, certain wags immediately started referring to it by its acronym. This quickly caught on and became a hashtag. While calling *My Kitchen Rules* 'MKR' or *Married at First Sight* 'MAFS' wasn't a problem, calling a food show 'POO' was. It did not make for the auspicious start we were hoping for.

In addition, some of the cooks just weren't up to scratch. In the first episode Ethan and Stew, the charming blokes who were representing Australia, struggled to make a potato mash. They were crushed by the talented Chinese team of Mandy and Chrys and their excellent biang biang noodles. We all knew that Aussie gold drove Olympic ratings success. Our boys weren't even close to bronze.

The arrival of COVID, and the Seven Network's concern about the health of the crew, saw the series cut dramatically. Even at the start, when the hugging, dancing and waving crowd opened our first episode, it probably seemed a bit off colour, given the fact that lockdowns were hurting so many around the country. We lasted four weeks and, not surprisingly, a second series was never commissioned.

MasterChef, on the other hand, with the reassuring presence of so many familiar and much-loved faces – and with new judges Andy Allen, Melissa Leong and the late Jock Zonfrillo – bounced back with a vengeance, eclipsing the series 10 finale two years earlier by some 200,000 people.

As with so many industries, COVID had a disastrous effect on hospitality. Almost overnight, businesses closed, and employees were out of a job. The pandemic also stripped my diary of all the plans I had for the rest of 2020. The TV show that had been greenlit in the UK was cancelled, and trips to do live shows in India and South Africa as well as all the festivals here in Australia evaporated. Luckily, interest in home cooking had never been greater, and like so many I pivoted. I bought myself some TV lights and a fancy wireless mic and started shooting simple recipe videos, which I put out for free on my social media channels. The reaction was encouraging. With everyone locked down there seemed to be a real hunger for simple and tasty recipes, so I set up a dedicated Instagram feed called @lockdownkitchen.com.au, which quickly attracted over 30,000 followers. I started sourcing videos from other cooks I love and within a couple of months it had grown to a resource of over a hundred video recipes. I didn't monetise the site because I wanted it to feel like an open-handed gift to people who were struggling, particularly in those places where *MasterChef* had been popular. My reward? It felt as though I had a sense of purpose – however small.

The skills I learnt filming those videos came in handy when I debuted more short recipe clips on TikTok and reconnected with that generation who grew up with *MasterChef* and were now in their twenties. Reading the comments to my first TikTok posts, it seemed once again I'd become Shrek, Humphrey B. Bear and Barney the Dinosaur. Along with dropping Aaron's pasta dish back in 2010, this probably had something to do with me popping up on those music festival doof sticks.

It has also changed the audience at my live shows. There is nothing better than getting on the road with my culinary offsider, and TV star in his own right now, Warren Mendes.

We've done dinners and countless live shows around the country, and overseas in locations from Pretoria and Mumbai to Kuala Lumpur and Abu Dhabi – often with 'the other Warren' in tow: chef Emma Warren – with audiences that range from hundreds to thousands of people. We all especially love the thrill of hitting a new city and finding inspiration for what to cook for dinners and for the demos we'll be doing in the markets and supermarkets, whether we are creating a malva pudding to celebrate ex-cricketer Kepler Wessels, or riffing on a local street snack that boasts a cult following.

These dinners have given us some of the biggest professional thrills because of the teams we've been able to work with – watching Emma Warren in Kuala Lumpar inspiring young Muslim women in the kitchen who have never worked with a female head chef before was uplifting.

The triple challenge of having to cook, entertain and impress on a stage, all while not forgetting the recipe, has been something I'm still trying to perfect, but the presence of this new generation of younger fans has made things a whole lot less sedate when we are headlining a food festival here or overseas. It's much closer to being in a rock band when you look out and see mobs of kids shouting raucously, wearing homemade T-shirts with your own mug on them. Certainly ironic, it's also very funny, and this is part of what makes events like the marvellous CheeseFest in Adelaide unmissable for me. Sure, it's all a bit of harmless fun, but secretly I am flattered – especially when the head of security at our last Pretoria shows told me the fans there were louder than the kids who were there to see rock band The Script the month before. Is food the new rock'n'roll?

After twelve years of never having enough time, constantly running to keep up with my commitments, COVID brought a welcome change of pace. I signed a contract with Penguin Random House Australia to write the food history book I'd always wanted to write. At last I had the hours in the day to deep dive into the history of a hundred or so dishes, write a suite of new and improved recipes, and bust a whole heap of food myths.

I spent forever lost in research papers. The gems I discovered were exhilarating. The first recipe for spaghetti bolognaise as we would recognise it did not appear in an Italian newspaper but in one from Adelaide. And I finally buried the myth that pavlova is a New Zealand invention – the recipe Kiwis always claim as their own was actually written by a cook from Sydney's Double Bay!

The book wasn't just full of history but nuggets of truth that informed and improved the recipes inside. Topping your tuna mornay with potato chips as my granny did is an old American idea, stroganoff was originally served with hot chips – delicious – and the first written recipes for Massaman curry were brightened with sour orange juice, the acidity of which lifts this Thai takeaway classic dramatically. The book was called *Matt Preston's World of Flavour*; if you see it in the discount bin, grab a copy . . . or head to the library and borrow one. My long-time recipe collaborator Michelle Southan (who's the food director at taste.com.au and with whom I've written recipes with for over a decade) is the one who ensured the food you'll cook from this is so darned tasty, and so darned easy to achieve.

After all the hard work, it was jolly pleasing when it was subsequently named the second-best Celebrity Cookbook in the World at the global cookbook awards. Some nice people from Lima won the category, but *Matt Preston's World of Flavour* is still one of my proudest achievements.

It's strange to think that I'm only writing cookbooks because someone at a publishing house liked my bolognaise recipe in the newspaper so much that she cut it out and stuck it up on the office pinboard at work, telling everyone to make it. It's a good recipe. In spirit it is my mother's recipe and it's been a regular feature – like a totem – tweaked, polished and amended over seven of my eight subsequent cookbooks it inspired.

When it comes to those cookbooks, I still think they all stand up and I still make recipes from each of them. I am, however, especially proud of the seventh one. *More* took three years of planning as Michelle and I quietly collated more than five hundred potential vegetarian and vegan recipes. Jennifer's bolognaise even makes an appearance, here made with lentils instead of mince.

The idea for the book was inspired in part by an experiment on my part, to eat a paleo diet for three months and then a strictly vegan diet for the same amount of time, as much as it was by those moments in the middle of the night when you wake with inspiration and reach for a notebook. Michelle and I picked one hundred or so of only the very best gems. I still reckon everything in the book – from homemade tater tots with leeks and a dusting of smoked cheddar, to a tray bake of pumpkin and potato in a peanut red curry sauce, to a carrot korma and a mushroom stroganoff – would (and did, and still do!) satisfy even the most rabid carnivores.

Even if I do say so myself, our idea of microwaving a whole cauliflower before baking it is still better than all the other options out there. The flavour isn't diluted by steaming or blanching, and the cauliflower ends up spoon-soft and creamy all the way through. It's also far quicker. It's the benchmark recipe for me, whether the cauliflower ends up golden under a rich blanket of torn bocconcini, grated parmesan, crème fraîche and plenty of black pepper, cacio e pepe style, or rubbed with olive oil and harissa before baking and served crispy-edged with hummus, yoghurt and cumin.

I've always been a fan of trying new things in the kitchen, but for the preceding twenty years my working life had always been about food – whether cooking, writing recipes, reviewing or talking about food on TV and radio. It was familiar and it had become easy.

This was about to change. I was about to step further out of my comfort zone than I had done at any time since joining the army . . . and this was actually going to be both scarier and harder, but ultimately far more satisfying.

60

For the two years I'd been contracted exclusively to Seven during the pandemic there understandably hadn't been much desire to launch new food shows. There were suggestions that I might like to jump the host/mentor/judge fence and become a contestant on some existing reality show, but I was resistant as my head was still buried in the food space with my old writing gig at News Corp. And to be honest, nothing else really appealed. I was probably also a little gun shy, and a little spent.

Making reality TV can be quite boring for the contestants, waiting around in (non-COVID) lockdown, and like everyone else, I'd had more than enough of that over the last couple of years. My mate Merrick Watts and I had a few chats both before and after he was on *SAS Australia* and his experiences scared me off.

At least for a while . . .

After finishing up from two years with Seven, I began looking to play in areas that interested me or that I thought might be fun. First cab off the rank had to be radio. Over the previous twelve years or so I'd done a lot of radio interviews, and I had co-hosted both on the ABC and on FM stations like Fox, Nova, Smooth and Triple M. I loved the immediacy – it was such an adrenaline rush – I loved the variety and, even better, as I had often been told, I had the perfect face for the medium.

However, it soon became apparent that I was happier doing some radio shows more than others. While the quick-fire nature of the early-morning breakfast slot can be fun, I grew grumpy and obsessive with the demands of filling in at the ABC. You'd arrive at 4 am and the show would still need to be pulled together. Coming from a magazine background, I was used to locking in ideas and stories months in advance of publication. The certainty that this gives you is reassuring. The seat-of-the-pants nature of breakfast radio on the other hand stressed me out. It has to be one of the hardest jobs in media and it's why I have such respect for the likes of the ABC's Sammy J or Nikolai Beilharz and Stacey Lee, 3AW's Russel Howcroft and the radio master Ross Stevenson. I don't admire them just for the brutal hours or the relentless pace they endure. It takes real journalistic talent to switch from a sensitive issue like a child abduction or refugee detention to chatting with a mealy-mouthed politician intent on obfuscation – or a shallow, self-absorbed TV star.

In the end I became so unbearable filling in on those weekday breakfast slots at the ABC that Emma put her foot down and issued the ominous words, 'I don't think breakfast radio is good for you.' When she said 'you' she actually meant 'us'.

Thankfully, soon after, I was offered Saturday mornings on the ABC and I jumped at it. There were lots of plusses: the show began at 8.30 am, so the hours were far more civilised than breakfast, and it could be planned in advance, which was definitely more my style. Doing radio just one day a week to keep my brain challenged and firing was the perfect way to start my long-awaited 'taper' into working less after years of stupidly long hours.

The long Saturday morning slot also gave me ample room to talk about all the things I hadn't got to talk about for fourteen years. I was also able to lobby for fresh voices to join me on air: people I admire and respect, like health and medical commentator Dr Vyom Sharma; Lisa Leong, who looks after Sunday's show; and of course Alice Zaslavsky.

Initially there was very little food talk. That would have been too predictable. Instead, it was all about music and gardening, nature and the theatre, along with regular health, pets and bird segments. We might talk to an expert about whether snakes have personalities, or whether ravens or bin chickens are the most evil of our avian companions. There was also the chance to do deeper, longer interviews with anyone who interested me and the producers (and who we hoped would interest others). Each week we'd navigate between big name guests like Tim Minchin or Sam Pang, Indigenous artist Richard Bell, the British band Wet Leg, or Nigella Lawson. It made for a joyous mix and kept me on my toes as the interviewer, especially as I have experienced how tedious it is to be asked the same question over and over again.

After fourteen years of recorded and edited TV, there is an intoxicating element to doing something that is truly live. There's something truly scary about the first time the light goes red and you are alone with a big fluffy mic in front of you and a big fluffy brain in your head that can only think about all of the people out there – and how any second of silence, drivel or hesitation will be pounced on. Relax. Smile. Hope that the maroon block on the text screen line doesn't explode into a blizzard of white type. Short texts are the worst. Short texts are invariably angry texts. And always ignore the texts in ALL CAPS – that's a big red flag.

And then you are off. You start talking and the guests you're speaking with are fascinating and I never knew I wanted to know more about sea shanties, or jonquils, or caterpillars that spit fire, or how the best way to eat a passionfruit is to cut off the top like it's a boiled egg. I've always been a curious person, someone whose enthusiasm is stoked by experts and obsessives. Then the blizzard starts but it's slow and steady – long texts, stories and insights from people listening that enhance the conversation and move it forward. Suddenly, two and a half hours have flown by and it's time to think about sport.

Right from the start I also was promised that I could spend the last hour of the show talking sport with my old friend and ABC journo Catherine Murphy. I am a total sports nuffie, whether it's soccer, AFL or rugby; netball or golf; cricket or even the hobby horse world championships. Catherine is the expert – albeit prone to moments of extreme naughtiness and occasionally quite rude about my love for Collingwood.

From the start we wanted it to be different. Here, some-thing my sister Eleanor once said inspired me. She spent over a decade as a top tennis journalist and it resonated when she bemoaned how little behind-the-scenes or colour-style sports journalism there was in Australia. It was as if sports talk here could only be team news, injuries and results. Catherine and I wanted to do something that would engage both passionate sports fans as well as those who weren't all that into people chasing or hitting balls. And that's the sweet spot – not just doing the obvious sports stuff, but also searching for the other 70 per cent that most sports people never get to show – and one never quite knows where this is going to go. This is in part because Catherine is a profoundly, and at times terrifyingly, mischievous co-host. Have a listen and see if we've succeeded. I may be biased, but I'm pretty stoked with it and I'm delighted that our audience is growing. It's sometimes known as the 'Cat and Matt Show' because, let's face it, I am a happy passenger here. It truly is a privilege to make.

That's not to say there haven't been challenges. The guest that texts to pull out at midnight the night before they're due to appear, the fact that stars always seem to die on a Friday night, requiring a completely new show to be drawn up and stocked with guests at 7 am on Saturday, or those moments of technological mayhem that always happen when only a skeleton tech crew is on call at the weekends. Those are the moments when your voice must be calm as a swan while the rest of you is frantically trying to work out why the mics aren't working or why we can't get Billie calling from Ballarat up on line one.

Doing radio once a week on a Saturday leaves me with plenty of time to take on other interesting projects. Sure, there are always a few potential TV pilots on the boil in the hope of catching lightning in a bottle again – so far we haven't but hope springs eternal – but I've also enjoyed trying my hand at acting and having someone else's words to say.

Back in 2015, our old executive producer at Network Ten, Rick Maier, had got me a bit part in *Neighbours* as he knew it was on my bucket list (and my mum would love it). The network had also managed to get me a small part in *Offspring* and *The Bold and the Beautiful* when the latter was filming in Sydney. *Offspring* was tremendous fun, but *The Bold and the Beautiful* was surreal. I got to play the part of Noah the wedding planner alongside some of the soap greats like John McCook, Thorsten Kaye and Ashleigh Brewer, and they were as generous with their advice as they were with their anecdotes. I've never been happier with a three-hour rain delay on set, as they were so inclusive, welcoming and happy to chat and share.

Mind you, I am under no illusion that my acting is any good. I once joked after playing a detective in Adam Zwar and Amanda Brotchie's *Lowdown* for the ABC in 2010 that the colour scenes magically turned to black and white, such was the leaden weight of my performance.

Not cowed by this lack of talent, in 2022 I hungrily accepted a tiny part on the ABC's comedy series *Aftertaste*. I enjoyed a sweet couple of days watching actors and crew at the top of their game. And I think my performance may have been a little better than previous efforts. It's probably still available somewhere online. As is the time I got to do an advert speaking Telugu in India. It was a promo for *MasterChef* and I had the great thrill of filming on one of the sound stages at Mumbai's Film City, home of Bollywood. Landing a small part as a baddie in a Bollywood movie is still an unchecked item on my bucket list and I hoped this would get me a step closer.

Playing baddies is something I discussed with friend and actor Lachy Hulme in between takes filming *Celebrity Gogglebox* in 2022. Sadly, I feel we are both too loquacious for a show that loves pithy soundbites, but I greatly enjoyed our chats – and Lachy's idea that he should also wear my wardrobe so we looked like matching twins onscreen. He is built like a more svelte version of me but has a similar mien, so much so he could be my younger, more talented and better-read brother. He's who I'd like to play me in the movie of my life. He actually once said – quite cruelly in my opinion – that my pomposity on *MasterChef* was part of the inspiration for his character Dr Martin Clegg on *Offspring*. Some might not see this as flattering, but more tellingly it might explain why his Clegg was always one of my favourite characters.

This new luxury of having time on my hands, paired with odd offers, resulted in a bizarre night in August 2022 when I was simultaneously on the three commercial TV channels at once. It was almost a reprise of the sort of overexposure I experienced in 2009. There I was in an ad for Uber on the Nine Network, debuting as a judge on *My Kitchen Rules* on the Seven Network (yes, we'll talk more of that shortly), and singing as part of the madness that is *The Masked Singer* on Network Ten.

I'd turned down *The Masked Singer* a couple of times before, but when I saw the gnome outfit that designer Tim Chappel had in mind for me – a huge, purple, twinkly-eyed cutie with a rotund belly and white beard – I was immediately smitten. It was also the biggest 'mask' Tim had ever designed for the show. Singing on TV was a scary prospect but, as you know, I'd made a pact with myself years before to pursue opportunities that seemed well outside my comfort zone.

The Masked Singer is a bizarre beast for a couple of reasons. Firstly, there's a crazy level of security that surrounds the guests. Maintaining the secrecy of each masked contestant's identity is paramount, so everywhere I went on set I was accompanied by my own personal security guard. He insisted that if I had to speak, I should whisper softly but in a high-pitched voice so no one would guess who I was. Of course, this might just have been a cruel prank. I never found out.

In fact, secrecy is so paramount (and might even be stipulated in my contract – or might not be: I couldn't confirm either way) that it is wisest if the following paragraphs of on-set *Masked Singer* insights are redacted.

████████████████████████████████████
██
████████████████████████████████████
███████████████████████████████████████
██
███████████████████████████████████████
████████████████████████████████████ twice
as much ███████████████████████████████
██████████████████ Chrissie Swan ██████████
███████████████████████ talented dancers
███████████████████ ████████████████████
██████████████████████████████████████
███████████ buckets ███████████████████████
██
█████████████ chicken shoes ██████████████
██████████████████ Osher's eyes █████████
██

████████████████████████████

████████████████████████████

████████████████████████████

████████████████████████████

moist ███████████████████████

████████████████████████████

████ steamed broccoli ████████

████████████████████████████

████████████████████████████

████████████████████████████

████████████ Good Times!' ████

████████████████████████████

████████████████████████████

████████████████████████████

██████

In the end, singing The Monkees' 'Daydream Believer' wasn't as hard as I thought it would be. Wearing the joyously outlandish costume removed any performance anxiety. This was a huge pay-off from doing the show.

The offer to guest judge one of the weeks of *My Kitchen Rules'* instant restaurant dinner parties during what would be their return 2022 season proved to be a slight conundrum. Manu Feildel was a friend, but the show had been our fiercest rival during my time on *MasterChef,* over an epic eleven-series slugfest, both of us had scored winning rounds. But the chance to see inside this opposition beast was too tempting for a TV food nerd like me to resist. And not only that, Nigella Lawson would be joining Manu for the first round so I'd be in good company.

On the surface, the skills required to judge *My Kitchen Rules* seemed very similar – basically translating the flavour of the dishes for the audience at home. However, while on *MasterChef* you had more opportunities to mentor the contestants, on *My Kitchen Rules* you got to know the contestants better because you spent so much time round the table filming with them. I enjoyed this facet of the show, eking out the contestants' stories so that they might become the sort of people whose adventures you'd want to follow.

If you failed to achieve this, you risked descending into reality TV clichés or relying on drama coming from the cook to propel the action. And it's far harder to get that sense of jeopardy with only one team at a time cooking in those opening rounds.

There were other unforeseen challenges too. While shooting in Albany, Western Australia, someone in production decided it would be a nice idea to dress our candlelit set with chillies. This looked spectacular, but placing Carolina Reapers next to the heat of the candles released the chillies' savage and volatile oils. Che Cooper and Dave Shorter's instant restaurant quickly turned into a crime scene. It felt as if there'd been a capsicum-spray attack; there were running eyes and people unable to speak without coughing. It was far funnier afterwards.

Although you got to know the contestants, the pace of the last series of *My Kitchen Rules* limited the amount of mentorship and development you could provide . . . especially because in those early rounds they were cooking a pre-set and (hopefully) practised menu that too much advice risked derailing.

Overall, though, it was a fascinating experience. As I'd found working with different producers with different approaches on

Plate of Origin, I learnt a lot from my weeks on *My Kitchen Rules*. There's a real strength in having contestant teams of two in terms of human warmth and the humour that comes from that closeness. The other upside was how relaxed Manu was when he was seated at the table. This really helped the happy mood of the show.

While we ate some excellent food, that old problem of occasionally casting people who can't really cook raised its ugly head again and I'm just too old and too grumpy to tell you something is 'cooked to perfection' when it's not, no matter how good a character you are!

The ratings for the second week of instant restaurants usually dipped, but ours actually included the highest rating episode outside of the finale. I took this as a bit of a win.

The other great thing about having more time in 2021 and 2022 was being able to get back to London to see my mum, Jennifer. She had been a regular, often annual, traveller to Australia each February, so I felt the loss of not seeing her during the COVID years even more keenly. During that time she had been diagnosed with Parkinson's, early onset dementia and a cancer of the blood plasma cells called myeloma. The doctor's cheering assessment of this last ailment was along the lines of, 'Don't worry, your mum is eighty-six, something else will get her before the cancer does.' I suppose he had a point.

As soon as I could, I headed back to the UK with my daughter Sadie in December 2021. I was immediately struck by how frail and small this once vital woman had become. A week into the trip, I managed to catch the dreaded COVID virus and give it to Sadie, my immune-supressed sister and, naturally, my vulnerable mum. I was terrified about what might happen. What if the virus took her as it had so many her age around the world?

Needless to say, I shouldn't have worried. We were all properly sick but my formidable mother presented with little more than a few sniffles. As we recovered, our isolation periods coincided so we could all be together. Sadie got Mum playing cards again and her ruthless killer instinct returned during games of Big Two and Gin.

This joint isolation also meant we could spend Christmas together. We decorated the tree as we always had with way too much gold lametta and tinsel. Just like my youngest sister Eleanor, Sadie is strong with the Christmas force. They share the lore that if you can see any part of the tree, you need to add more sparkly stuff. I roasted turkey and made bread sauce. Everyone except Jennifer ate too many brussel sprouts.

After lunch, my other sister Katie and her family came over to sit on the other side of the bay window, chilling outside like Dickensian orphans, for a little more shared Christmas cheer. We were divided by the glass – and the fact that we were all rather toasty inside by the open fire and they weren't – but we were together. We didn't know it was to be our last proper Christmas with our beloved mum.

I came back twice more the following year to spend time with her. On each occasion she slipped a little further away, although she'd always rally when I was there. I'd take her for walks in her wheelchair across the Common and for coffee at the local hipster cafe in the spring sunshine. We'd talk about her life and those of the family who had gone before. But she was always cold. Even with the blow heater on full, her papery hands felt like ice.

Her beautiful carer Justina would, unprompted, insist on putting lipstick and a little blush on her for those outings. Remembering Justina do this – all gentle care and commitment to dignity – as my mother grumped about the fuss is still emotional, though more poignant than painful. Writing this now, I'm crying.

We'd watch Fulham together on the telly and I'd tease her about her crush on Les Strong and her protective streak when it came to Rufus Brevett. She had had a bit of a thing for Fulham left backs over the years. And, of course, she'd make me watch *Strictly Come Dancing* (the UK version of *Dancing with the Stars*). It was her favourite show and I couldn't avoid it when I was there.

In time, she started to sleep more and lose interest even in her football team. *Strictly Come Dancing* was her constant passion, and really the only thing, other than the visits of loyal friends, that she looked forward to. She avidly tuned in to the finale with Justina, a fellow *Strictly* tragic, on that last Saturday before Christmas 2022.

61

On Boxing Day morning, at the age of eighty-nine, my mother Jennifer breathed her last. She was in her own bed with her cat curled up at her feet with one of my sisters by her side. She wasn't in pain and there was a sense among those who saw her in her last weeks that she was ready to go. My sisters, Katie and Eleanor, and Justina, had found ways to keep her out of the hospitals she hated and the hospices she dreaded. This had made a huge difference to the final years of her life.

Of course I was sad at her passing, but I also felt incredibly fortunate. Not just because she had been my mother and had fought to keep me no matter how hard she knew that would be, but because I'd had three years to say goodbye to her. When she'd left Australia after her final visit in 2019, I had farewelled her knowing that it could very well be the last time. Post-COVID I got to see her again and spend time with her, and after each time the sentiment was the same. I was blessed with time to appreciate her, to ensure that there was nothing unsaid or unasked, and to say thank you and tell her that I loved her.

*

All the family flew to London for the funeral. We were sombre as we quietly clopped through the streets of Fulham, the place she'd called home for almost sixty years, padding along behind the glass-sided hearse drawn by a team of black horses with funereal black ostrich plumes on their heads. Mum had always said she wanted to be taken out that way. She wouldn't have expected, however, the way builders on scaffolding along the road stopped and removed their hardhats, or that an office worker scurrying for the Tube would turn and make the sign of the cross.

Two months after the funeral, I received a call from my manager, Henrie Stride, asking if I'd like to appear on *Dancing with the Stars*. I felt my mother's hand in this. Not because she thought I was a good dancer, nor because *Strictly Come Dancing* was her favourite show, but because looking down I knew she'd be laughing as Craig Revel Horwood mercilessly ripped into me.

This seemed like a fitting final tribute.

Epilogue
Eulogy for my mother

This book has been so much about my mother, so it seems fitting to end it with the eulogy I delivered at her funeral on Friday 3 February 2023.

For those of you who don't know me, I am Jennifer's oldest child, and on behalf of the family we are so happy that you are all here today.

Jennifer loved people and she'd be delighted to see such a full church. It was one of the most firmly underlined instructions from the fulsome funeral wishes that she left – organised to the last. 'Tell everyone. Fill the church!'

She would love this – or, should I say, she *is* loving this, because her Christian faith was strong and she was a firm believer that a better place waited for her.

This feeling of her continued presence is why my son William told us yesterday that he was on his best behaviour around the house, just in case Jennifer was watching!

Our mother could be mischievous, funny and occasionally a little bit scary, but above all she *loved* people. Right till the end she loved it most when people visited, walked past and waved, dropped a line or called. If that was you, know that the joy brought by your visit lingered long after. So, from all the family, thank you.

Before we chat about Ma's life, we also all want to thank the formidable and gentle Justina and her team of carers who helped keep Jennifer in the home that she loved right until the end, and who looked after her so beautifully, bringing both care and dignity to her last days.

And I must acknowledge the amazing love and support that Eleanor and Katie (and Mark and Paul) have been – not just recently, but always. Jennifer always appreciated this – even if she might not always have expressed it verbally! Praise was seldom – heck, let's say never – something you heard from our mother. At least until it filtered back second- or third-hand – but then, it was also fulsome!

So, Anne Jennifer Preston. Friend, colleague, mother, wife, grandmother, Roman Catholic, Fulham fan – but above all, Jennifer was a teacher.

This underpinned so much of her life, and her famed ability to connect with young people from everywhere.

After a stint at the London Library, she started off teaching at The Vale in Chelsea. So began a lifelong love affair with helping children – not just as a teacher but as a school governor, tutor and educational specialist for kids who needed extra help. She worked on a number of projects for children with partial hearing and learning difficulties, where her warmth and generosity of spirit bloomed.

With Holly Sandys, she pioneered the independent mock entrance exams that are so common these days, and – after the death of our brother, William – she channelled her pain into setting up, with other parents who had lost a child to epilepsy, a charity that provided support for bereaved parents and helped young adults living with epilepsy.

Jennifer's way was to just do it, and in this she wrought the change she felt was important. She was an action woman who, in ways both small and large, leaves the world a better place.

This teaching didn't stop at the door to her classroom. We all learnt so much from her.

I remember my wife, Emma, and I queried why, after reading our daughter, Sadie, her bedtime story, Jennifer left a book in the cot for her to read. She was only eighteen months old. We understood a little later when we looked in on her . . . Sadie was sitting up happily murmuring to herself over the open pages.

And it was actually Ma's bolognaise recipe which she taught to me that was responsible for getting me my first cookbook deal. It was that good.

She was a good cook, but an even better seamstress and knitter, whether quilting, knocking up a jumper for her, or our, friends' new babies overseas, or making our son Jonathan a magnificent dinosaur costume when he was obsessed with *T-Rex*.

Put simply, Jennifer loved the young but she wasn't a fan of old people . . . perhaps because she never saw herself as any older than twenty-five.

Sometimes it felt as if she wanted to turn her Fulham home into an embassy for youth. Whether it was our friends here, or her new young friends from around the world, there was always space at the table for dinner, or a bed for a night or two.

Living on the other side of the world, my family and I were lucky that she loved to travel – circumnavigating the world some thirty times and visiting everywhere from Cuba and Lebanon to South Africa, the US and of course Australia many times.

Early on she lived in Rome and Paris – and returned to study at the Sorbonne, living with her Aunt Betty – another formidable character who, with her girlfriend, hosted a sort of salon on the Left Bank for expats, artists and society academics, including the likes of Nancy Mitford. Nancy described Betty in her obituary as being 'gifted in the art of friendship' and the same can be said of Jennifer. We were also remarking that this was pretty much how her home on Crondace Road could be – although the conversation would have been less about Descartes and more about playing cards.

Gee, she loved to play cards but gee, she hated to lose!

She became just as animated while watching Fulham, and it's a little-known fact that she particularly warmed to their left backs over the years. In that era when Fulham tasted European glory, Rufus Brevett was her favourite. I remember a game when she loudly berated an opposition player after a particularly robust tackle on the Whites defender . . . 'Leave my Rufie alone!' she bellowed. As my sister Eleanor will tell you, this was *not* a one-off occurrence. If she'd been using a walking stick back then, she undoubtedly would have brandished it threateningly.

She had a gentler nature when it came to animals. Her love of cats is well known, from Emma through to Lulu, and early on, of dogs. Of hamsters. Of guinea pigs. Of rabbits. And of horses.

When I was contemplating buying a share in a racehorse, my despairing wife turned to Jennifer for support to stop this madness. 'Oooh,' she exclaimed 'Wouldn't that be fun?'

Needless to say, her response was not what Emma expected. My mother loved fun!

We remember her laugh, her severe looks, her disapproving 'What?!', her mischievous sense of humour, her ability to hear whispered conversation across a room but to blame her hearing aid at all other times when it was something far closer that she didn't want to hear, her love of ice cream in her later years, her supreme distrust of vegetables, her forthright views, her love of crosswords and Words with Friends, and her intense love of her grandchildren.

Each person is a tapestry woven of a thousand threads like these.

Over the years, threads can snag and the colour can fade, but Jennifer was one of those fine individuals who continued to add more threads right till the end. We'll miss her.

Bye, Ma! Enjoy wherever it is your new travels take you . . .

Her next journey would in fact take her in the horse-drawn hearse for a 5-kilometre trot to the cemetery – bizarrely, passing Gary Lineker as he paused to cross the road when the funeral procession passed in Barnes. Jennifer always rather liked Gary Lineker talking football on the telly. It seemed fitting.

Once at the cemetery, we lowered her into the ground to join her son William and her husband Antony. It's a quiet spot and it was a poignant moment.

I think about where they all are now together when I'm cooking. Perhaps while stirring the recipe for her bolognaise as it bubbles away in that same white enamel pot she always used to use, but now on a hob on the other side of the world, cooking to feed my family and her grandchildren.

Acknowledgements

MY FAMILY

Forgive me if I turn the usual order of acknowledgements, which tends to start with the team behind the book, on its head, as this book wouldn't have happened at all without the support, advice and reminiscences of my sisters, Eleanor and Katie. So much of this story is theirs too – well, apart from the bits where I exhibit my signature rubbishness. This is memoir so by its very definition it's a collection of my memories and may not reflect others' truths, but I wanted to ensure that they at least recognised the plot. Enormous gratitude to them also as they bore the load of looking after my mother in her final years – along with the support of their partners, Mark and Paul. Thanks, too, to my nephew and niece, Gabriel and Nelly, whose visits always gave my mother such joy.

My own tight little family of Emma, Jonathan, William and Sadie have also contributed to this story. Emma's support has been invaluable and immeasurable to keep me on an even keel through the emotional rollercoaster of the learning and the telling. They are consistent in egging me on, supporting me and keeping my feet on the ground; I hope I'll measure up if they ever write their own memoirs.

There's one other member of my extended who never gets enough credit, and that is Henrietta Stride. From casting me in *MasterChef* to sharing all the subsequent crazy adventures as my manager, Henrie is equal parts friend and third sister. She pushes me and I like that, and I often need it! She's been with me for over fourteen years and she's made my life immeasurably better. Thank you, Henrietta!

Henrie's hard work has been supported by David Vodicka and Yasmin Neghavi, who have been my lawyers since this whole crazy TV ride began, keeping me out of trouble and going in to bat for me when required. Love 'em both. As I do long-term accountant Aaron Hurle. Charlotte James started looking after my social media before social media began (and through her I met Catherine Murphy, my sports co-host on ABC radio's 'Cat and Matt Show'). Thanks so much to this brains trust for everything. It's been a wild ride!

MY BOOK FAMILY

The team at Penguin Random House Australia have been brilliant through the almost three-year process of creating this book. Publisher and muse Alison Urquhart has led the charge; she published my first-ever book fourteen years ago (*Cravat-a-lious*, don't cha know) so it's beautiful and right she has brought this one to fruition. Her advice and insight have been invaluable. Editors Rod Morrison and Kathryn Knight had the momentous task of wrestling the 200,000+ words I filed into something that wouldn't damage you if you feel asleep while reading it in bed and dropped it on your head. They have immeasurably improved what you've read. Managing editor Catherine Hill came on board at the end to marshal the book to print. I thank her too.

Adam Laszczuk designed the arresting cover and Julian Kingma shot the photo with his usual ability to ensure that the camera does lie. The brilliantly talented Maureen Moriarty did my hair and make-up (just like she did over seven years of *MasterChef* in Melbourne), and my style guru from that time, Charmaine de Pasquale, inspired me to be brave with a neckerchief rather than a cravat. Love I still get to work with these legends.

Midland Typesetters made everything ~~legidible~~, ~~legerbil~~ legible and Bella Arnott-Hoare was back to drive the publicity on this book with her usual mix of alacrity and humour.

MY FOOD FAMILY

Food is so much of who I am and what I do, and this has only been possible thanks to some amazing people. Marnie Rowe and Kate Quincerot were there at the start when it all seemed so daunting. They made it less so and came up with brilliant ideas for my cookbooks. Warren Mendes and Emma Warren are there still when the hairiness tends to come – on bumpy overseas trips as much as shooting one of my books. Frankly I couldn't do it without them. All four are inspirational cooks, and I couldn't be more thrilled by the exciting turns their lives are taking.

The fifth member of this informal posse is Michelle Southan, who has been a recipe collaborator and colleague for almost a decade. Every conversation with her is an opportunity for learning and I love the videos we've started collaborating on for taste.com.au. I think 'crispy pork belly bites' stands at over five million views now.

This combination of over twenty years writing for *delicious*.magazine and taste.com.au, and in *Stellar* and *Escape* in newspapers like the *Daily Telegraph*, the *Herald Sun*, *Courier Mail* and *Advertiser* means there are loads of people to thank here too. Let's start at the top with editorial director Kerrie McCallum and food czar Fiona Nilsson, who are the power team that drives three of these four brands. I've worked in publishing for four decades and I can't think of any who could match them for vision, execution or inspiration. Then there's editor of taste.com.au Brodee Myers Cook; Jana Frawley and Toni Mason at *Escape*; Krysia Bonkowski, Lucy Nunes and John Hannan at *delicious* (as well as predecessors like Danielle Opperman, Sam Jones, Shannon Harley, Phoebe Rose Wood, Neale Whitaker and Trudi Jenkins), all of whom make me happy that the words 'food writer and recipe developer' are my day job. Huge also in bringing joy are collaborators and formidable food knowledge banks like Anooska Tucker-Evans at the *Courier Mail*, Kara Monssen at the *Herald Sun* and Jess Galletly at the *Advertiser* – they are best in their field and I am proud to call them friends and colleagues.

Also, a special word of thanks to the team at *Stellar* for my weekly column, in particular chief sub Katie Hendry who makes everything better, and editor-in-chief Sarrah le Marquand (who I'm still a little intimidated by after all this time).

Of course, when it comes to food family, I need to mention and thank Natalie O'Brien, Ann Houlihan and Ute Biefang, whom I worked with at the Melbourne Food and Wine Festival and who helped my life in food be even more fun, exciting and satisfying.

TELEVISION FAMILIES

The initial and continued success of *MasterChef* was dependent on the drive and vison of gurus like David Mott, Beverley McGarvey, Mark and Carl Fennessy, Paul Franklin and Jono Summerhayes, and of course the crew who worked on the series. It's a weird thing that for legal reasons I can't say all the positive things I wanted to about Marty Benson, David McDonald, Peter Newman, Caroline Spencer, Margie Bashfield, Tim Toni, Rick Maier, Karen Warner and the world-beating producers and crew who worked across the eleven years of *MasterChef*. These people were crucial to the success of an amazing show.

As crucial were the contestants, who trusted their food dreams to us. I've consciously included no contestant photos, in part because I didn't want to single out anyone – they were all vital, but the gift was that there are so many I love and now count as friends. They know who they are.

It's been a crazy few years for me, and I'd like to thank James Warburton and Andrew 'Backers' Backwell who both made my time at Seven, and after, so fulfilling and often fascinating. They were also responsible for me meeting my new sister, Jess Raffa, when they signed me up for *Dancing with the Stars*. In fact, I should thank (and apologise to) anyone whose stage or soundstage I've stunk up as I chased new experiences and challenges!

MY RADIO FAMILY

My newest family is at ABC Radio. I relish my 3.5 hours live on air every Saturday. I love the people I've met through it and that it's such a warm, personable way to connect. And I love how much people we meet seem to enjoy it too. What's that secret about how to never work a day in your life? I love chatting about everything from gardening with Carolyn Blackman and Stephen Ryan, health with Dr Vyom Sharma, pets and nature with Dr Diana Barker, wonderbirder Matthew Crawford and Dr Ken Walker, to music with Will Ewing. I love that people like ABC newsreader Mary McDonald and Jo Toscano are willing to be part of the show each week; I've been learning so much from all of them. I wouldn't have been there without Dina Rosendorff, Shelley Hadfield, Mary-Jane Fenech and Warwick Tiernan, so big thanks to them. Even bigger thanks to brilliant exec producer Virginia Millen, who was handed the reins of this runaway stagecoach by Nadia Hume before handing them on to Patrick Hills. And thanks to those who have helped so much along the way, including new producer Pat, who has a similarly skewed view of sport to myself and Catherine Murphy, and the likes of Tyson Whelan, panel op, producer and prodigious baker Andrew Kelso, and Rowena Murray. A big shout-out to the ABC's audio tech boffins Kon Karamountzos and audio legend Lee Deadly O'Keefe. It gave me no little pleasure when he joined us at the ABC after he'd made me sound good for years on *MasterChef*.

My final thanks are to the various coteries to which I am attached, which bring me joy and succour in equal measure, whether it's the culinary luminaries of the Road Trip Club, who are willing to take food story-telling to the highest levels on our *in camera* meals together; my fellow Collingwood tragics who make up the charitable institution that is The Phungs; the Golf Trippers and The Dix Allen Shufflers; and everyone back in the UK who are so much a part of this story, from the dance halls of West London and the terraces of Stamford Bridge to late nights in the West End and the life-changing moments from my youth onwards. I'll see you all for a beer in the Churchill or the Neptune, the Harwood or the Fox and Pheasant.

*

PHOTO CREDITS

All images are courtesy of and supplied by Matt Preston except for:

Photographs of Matt and his family © Julian Kingma
Matt with Henrietta Stride © Mark Roper
Gary, Matt and George with (then) Prince Charles © Kelly Gardner/EndemolShine Australia
Matt with the cast of *Neighbours* © Ray Messner/Fremantle-Media Australia
Matt with René Redzepi © Brett Stevens/*delicious.*magazine
Matt as the Statue of Liberty © Jeremy Simons/Newspix
Matt in *The Masked Singer* © Brett Symons/Warner Bros
Matt and Erik Thomson © Ian Routledge/Closer Productions
Matt with his ABC Melbourne radio team © Rebecca Michael, courtesy of the ABC
Matt in *Dancing with the Stars* © Stuart Bryce for BBC Studios